PERGAMON INTERNATIONAL LIBRARY
of Science, Technology, Engineering and Social Studies

*The 1000-volume original paperback library in aid of education,
industrial training and the enjoyment of leisure*

Publisher: Robert Maxwell, M.C.

Pergamon Titles of Related Interest

Cartledge/Milburn   TEACHING SOCIAL SKILLS TO CHILDREN:
Innovative Approaches, Second Edition

Conoley/Conoley   SCHOOL CONSULTATION:
A Guide to Practice and Training

Eisenson   LANGUAGE AND SPEECH DISORDERS
IN CHILDREN

Kirby/Grimley   UNDERSTANDING AND TREATING
ATTENTION DEFICIT DISORDER

Morris/Blatt   SPECIAL EDUCATION: Research and Trends

Plas   SYSTEMS PSYCHOLOGY IN THE SCHOOLS

Related Journals
(Free sample copies available upon request)

JOURNAL OF CHILD PSYCHOLOGY AND PSYCHIATRY
JOURNAL OF SCHOOL PSYCHOLOGY

PERGAMON GENERAL PSYCHOLOGY SERIES
EDITORS
Arnold P. Goldstein, Syracuse University
Leonard Krasner, SUNY at Stony Brook

Behavior Management In The Schools
Principles and Procedures

Richard M. Wielkiewicz

Fargo Public Schools
Fargo, North Dakota

PERGAMON PRESS

New York • Oxford • Beijing • Frankfurt
São Paulo • Sydney • Tokyo • Toronto

Pergamon Press Offices:

U.S.A.
Pergamon Press, Maxwell House, Fairview Park,
Elmsford, New York 10523, U.S.A.

U.K.
Pergamon Press, Headington Hill Hall,
Oxford OX3 0BW, England

PEOPLE'S REPUBLIC OF CHINA
Pergamon Press, Qianmen Hotel, Beijing,
People's Republic of China

FEDERAL REPUBLIC OF GERMANY
Pergamon Press, Hammerweg 6,
D-6242 Kronberg, Federal Republic of Germany

BRAZIL
Pergamon Editora, Rua Eça de Queiros, 346,
CEP 04011, São Paulo, Brazil

AUSTRALIA
Pergamon Press (Aust.) Pty., P.O. Box 544,
Potts Point, NSW 2011, Australia

JAPAN
Pergamon Press, 8th Floor, Matsuoka Central Building,
1-7-1 Nishishinjuku, Shinjuku-ku, Tokyo 160, Japan

CANADA
Pergamon Press Canada, Suite 104, 150 Consumers Road,
Willowdale, Ontario M2J 1P9, Canada

Copyright © 1986 Pergamon Books, Inc.

All rights reserved. No part of this publication may be reproduced, stored in a retrieval system or transmitted in any form or by any means: electronic, electrostatic, magnetic tape, mechanical, photocopying, recording or otherwise, without permission in writing from the publishers.

First printing 1986

Library of Congress Cataloging in Publication Data

Wielkiewicz, Richard M.
   Behavior management in the schools.

   (Pergamon general psychology series ; 140)
   Bibliography: p.
   Includes index.
   1. Behavior modification. 2. School children--
Discipline. I. Title. II. Series. [DNLM: 1. Behavior
Therapy--in infancy & childhood. 2. Child Behavior
Disorders--therapy. 3. Schools. WS 350.6 W646b]
LB1060.2.W54 1986   371.1'024   86-4932
ISBN 0-08-032364-2
ISBN 0-08-032363-4 (pbk.)

Printed in the United States of America

To my parents, Michael and Mary Wielkiewicz

CONTENTS

PREFACE

The purpose of this book is to provide a sound introduction to the principles of behavior modification along with practical information and specific procedures necessary to successfully apply these principles. The book is addressed to school personnel, particularly regular and special education teachers, counselors, social workers, and school psychologists. Others who are associated with school systems such as administrators, school principals, community psychologists, parents, or parent advocates, should also find the book helpful.

My motivation for writing the book was the realization that there is often a large gap between theoretical knowledge gained in classes on behavior management and the practical limitations imposed upon school personnel by the reality of their environment. Most of the existing books in this area focus upon underlying theory and general principles, which leaves the reader without the practical knowledge needed to apply techniques in the real world of the classroom. My book attempts to close the gap between theory and practice by describing techniques for managing child behavior in a concrete, step-by-step manner. The techniques vary from simple to highly complex and are intended to provide a wide range of options for handling various problems. By providing step-by-step procedures for attacking many specific behavior problems encountered in the schools, I hope that the reader will gain both a sound theoretical background in the use of behavior management and practical guidance in how to apply these principles in the school.

The book has two parts. Part 1 is concerned with the general principles of learning and behavior management, which are covered in Chapters 1, 2, 3, and 4. Chapter 5 addresses the issue of how the home and school interact to influence a child's behavior and how the home can influence the outcome of school-based behavior management programs. The first chapter of Part 2 describes the behavior problems most likely to be encountered by school personnel. The remainder of

Part 2 provides specific, step-by-step procedures for managing common behavior problems encountered in schools.

I would like to acknowledge several individuals who contributed to the evolution of this work. I owe a great debt to my colleagues Phillip Rice, Cheri Gess, Lori Jorgensen, Betty Torgrimson, Sharon Hall, and Kathy Stigman for providing a supportive professional environment in which to learn about the needs of the school-age child. The editorial assistance of Phillip Rice and Anne Mary Wielkiewicz is also greatly appreciated.

PART 1
PRINCIPLES

chapter 1

THE HOW AND WHY OF CHILD MANAGEMENT

The question of how to help children with behavior problems is particularly important in the schools, where efficient and effective ways of remediating problem behavior are needed. In American society, education has always been viewed as a means of improving one's life situation. The child who fails to gain maximum benefit from school will often have a limited future. Consequently, school practitioners must be experts in behavior change techniques that will enhance the benefits children receive from their schooling.

INTRODUCTION TO BEHAVIOR MANAGEMENT

One of the most successful models for producing behavior change is the behaviorist or learning model. Its basic assumptions are that both adaptive and maladaptive behavior are learned and that the best strategy for remediating problem behavior is to structure the child's environment to provide supportive feedback for desirable behavior. The model is known by a number of terms including *behaviorism, behavior therapy, behavior modification, and social learning theory.* The purpose of this book is to provide a thorough grounding in the fundamental principles of learning and their application to changing children's behavior in school. The general term, *behavior management,* will be used to denote the process of applying the principles of learning to remediating children's problem behavior.

Successful behavior management does not depend solely on school practitioners, however. The typical child spends most of his or her time in *two* environments: the home and school. Neither environment is more important than the other. Each makes crucial contributions to the child's physical, behavioral, and cognitive growth. In the broadest sense, behavior problems observed in school really involve the entire system including the child, the home, and the school. In order for a problem to be resolved successfully the components of the system will need to balance in some way. Most of the time, the balance requires that the child's parents acknowledge the existence of a problem and actively cooperate to help remediate it. Thus, both the school and home adjust to support the behavior management goals. Unfortunately, it is not always the case that the components of the system can accommodate needed changes.

For example, a child's aggressive behavior in school may be related to the modeling provided by abusive, unskilled parents, or academic failure may be related to the emotional turmoil surrounding the divorce the child's parents. Within school it is possible that undesired behavior has inadvertently been rewarded or that an unidentified learning problem has been causing the child intolerable frustration in the classroom. In such cases, focusing exclusively upon the child's behavior may solve the *school's* problem but might ultimately fail to help the child, if the relationship of other components to the child's behavior is ignored.

Instead, one must examine the influence of all components of the system upon the child's behavior, ensuring that the entire system including parents, teachers, siblings, administrators, and peers, is able to successfully accommodate and support desired changes. Behavior management techniques should not be used in ways that *increase* conflict within the system. In many cases, resolution of a problem situation may require a team effort involving teachers, parents, administrators, special education staff, social service representatives, and psychologists. Regardless of the complexity of a problem, the needs of the child should take precedence over other system problems.

The perspective taken in the present book is that children behave within the confines of a system consisting mainly of the school and home environments. Although the book is addressed to school personnel, its scope is not limited to management of behavior that occurs in school. Instead, the entire system in which the child functions is considered the potential focus of intervention. The reality of working within school systems is that many events relevant to the child's adjustment are outside the control of school personnel. Yet, this should not prevent personnel within the school system from trying to understand the entire system in which the child functions, because there are many opportunities for helpful, and in some cases, legally mandated, interventions. Chapter 5 elaborates this perspective.

Basic Behavior Management

When a behavior problem has been identified and it is agreed that it would be beneficial to modify the behavior, a working model of appropriate techniques is needed to guide the intervention plan. The model presented in this book, given the generic label *behavior management*, is based primarily upon the principles of learning theory. Its roots are in the work of the great American psychologist, Edward L. Thorndike. In a series of experiments with cats, Thorndike observed that responses followed by "satisfaction" (food, in this case) tended to be more likely to recur in the same situation. Responses followed by "discomfort" were less likely to recur in that situation. Thorndike theorized that changes in the probability of responses were the result of strengthening and weakening of "bonds" between the stimulus and response. This is the well known Law of Effect.

The Law of Effect is both a theoretical statement and a summary of empirical observations. However, in either its theoretical or empirical form, the statement remains a *law*. Behavior is affected in a predictable manner by its consequences. This fact forms the basis of modern principles of child behavior management. Furthermore, being a law, it is not possible to circumvent or repeal it. Whether or not one chooses to apply these principles in a conscious manner, research demonstrates that they do, in fact, influence behavior.

Consider a few examples. Brown and Elliott (1965) studied aggressive behavior in a nursery school class. Physical and verbal aggression were tallied separately. They found that the number of aggressive acts was cut in half when teachers were instructed to ignore aggression and attend only to cooperative behavior. Interestingly, it was very difficult for the teachers to ignore physical aggression so the number of physically aggressive acts almost returned to the original level when compliance with the management plan was no longer monitored by the researchers. The number of verbally aggressive acts continued to decline. Adult attention directed at undesired behavior frequently serves to reward that behavior rather than decrease it, contrary to the expectations of adults. Conversely, academic productivity can be increased when teacher attention is directed at students who are on-task while off-task behavior is ignored (Hall, Lund, & Jackson, 1968; Madsen, Becker, & Thomas, 1968). (see Ross, 1981, p. 211ff; and Ullman & Krasner, 1975, for further discussion).

The behavior of adults who attend to and incidentally reward undesired behavior can also be viewed as learned. In the typical classroom, when a child behaves in a disruptive manner the teacher is distracted from the job of teaching children. To eliminate the distraction and interference, the teacher typically resorts to some sort of verbal admonishment. Usually, the admonishment is effective to the extent that the disruptive child immediately ceases the annoying behavior and the teacher is thereby rewarded (more precisely, negatively reinforced) by the immediate removal of the annoying behavior. Unfortunately, while the teacher has obtained immediate relief, the overall frequency of disruptions, measured over days or weeks, does not necessarily decline. Instead, it may remain constant or even increase if adult attention is rewarding to the disruptive child or children. This is why objective counts of target behaviors play a central role in behavior management programs. Objectively counting occurrences clearly shows what is happening to a particular behavior, and how it is being influenced by adult responses.

Dobson (1970) provides a more humorous example of the same principle. He reports a classroom teacher who would yell and scream at her students when they were uncooperative. When this failed to bring order to the class, she resorted to climbing upon her desk and blowing a whistle. The children enjoyed this so much that they would plot ways to annoy the teacher. One can be fairly certain that such a production got the attention of the children to a sufficient degree that disruptive behavior temporarily ceased, but the overall effect on the classroom climate was to *increase* disruptions and off-task behavior. Thus, because of the effect of child behavior upon adult behavior, it is easy for adults to fall into a pattern in which their behavior has an unintended effect upon the children they wish to teach and manage.

At home, similar patterns of parent-child interaction may develop. Patterson, Cobb, and Ray (1973), for instance, described patterns of parenting observed in the course of research and intervention with families of aggressive boys. One of the parenting patterns they labeled the *diffusion parent.* According to their description, the diffusion parent does not attend to low amplitude aggressive behaviors, such as teasing or yelling, which may be the beginning of a chain of behavior leading to high amplitude aggressive behavior, such as hitting. However, the diffusion parent does respond to high amplitude aggressive behavior by nagging or yelling. The net result is that aggressive behavior continues at a high rate because of the rewarding properties of adult attention. Diffusion parents are characterized by generally poor and inconsistent child management techniques that allow aggression to be rewarded and positive, prosocial behavior to go unrewarded. Thus, the parental reaction to aggressive behavior contributes to its persistence in this type of family. Such mothers also experience great difficulty in changing their patterns of interaction with their children (Wahler, 1980).

It is possible, then, that parent and teacher goals for children's behavior are not always congruent with what they accomplish. Often, this can be due to the rewarding effects of adult attention. In addition, adults are rewarded by the immediate effects of their attention since the annoying behavior of the child temporarily ceases, although it may remain at a high overall frequency. On the other hand, the influence of positive adult attention upon desirable behavior is often not immediately evident. Instead, the positive effects may be observed only over a long period of time as the child slowly acquires complex skills. In order to ensure that children's behavior is consistent with the goal of significant adults such as teachers and parents, it is important that school personnel be thoroughly familiar with the techniques and principles of child behavior management.

Reward and Punishment

Thorndike's early research and observations are mainly of historical interest because much has been learned about human behavior since his time. However, the basis of behavior management remains the same as it was in 1898, when

Thorndike first published his findings. Reward and punishment are still the primary techniques of controlling behavior. As observed by Thorndike, behavior is affected by its consequences, that is, the events that follow it. However, the effect is upon the *future occurrence* of the behavior under the same or similar conditions. Consider a simple example:

A parent is shopping for groceries at the local supermarket. She has with her a somewhat tired 4-year-old. About halfway through the shopping trip, the child begins to cry and whine which is a sure signal to the mother that a tantrum will begin soon, but she decides to ignore the behavior and continues shopping. Minutes later, the crying is louder and the child is kicking and hitting at the grocery cart. In desperation the mother gives the child some candy "to quiet him down." Not surprisingly, the child becomes quiet and the mother is relieved. Both mother and child are "satisfied." However, what has been learned?

While the immediate problem of the child's annoying behavior has been solved, this parent may be on the way toward creating a more difficult problem for the future. The next time that the child is in the same or similar circumstances, the candy reinforcement has made it *more likely* that a tantrum will occur. *Reinforcement following a behavior operates on the likelihood of future occurrences of that behavior under the same or similar circumstances.* The proof that an event is reinforcing lies in demonstrating that the behavior becomes more likely in the future, although it may require several reinforced instances of the behavior for an increase in its likelihood to become apparent. It is the gradual change in the frequency of the behavior that demonstrates the operation of reinforcement.

Punishment operates in a manner similar to reinforcement, but its effect upon behavior is the opposite. When a behavior is followed by an event that is punishing, the chances of the behavior recurring under the same or similar circumstances are decreased. Few examples of the operation of punishment in its "pure" form exist, but consider the curious child who touches and explores everything in sight. Imagine that the child is about to touch a hot dish when his mother says, "No! It's hot!" However, the child ignores the warning and touches the dish anyway receiving a painful burn. The next time the parent gives a warning that something is "hot," the child will be less likely to touch it. This is how punishment operates on behavior.

While punishment is probably the most frequently used method for trying to change child behavior, its use has several problems. As noted in earlier examples, a major problem is that events presumed to be punishing often turn out not to be. Another problem with the exclusive use of punishment is that the behavior problems of children are most often the result of both the *presence* of annoying behavior and the *absence* of desired behavior. Using punishment to eliminate the annoying behavior still leaves the child without the necessary skills to behave appropriately in the problem situation. Thus, the focus of behavior management should usually be upon teaching and rewarding *new* skills. For instance, hyperactive children must typically learn to be less disruptive *and* to exhibit the prosocial skills which they are lacking. Such learning is best accomplished using reinforcement rather than punishment.

Punishment and reinforcement make up the core of child behavior management techniques. The details and terminology of these techniques will be reviewed in Chapters 2, 3, and 4. Before moving to the specifics of behavior management techniques, however, one often neglected aspect of child management will be considered. It concerns the way that adults interact with children.

ASSERTIVE BEHAVIOR AND CHILD MANAGEMENT

Adults are in a position of great authority over children, and they are free to exercise this authority using virtually any style of interaction they choose. At one extreme, it is possible to be very timid, while at the other extreme it is possible to be very aggressive. Of course, neither extreme is optimally effective. In the context of applying behavior management techniques with children, a style that represents the middle ground between these two extremes is necessary. This is known as behaving *assertively*.

Assertive behavior lies in the middle of a continuum of behavioral styles anchored at one end by nonassertion and at the other end by aggression. *Nonassertion* involves violating one's own rights by failing to express honest feelings, thoughts, and beliefs, or expressing one's thoughts and feelings in such a timid, apologetic, diffident, or self-effacing manner that they can easily be disregarded or ignored. Often, behaving nonassertively involves an underlying desire to avoid conflict at all costs, to avoid hurting the feelings of others, or to avoid losing the affection of others. By behaving in such a manner, one indirectly shows lack of self-respect by allowing one's own rights to be violated. One also shows lack of respect for the ability of others to handle disappointment, responsibility, or the consequences of their own behavior.

At the other end of the continuum is *aggression*. Aggression involves directly standing up for one's rights and expressing oneself in ways that are often dishonest, usually inappropriate, and always violate the rights of others. The usual goal of aggressive behavior is domination or winning, accomplished by humiliating, degrading, belittling, or overpowering other people so they become weaker and less able to express and defend their own rights and needs.

In the middle of this continuum of behavioral styles is *assertion*. Assertion involves standing up for one's personal rights and expressing thoughts, feelings, and beliefs in direct, honest, and appropriate ways that do not violate the rights of others. Messages are conveyed without dominating, humiliating, or degrading the other person. Assertive behavior is a positive approach to communication that involves respecting oneself and the adult or child with whom one is communicating.

The adult who behaves assertively is at a distinct advantage over those who behave nonassertively or aggressively. Those who behave nonassertively are likely to find that they are not really in control of their children or classrooms and that their sincere desire to create an effective, pleasant learning environment is not fulfilled. Those who behave aggressively may be in complete control but it is at the expense of their pupils or children who are likely to feel belittled, inferior, uninterested in learning, and perhaps dumb. On the other hand, an assertive style of child management allows for the honest and direct expression of the caretaker's wishes. Rules are clearly stated and consequences of behavior are administered without belittling or insulting the child. In short, the caretaker is responsible for the rules and the child is responsible for his or her behavior.

In order to successfully apply the techniques discussed in this book, an assertive style of behavior is essential. The techniques all involve administration of consequences (reward or punishment) for appropriate or inappropriate behavior. Success is dependent upon clearly and directly stating the rules followed by consistent and firm administration of consequences. If rules are stated apologetically or timidly, the likelihood of their being ignored or violated increases, while the likelihood of successful child management decreases. If one applies these principles in an aggressive manner, the rights and responsibilities of the children are sacrificed. Thus, a prerequisite for successful child management is the willingness and skill to assertively take charge of the children, clearly setting rules and limits for them.

Table 1.1 presents examples of assertive, nonassertive, and aggressive behavior. For those who would like to pursue the topic further, the books by Alberti and Emmons (1978) and Silberman and Wheelan (1980) are recommended.

Table 1.1.   Examples of Assertive, Nonassertive, and Aggressive Characteristics

Assertive	Nonassertive	Aggressive
persistent	evasive	nasty
good listener	flustered	deprecating others
politely refuses requests	too nice	makes accusations
makes clear, direct requests	is taken advantage of	teases others
empathic	creates unclear expectations	tricks, puts down others
honest	inhibited	nags
accepts other's feelings	anxious	gives harsh punishment
fair	self-blaming	hurts others
gives sincere compliments	is treated unfairly	discredits others
accepts compliments	begs	engages in power struggles
active	passive	mean

CHILD RIGHTS, PARENT RIGHTS, AND TEACHER RIGHTS

The word *rights* invokes those qualities of a behavior management program relating to its acceptability from a moral, ethical, or legal perspective. The use of behavior management procedures in the schools demands consideration of a number of issues relating to the rights of the child, the child's parents, and the child's teachers.

In the United States, the foundation upon which human rights are based is the Constitution. Bersoff (1982) points out that the conduct of school administrators and practitioners often "directly and sharply" invokes Constitutional principles. The Constitutional principles that are most often entailed include rights to equal protection under the law, to due process, to privacy, and property rights.

The right to equal protection has been interpreted as meaning that children, regardless of race or handicap, should have equal access to an education at public expense. The right to a free public education has been defined by court decisions as a property right guaranteed by the Constitution.

The due process guarantees of the Constitution prohibit schools from denying access to educational privileges unless procedures are followed that are fundamentally fair and impartial. This includes the process of labeling individual students to provide them access to the rights granted handicapped students. To protect children from the stigma that could result from being labeled *handicapped*, schools are required to follow fair procedures and conduct impartial hearings, in which all interested parties have input into the decision. The need to conduct fair and impartial procedures is largely responsible for the flood of paperwork that accompanies the special education process. The purpose is to create a record, documenting the need for special services and assuring that procedural requirements of fairness and impartiality have been followed.

The remainder of this chapter will be devoted to specific ethical concerns that may be involved in the use of behavior management procedures with schoolchildren.

Rights of the Child

Children are generally not regarded as capable of protecting their own rights. Thus, school practitioners and parents are obligated to do their best to see that the child's rights are adequately protected. With respect to behavior management procedures, just what are some of the important ethical concerns?

Assure That Treatment Is in the Child's Best Interests. The primary ethical concern is to conduct behavior management programs that are in the best interests of children. It is usually desirable that children deport themselves well and complete assigned work. Under most circumstances, it is a simple matter to design behavior management programs for children whose behavior does not meet these standards. However, it is also important to consider whether a behavior management program is truly in a child's best interests. Perhaps the child's behavior would be more acceptable if the other components of the system were modified to accommodate the child's needs rather than vice versa?

A behavior management program also might not be in a child's best interests when conditions outside of the school underlie problem behaviors observed in school. Although it is possible to apply behavior management principles without reference to other underlying problems, doing so could result in outright harm or continuation of a harmful situation. For instance, hyperactivity and inattention are very common behavior problems observed in the classroom. These problems can exist in isolation but have also been associated with childhood depression, sexual and physical abuse, parental divorce, and other family problems. Conducting a behavior management program while ignoring the possibility that more serious problems underlie the child's behavior would certainly not be in his or her best interest. In order to avoid problems such as this, a thorough assessment of the problem situation is needed. A procedure for conducting behavioral assessments is described in Chapter 3.

Behavior Management Programs Should Be Competently Conducted and Effective. Although the basic principles of behavior management are very straightforward and even easy to understand, the more advanced principles that play an important role in many behavior management programs are often not as well understood. For instance, almost all those who teach children have had occasion to implement reward programs involving notes to parents, stickers, access to privileges, or other rewards available within the school. Yet, many of these programs fail because it is not known how to promote generalization of the program, so the desired behavior occurs after the program is discontinued. In addition, practitioners may not know how to modify a program if, at first, it does not succeed.

When a behavior management program is contemplated, the child has a right to competent treatment. That is, the practitioner should be familiar with all the principles that might influence the success of the program, including how to modify the program if it does not work initially and how to discontinue the program while maintaining the behavioral gains. In this book, each program is accompanied by suggested modifications that can be tried if the program does not work initially. Also, each program includes specific techniques for increasing the probability that behavioral gains will continue after the program is discontinued. It is the obligation of those who attempt to use these programs to develop a thorough understanding of both the mechanics of conducting the program and the principles that underlie it.

On a more concrete level, those who employ behavior management techniques should obtain training in both the general principles of learning and the specific techniques they wish to employ. Adequate course work and supervised experience in the application of these techniques to children is needed. Part 1 of the book provides a solid introduction to the basic and advanced principles of behavior management, and those who go on to apply these principles will find more than adequate guidance in Part 2. Yet, the practitioner is obligated to be sure that he or she has developed a solid understanding of the contents of these chapters before attempting to apply what has been learned. In addition, those in the schools should not attempt to conduct interventions that are beyond their competence. The practitioner who does not feel competent to conduct a particular behavior management program should obtain consultation and supervision, try a different approach, or refer the child to individuals who have the needed skills.

A child who is subjected to a behavior management program also has a right to effective treatment. This does not mean that the practitioner must select a procedure that will work the first time it is applied. Rather, it is important that the effects of any behavior management program be monitored carefully. Programs that do not have the predicted effect should be modified.   This implies that a behavior management program should include clearly defined goals and that progress toward these goals should be measurable.

If clear goals are not established, the danger is that a child will be subjected to a management program that does not work yet places a costly burden upon the child such as making up lost instructional time. It is extremely important that a behavior management program that takes away instructional time be cost effective in the sense of improving the child's long term academic success.

Ineffective treatment may also result when the original goal of the behavior management program is not valid. As will be pointed out in subsequent chapters, the current behavior management goal for a child represents a potential solution to problems as they are understood at that time. However, new information may be obtained at any time or a program may be without positive impact. In such a case, a revision of one's understanding of the child's behavior problems may be necessary. The result may be that the approach to remediation also undergoes repeated revision. However, in the long run, the child is spared the costs of being subjected to an ineffective treatment. These costs may range from an inconsequential loss of time to extreme stress resulting from attempts to cope with impossible family situations or academic handicaps such as retardation or a severe learning disability.

Effective intervention also includes constructing a classroom climate that is conducive to behavior change. McClannahan and Krantz (1985) discuss some components of effective learning environments for developmentally disabled children, which are relevant to any child with behavioral problems. First, the activities of both children and instructors need to be scheduled appropriately so that instructional time is maximized. Second, the responsible teacher needs to be present in the instructional area as much as possible. Third, teachers should be selected or trained to have low tolerance for deviant behavior. Instead, when deviant behavior is observed, appropriate instruction to eliminate deviant behavior should be conducted. Fourth, learning environments should be pleasant, in that a high rate of specific, rewarding praise is delivered. Finally, McClannahan and Krantz point out that instructors must be masters of the basic principles of rewarding and shaping behavior.

Children Have a Right to Participate in Decisions About Their Treatment as Much as Possible. Generally, children are assumed to be incapable of knowing what is in their best interests. Consequently, adults make most of the decisions regarding how they should behave and, when behavior goes beyond the limits set by adults, it is their responsibility, not the child's, to determine an appropriate course of action. However, there are several advantages to allowing children to participate in planning of behavior management programs as much as their age and maturity allow.

One clear advantage is that the chances of success increase when the child participates. Even the youngest kindergarten child is capable of expressing preferences for various activities or rewards, which could be very useful if used in the context of behavior management programs. Furthermore, it is even possible that children can contribute to formulating a program's goals. As children become older, the success of a behavior management program may hinge upon the child's successful participation in the initial planning stages. When children reach adolescence, it may be next to impossible to conduct a successful behavior management program in the school without their input. The essence of behavioral contracting, which seems to be the most useful technique with adolescents, is that both parties in the contract are assumed to contribute to the final product. Each side agrees to meet some need of the other party so that the final product specifies the mutual exchange of privileges, rather than the imposition of rules upon the child by adults.

Another advantage of allowing children to participate in planning behavior management programs is that they can learn increased responsibility and independence. Furthermore, their input may lead to revisions of how the child and his or her problems are viewed. This is consistent with the trend to allow children, particularly adolescents, more responsibility in making important decisions and independence from their parents as they near the age of majority.

The Right to Treatment and a Free and Appropriate Public Education. A wide range of behavior problems may be targeted in a behavior management program. At one end of the continuum lie innocuous but slightly annoying behaviors which may disappear when adults begin to ignore them. At the other extreme are serious behavior problems that require detailed assessment, highly structured management programs, and considerable professional time to remediate. The more serious the problem, the greater the likelihood that a successful behavior management program will, at least temporarily, interfere with the child's regular classroom instruction. In general, practitioners must be cautious that behavior management programs either do not interfere with regular classroom instruction or do so to the minimum extent necessary to remediate the behavior problem.

On the other hand, children who show a problem that prevents or interferes with their ability to benefit from regular classroom instruction also have a right to receive an "appropriate" education, which meets their individual needs. This may include even the most structured behavior management programs conducted away from the child's regular classroom. The line that divides the "right" to appropriate treatment from the "right" to be left in the regular classroom free from interference is whether the child can be labeled as *handicapped*.

Children labeled *handicapped* simply have more rights than nonhandicapped children, although these rights are really the prerogatives of the child's parents until age 18. The precise nature and meaning of these rights will be discussed in the next section, Parent Rights. In this section, the focus is upon the issue of where and how behavior management programs are conducted without violating the child's rights.

It seems that the best way to approach this issue is to proceed from the simplest to the most complex situations with regard to both the nature of the behavior problem and the behavior management program employed to remediate it. Typically, the simplest case that might require a behavior management program would involve the classroom teacher who identifies a behavior problem and takes steps, independent of other school personnel, to remediate it. Such steps could range from imposition of a more structured approach to classroom discipline to employing a simple behavior management program targeted at the individual child. Teachers, acting independently within their own classrooms, are generally considered to have the freedom to plan and implement interventions to improve the academic performance and behavior of their students.

When a child is singled out for special attention, even while remaining within the regular classroom, the nature, severity, and resistance to change of the problem behavior become important considerations. Some problems such as autism, severe childhood depression, cerebral palsy, retardation, and learning disabilities that interfere with educational progress would make the child eligible for special services as a handicapped child. When such a child is found, a complete psychological and educational evaluation must be completed (if the child's parents consent) to determine the child's needs and how they can be met by the school district. The individual teacher's principal will be able to assist in making the appropriate referral and starting the process of identification, if it is needed. Some problems do not, in themselves, create a need for handicapped services and the initial attempt to remediate them should be made in a regular classroom. This would include many of the common discipline problems faced by the classroom teacher, such as being off-task, not completing assignments, and disruptive behavior.

The severity of a behavior problem depends upon such considerations as its intensity, duration, frequency, and the degree to which it disrupts the class. Less severe problems are likely to be resolved within the classroom without a need for handicapped services. The most severe problems may require immediate attention of those who provide services to the handicapped. This is especially true if the behavior interferes to a significant degree with the education of other children or is dangerous to the child or others. Within these extremes are behavior problems that are annoying, may interfere with normal classroom functioning, and occur fairly often, but that do not clearly fall into either the "minor problem" or "handicapped" categories.

These children often need formal behavior management programs conducted within the regular classroom. This can be very difficult for a busy teacher working with a classroom of 20-30 students. Adding to the complexity of this situation is that it is unknown whether the student will eventually need services for handicapped students. Consequently, it is important to be aware of the child's right to remain in a regular classroom, if possible, and the right to receive special services for handicapped children, if they are needed. What this amounts to is a double bind, in which the best solution is to document what is done in attempting to solve the problem and to establish contact with the child's parents.

Regardless of the circumstances, behavior management programs that result in the child being treated differently than other children in the classroom should probably be conducted with the active cooperation of the child's parents. Procedures which employ home-based rewards (see Chapter 10) are a very effective method of actively involving parents. In addition, detailed records of attempts to remediate a problem should be kept. These records should describe the behavior management program and its effects upon the problem behavior. This documentation will be very useful in establishing whether a need for handicapped services exists.

If a behavior management program has been implemented for a reasonable period of time, appropriate modifications have been attempted, and positive changes have not occurred, it would be prudent for the classroom teacher to obtain the consultation of the school's principal, a special education teacher, or a school psychologist. At this point, numerous options are available, some of which would invoke student rights as spelled out in Public Law 94-142. These options would basically begin with a thorough assessment of the problem behavior by special education personnel and would require the informed written consent of the child's parents. Following assessment, the special education team, including the child's parents, would determine whether a need for special services for handicapped children exists. If such a need is found, the team would then determine the best way to meet that need.

Another option, prior to special education assessment is for consultants to assist the classroom teacher in managing the behavior problem within the classroom. However, there is still the double bind of deciding whether it is more appropriate to maintain the child in a regular classroom versus providing handicapped services, if they are needed. There is no simple resolution to this situation. However, thoroughly documented efforts to resolve the problem within the regular education classroom are consistent with Public Law 94-142, which states that education for handicapped children should take place in the "least restrictive environment" available to meet that child's needs.

What this means is that handicapped children should be educated with non-handicapped children to the maximum extent possible and that removal from the regular classroom should occur only when education in regular classes cannot be achieved satisfactorily due to the nature or severity of the handicap. Documented attempts to resolve the problem within the regular classroom, which involve parents to the greatest extent possible, are probably the best way to ensure that this provision of the law has been satisfied. In rare instances, parents will refuse to cooperate with intervention efforts or allow school practitioners to intervene with a behavior problem. In such cases, consultation at the highest levels of school administration may be necessary to determine an acceptable course of action.

To summarize briefly, behavioral interventions can be considered to take place at three different levels within a classroom environment. At the first level are interventions conducted by the classroom teacher as part of normal discipline procedures. At the second level are interventions that focus on a particular child, who is treated at least somewhat differently than other children in the class. At the third level are interventions that are performed as part of a plan developed to meet the needs of a handicapped child who is in a regular classroom for at least part of the school day. While a child's rights are important at all three levels of intervention, they become more clearly articulated at the second and third levels because of the actual or potential need for services for the handicapped.

The next section, on parents' rights, will provide a detailed review of the rights of handicapped children and their parents. This discussion will clarify many of the issues already introduced.

Parent Rights

Children themselves have few rights, except those allowed them by adults. For the most part, prior to age 18, a child's educational rights are held by their parents or guardian. The clearest articulation of these rights is included in Public Law 94-142, The Education of All Handicapped Children Act. An abridged copy of the rules and regulations for the implementation of this act is included as Appendix C of Reynolds and Gutkin (1982). What follows is a discussion of parent rights as described in Public Law 94-142. While it is possible to conduct most behavior management programs without involving the child in services for handicapped children, a significant number will directly involve such services and they will at least be considered in the majority of the other cases.

The Right to a Free and Appropriate Public Education in the Least Restrictive Environment. This right is the central feature of Public Law 94-142, which is essentially a grant-giving statute that contributes toward the cost of educating handicapped children. A handicapped child is one who has been evaluated in accordance with accepted procedures and found to be mentally retarded, hard of hearing, deaf, speech impaired, visually handicapped, seriously emotionally disturbed, orthopedically impaired, other health impaired, deaf-blind, multi-handicapped, or as having specific learning disabilities and who needs special education or related services. As noted in later chapters, almost any of these handicaps may be a causal factor when a child's behavior in school leads to contemplation of a behavior management program. Some of these conditions would contraindicate behavior management approaches until the precise nature of the child's handicap is understood and other strategies have been implemented.

For instance, the academic performance of a child with an undiagnosed hearing deficit is not likely to improve when a behavior management program to improve academic performance is implemented. Instead, medical intervention should be given priority. Thus, it is always important to remember that a behavior management program is only one of several potential responses to problem behavior. Another way of responding is to conduct a more detailed assessment to determine whether another handicapping problem exists, which is interfering with academic progress. This problem is discussed in greater depth in Chapters 3 and 6. However, when a child experiences difficulty in school, one possibility is that the child is handicapped. Public Law 94-142, related regulations, and court decisions have established that a handicapped child has a *right* to a free and appropriate public education. This right is balanced by procedural safeguards designed to prevent the mislabeling of a child as handicapped when, in fact, no handicap exists.

Although the appearance of problem behavior may be a signal that any of a number of problems may exist, the most likely category of handicap for a child with behavioral problems is seriously emotionally disturbed. The definition of *seriously emotionally disturbed* in the regulations of Public Law 94-142 covers a fairly broad range of conditions, which have existed "over a long period of time and to a marked degree." These conditions include an inability to learn not explainable by other factors, an inability to establish or maintain satisfactory interpersonal relationships with peers and teachers, inappropriate behavior or feelings, unhappiness or depression, and physical symptoms or fears associated with personal or school problems. This definition includes schizophrenic children but not those who are autistic. The latter are categorized as other health impaired.

The definition of seriously emotionally disturbed includes a very broad range of childhood behaviors, many of which might be considered as potential targets of behavior management programs. Consequently, when a behavior management program is contemplated, it is possible that the child may be handicapped and therefore in need of special services for the handicapped. The key to the process of identifying and serving handicapped children is the Individualized Education Program, or IEP. Once a potentially handicapped child is identified and evaluated, the education team writes a statement of how that child is functioning in school, a statement of goals for improving that level of functioning, and a statement of what special education services the child will be receiving. The resulting document is the IEP. The process of evaluating a child and writing the IEP must actively involve the child's parents in a number of ways that will be discussed in the next section. Of greater importance in the present context is to discuss the concept of least restrictive environment as it applies to special education.

While it is true that Public Law 94-142 mandates that all handicapped children be identified and served, this requirement is balanced by a requirement that special education take place in the least restrictive environment. This means that handicapped children must be educated with nonhandicapped children to the maximum extent possible. In addition, handicapped children are to be removed from the regular education environment and placed in a special class only when the nature or severity of the handicap is such that education in a regular classroom with supplementary aids and services cannot be achieved satisfactorily.

Behavior management programs can be very important techniques for educating handicapped children in the least restrictive environment. This is especially true for children who may be labeled *seriously emotionally disturbed.* Their IEPs could be written to include behavioral goals to be accomplished using formal behavior management programs. Furthermore, by using a behavior management program prior to the formal assessment process, it may be possible to avoid labeling the child as handicapped at all. Although the right to receive services, if needed, is important, the bias of placement should be toward the least restrictive environment, which would imply that placement is to be avoided, if needs can be met in the regular education environment. A well-designed behavior management program may play a crucial role in keeping the child with behavior problems in a less restrictive environment.

Parental Rights to Participate in the Entire Process of Identifying and Placing Handicapped Children. Basically, Public Law 94-142 and its associated regulations require that a child's parents be an integral part of the team that makes decisions about the child. Their participation begins when the child is initially identified as potentially needing special services. Before an evaluation can be carried out to determine whether the child is handicapped in some way, the informed, voluntary, written consent of the child's parents is necessary. By informed, it is meant that the parents are made fully aware of the purposes of the evaluation. By voluntary, it is meant that no benefit to the child may be made a condition of providing consent. Finally, the consent must be in writing and describe the evaluation activity that the school district intends to perform.

Once consent for an evaluation has been obtained, the evaluation itself must conform to high standards. The instruments employed must be selected and administered so as not to be racially or culturally biased. Instruments must be administered in the child's native language or other mode of communication, unless this is impossible. Instruments must be valid, administered by trained people, focus on the child's individual needs, and be administered so as to ensure that any sensory impairments do not adversely affect the results, unless the effects of the sensory impairment are being measured. In addition, evaluations must not depend upon the results of a single assessment procedure, must be performed by a multidisciplinary team, and must assess all areas related to the suspected disability, "including, where appropriate, health, vision, hearing, social and emotional status, general intelligence, academic performance, communicative status, and motor abilities" (Reynolds & Gutkin, 1982, Appendix C, p. 1153).

It is up to the professional who is considering a behavior management program to determine the extent to which parental rights are invoked. If it is believed that the eventual result may be a placement in special education, then the practitioner should be cognizant of parental rights at all times. Assessment activities should be delayed until written consent from the parents has been obtained. It would seem prudent to gain parental cooperation and have at least oral permission to conduct any preassessment interventions. This would be especially important if the behavior management program generates written documentation. Informal behavior management programs that do not result in a record of behavioral observations would not be as likely to invoke parental special education rights.

As the process of special education placement continues beyond the preplacement assessment, parental rights to have input into the process also continue. Briefly, these rights include the right to consent to or refuse special education placement for their child; the right to obtain an independent educational evaluation, should they disagree with the results of the school's evaluation; the right to know where their child's records are kept and to know who has access to them; the right to be notified when a change in a special education program or placement is considered; the right to participate in two progress report meetings each year and to participate in future education planning for their child; the right to have their child's records maintained confidentially; and finally, if the child's parents and the school district disagree with actions that are proposed, the parents have a right to request a due process hearing conducted by an impartial officer with free or low cost legal services made available.

The practice of behavior management in schools invokes numerous considerations of both parental and student rights. There are a mass of statutes, court decisions, and generally recognized principles that can influence the practice of those who wish to conduct behavior management programs in the schools. However, as with many complicated endeavors, adherence to a few simple principles can help greatly in avoiding potential pitfalls. With respect to the use of behavior management programs in schools, I suggest that the following be kept firmly in mind and that, when some doubt arises, consultation with experts be sought before any program is begun:

1. Do not conduct procedures that have the potential to deny educational privileges to a child.

2. Use procedures that are effective. More specifically, keep track via formal data collection or informal observations of the results of any behavior management program that goes beyond normal classroom procedures.
3. Begin with the simplest behavior management procedures and proceed to more complex procedures only if they are needed. When initial programs fail, consider whether the child might be categorized as seriously emotionally dis-turbed, therefore being in need of special services for the handicapped.
4. Seek the active cooperation of parents in behavior management programs. If parents balk at the implementation of a particular program, obtain consultation.
5. When detailed assessment of the child seems warranted, obtain parental permission, consult with special education staff, and assemble an assessment team before proceeding. At this stage the child's parents should be actively involved.
6. Always remember that behavior management programs are to be conducted in the interest of serving a child with problems at school.
7. Allow the child to participate in the planning of the behavior management program to the maximum extent possible.

Rights of Teachers

Teachers are at the core of the educational process. It is important that those supervising or directly implementing behavior management programs, including teachers themselves, be aware of the needs of classroom teachers. One of the basic rights of teachers is to have a classroom environment free from disruptions that consistently interfere with teaching. Even Public Law 94-142 states that when a handicapped child is so disruptive in a regular classroom that the education of other children is seriously impaired, placement in a regular classroom would not be considered appropriate. Thus, it should never be necessary for a teacher to sacrifice the educational progress of the majority of students in a classroom to the needs of a single student.

Behavior management programs should generally be simple but effective. Teachers are frequently the administrators of behavior management programs. When asked to fulfill this role, all who are involved should be aware that teachers cannot afford to be burdened with complicated record-keeping procedures or time-consuming programs that decrease instructional time for the remainder of the class. If a program is needed that requires detailed monitoring of the child's behavior, removal of the child from the classroom, or physical control to prevent injury to the child or others, it must be questioned whether a regular classroom is the appropriate setting for that child. Instead, a referral to special education personnel, such as the school psychologist, or hiring of a classroom aid is needed.

Another right of teachers is to have their opinions and impressions respected. This is important for both teachers themselves and those school practitioners who work outside the regular classroom to remember. For those who work outside the classroom, it is important to remember that a child's classroom teacher has had more hours of contact with the student than any other person in the school. Therefore, the teacher is likely to be a very valuable source of information whose participation should be actively sought in the process of planning behavioral interventions. For teachers themselves, it would be important to remember that the best interests of the child may not be served unless the time and effort are taken to add their input into the planning process. Even if a teacher is unfamiliar with the technical aspects of a particular behavior management program, his or her knowledge of the child can save time and effort and greatly improve the team's chances of successfully remediating the problem.

In sum, the classroom teacher is an invaluable part of the team when behavior management programs are implemented. Both those who work in the classroom and those who come into the system from outside the classroom must cooperate to the greatest extent possible to ensure the maximum chances of successfully remediating problem behavior. Mastery of the basic principles and specific procedures of behavior management by all who work in school systems can contribute greatly to the overall academic and personal success of children in school.

SUMMARY AND PLAN OF THE BOOK

The first half of this chapter was aimed at presenting a general introduction to the principles of learning and behavior management. The principles of learning were illustrated with examples of the use of reinforcement and punishment. It was also pointed out that, often, adults behave in ways that lead to unplanned effects upon children's behavior. Thorough knowledge and skillful application of behavior management techniques may be helpful in avoiding such occurrences. It was also argued that skillful application of behavior management techniques requires an assertive personal style of interacting with children. The remainder of the chapter discussed the rights of parents, children, and teachers, focusing on Public Law 94-142, The Education for All Handicapped Children Act of 1975, which has a ubiquitous influence on the conduct of school personnel.

The remainder of the book is divided into two parts. Part 1 consists of this chapter plus Chapters 2, 3, 4, and 5. Chapters 2 and 4 present an overview of the basic theoretical principles of behavior management. Chapter 3 presents general step-by-step procedures for assessing and managing problem behavior. Chapter 5 is concerned with cultivating positive relationships with parents, who are viewed as playing a key role in the management of problem behavior. Chapter 5 also discusses the effects of family conflict on the behavior of children.

Part 2 begins with a chapter on the specific problem areas likely to be encountered by school personnel. This chapter covers a broad range of problem behaviors including hyperactivity, childhood depression, childhood alcoholism, and child abuse. The purpose of the chapter is not only to introduce the behavior problems which can be effectively dealt with using behavior management strategies, but also to discuss other common problems that might interfere with school performance such as child abuse and family alcoholism. These latter problems require both school and family intervention for satisfactory resolution and can interfere with the success of behavior management programs conducted in the school.

chapter 2

BASIC PRINCIPLES OF CHILD MANAGEMENT AND BEHAVIOR MODIFICATION

The purpose of this chapter is to introduce the basic principles of child behavior management. Three topics are covered: child development, basic techniques of managing behavior, and use versus misuse of punishment.

BASIC PRINCIPLES OF CHILD DEVELOPMENT

Development refers to the marvelous process of growing. It begins when a child is born as a totally dependent organism and does not end until death. Child behavior management should be viewed in a developmental context for two reasons. First, one's view of problem behavior needs to be tempered with knowledge of what is appropriate at each age level. For example, a high rate of activity and short attention span are typical of preschool children but might be considered a problem in a fourth-grade child. In addition, a child's ability to interpret particular situations, such as parental divorce, will be different at the various developmental stages. This, in turn, will lead to different expressions of that problem in the child's behavior. An awareness of developmental issues will enable the practitioner to interpret behavior more accurately.

A second reason for maintaining a developmental perspective in child behavior management is that behavior management techniques vary widely in complexity. If one indiscriminately applies techniques without considering the age of the child, some unnecessary failures are likely to result. In selecting an appropriate behavior management strategy, the age and intellectual ability of the child must be considered. Complex procedures with long delays between behavior and its consequences are generally most appropriate for older children. Simple procedures with concrete and immediate consequences are generally most appropriate when managing the behavior of younger children.

The goal of this section is to acquaint the reader with a few basic generalities of child development via the theories of Piaget, Erikson, and Kohlberg. This information is presented to provide a perspective on applying child management techniques across the age span.

Early Childhood

Early childhood runs from about age 1 to age 6 or 7. At the beginning of this period, the child begins to walk without being supported and to say his or her first words. By the end of this period, the child is showing adultlike motor skills, has a vocabulary of about 3,000 words, and is learning to read and work simple arithmetic problems in school. In terms of the child's cognitive development, that is, the ability to think and reason, the child progresses from being extremely concrete to being able to use abstract symbols within this time span.

According to Piaget, cognitive growth from birth to age 2 is characterized by learning that objects are permanent, that is, they are still sought even when they can not be seen, and that actions have consequences. As children get older, they become capable of using symbols (language) to represent objects in the world, but they do not have the skill to mentally retrace or reverse a physical demonstration so as to derive logical conclusions about it.

Erik Erikson views a child's psychosocial development as a series of stages in which successful adjustment depends upon the previous stages. In early childhood, the child must resolve three issues: trust versus mistrust, autonomy versus shame and doubt, and initiative versus guilt. Positive resolution of these issues means that the children acquire the beliefs that their mother, and eventually others, will love and care for them, that they are competent and in control of themselves and their fate, and that they can initiate activities and carry them through to completion. According to this theory successful adult adjustment depends upon the feelings of trust, competence, and initiative that develop during childhood. Obviously, parents play a key role in fostering successful adjustment.

Kohlberg's theory proposes three levels of moral development. In the first level, which consists of two stages, rules are set down by others and the goodness or badness of actions are determined by their physical consequences. The emphasis of the child is upon his or her own needs, although the beginnings of the concepts of fairness and reciprocity are present in some actions taking place in the second stage. Again, it must be apparent that parents and other caretakers influence the moral development of the child via their role as rulemakers and providers of rewards and punishment.

The common theme that emerges from the theories of Piaget, Erikson, and Kohlberg is the importance of the child's concrete and observable interactions with his or her environment in early childhood. Through such interactions the child develops cognitively, socially, and morally. Consequently, the types of behavior management programs likely to be successful with children in early childhood would emphasize concrete goals, immediate consequences, and material rewards.

In contrast, one would predict that most children in early childhood would not respond well to programs with long delays or complicated relationships between behavior and rewards. Subtle moral arguments, such as the difference between "accidental" actions and "purposeful" actions are not likely to be understood, only the physical consequences that result from actions. Thus, in planning a behavior management program for a child showing frequent aggressive behavior, one would not be likely to find success if an attempt was made to discriminate among the various circumstances that lead to aggression. Basically, all aggressive acts should meet with the same consequences. As the child's cognitive skills grow, more complicated social skills can be learned. The young child is dealing with social issues on a much more basic and concrete level than adults.

Middle Childhood

Middle childhood can be loosely defined as encompassing the time between ages 7 and 12. This is a period dominated by development in the social arena provided by schoolmates. School and school-related activities occupy much of the child's time. Physical development is relatively quiescent compared to the changes that will dominate the child's adolescent years. The emerging theme of this period concerns the child's increasing mastery and understanding of the physical environment.

Piaget calls the period from 7 to 11 years the *concrete operations stage*. It refers to a period in which the child can perform many complex mental operations but is restricted to performing them upon concrete objects, which can be handled or imagined. Children in this stage are capable of retracing their thoughts, correcting themselves, and mentally reversing operations. They now realize that a change in the shape or container of a substance does not alter the amount that is present, and they can focus on more than one dimension or aspect of an object in drawing conclusions about it.

Socially, according to Erikson's theory, the child within this age-span must resolve the issue of developing a sense of industry versus a sense of inferiority. A sense of industry is characterized by development of basic competence through social and academic experiences. The key event is entry into school where the child is exposed to the technology of our industrialized society. Success at mastering the social and academic tasks presented by school produces a sense of competency, mastery, and industry that encourages the child to do things well and take projects through to completion. Failure at these tasks produces a sense of incompetency and inadequacy. The child will then not conform with society's expectations and will experience great difficulty during adolescence.

According to Kohlberg, moral development in middle childhood continues to be strongly influenced by the consequences of actions. That is, the experiences of rewards and punishments shape the child's "morality." However, as the child approaches adolescence, internal standards (rules) of right and wrong begin to develop, but they are based primarily upon approval of other individuals, family, and society.

Thus, the theme in the middle years of childhood is the growing cognitive ability of the child and how it interacts with the increasingly complex environment to which the child is exposed. Yet, a great dependence upon external experience still exists so the child is greatly influenced by environmental events rather than internal rules, standards, and reasoning. What are the implications for development of behavior management programs?

First, more complex behavior management procedures can be employed. This would include fairly complex token reward programs in which the child earns points for good behavior that can be exchanged for various material rewards. Home note programs, in which the child's teacher rates classroom behavior on a daily or weekly basis and the child's parents provide rewards contingent upon the quality of the ratings, are also likely to be effective. Second, it has been my experience that it is important to "reach" troubled children at this stage to help them control their behavior within the bounds set by society. Many adolescents referred for severe behavior problems have histories extending to their middle childhood. Unfortunately, at adolescence, it is very difficult from a practical and legal standpoint for behavioral control to be exercised by schools. For children of middle childhood, the entire range of common behavior management procedures is likely to be effective if appropriate individual adjustments are made. Consequently, one might predict the greatest behavior management success with pre-adolescent children.

Adolescence

Adolescence has often been characterized as a period of great "storm and stress" in a child's life. The period runs from about age 13 to young adulthood or when the child leaves home to work, attend college, or marry. Great physical changes occur within this time span, as the child approaches physical and sexual maturity.

According to Piaget's notions, the 11- or 12-year-old enters the stage of formal operations. In contrast to the concrete operations stage in which the child's thought processes are tied to concrete events, the child in the formal operations stage becomes capable of abstract, logical thinking and hypothesis testing. When this stage is achieved, the child's thinking resembles that of the scientist, who generates theories and then tests them against reality. With the development of these skills, the adolescent becomes capable of pondering such problems as what others are thinking and moral or political issues, all from a variety of perspectives.

The culmination of psychosocial development, in Erikson's view, is the resolution of the crisis of finding an identity versus experiencing role confusion. The task at this stage is to integrate all of the roles that are taken by the child (son or daughter, friend, student, etc.) into a single identity. The term *identity crisis* has often been used to characterize the indecisiveness of this period. Societal, peer, and family demands all tend to force the adolescent to consider a variety of roles while making educational and occupational decisions. Negative outcomes at this stage include making an early decision regarding one's identity (foreclosure), thereby not experimenting with the variety of available roles, or failing to evolve an integrated identify (identity confusion).

Adolescent moral development, according to Kohlberg, parallels cognitive development. The two levels of moral development through which the adolescent may pass are the conventional and postconventional levels. The conventional level, as noted earlier, is marked by the adoption of rules that derive from external sources, such as society, peers, and family. In the postconventional level the individual follows ethical principles rather than rules.

Moral reasoning at all levels of Kohlberg's sequence is likely to be shown by any individual. The important developmental theme is the reliance upon externally imposed rules, which occurs in early childhood, as contrasted with the ability to view a situation from the perspective of internal ethical standards, which occurs in adolescence. The unfortunate fact is that some individuals fail to develop any sense of internal moral standards and tend to respond to either the immediately obvious, externally imposed restrictions upon behavior or to virtually no standards at all. These children represent a great challenge to the school system, often requiring firm consistent consequences for behavior carried out over exceedingly long periods of time (see Shaw, 1983, for a discussion). Such programs are likely to require very concrete contingencies and goals as might be typically employed with children in early or middle childhood.

Adolescents, whether or not they have developed internal standards of conduct congruent with societal expectations, will normally have developed advanced cognitive skills. Along with advanced cognitive skills comes a desire for independence from adults. Consequently, adolescents are likely to respond best to programs in which they have a major say. Probably the most common approach with adolescents is behavioral contracting. The key element in such contracts from the adolescent's perspective is that it allows them input into the process. In fact, good behavioral contracts specify that both parties signing the contract are to both receive and grant privileges to the other party. With this technique the adolescent has the opportunity to effect changes in his or her own behavior as well as in significant others. Behavioral contracts, then, are appropriate to the advanced skills of this age group.

School Readiness

Although the above mentioned theorists provide a picture of how one might expect a child's cognitive skills to develop, it is important in this context to consider some of the specific behaviors a child needs to succeed in school. Many educators place a great deal of emphasis upon the notion of "readiness." Readiness refers to having the prerequisite skills to begin benefitting from formal instruction. Staats (1971) named the generic set of skills necessary to benefit from academic instruction *the basic behavioral repertoire.* The repertoire consists of the attention-discrimination behaviors necessary for school success. More specifically, in order to learn the facts presented in school, such as the letters of the alphabet, a child must acquire the habit of attending to the relevant information. This means responding to requests such as *look* or *listen* in order to see a letter or hear its name pronounced. This task is more difficult than it may seem, because it is not obvious from the child's point of view that the lines representing a letter are the stimuli to which he or she is supposed to attend. The shape of the paper, tone of voice, toys that are in sight, an itch, or anything else the child can see, hear, or touch are all competing with the letter for the child's attention.

Fortunately, even the very young child's environment is full of tasks that require attention to particular stimuli so that the typical child has learned to attend to stimuli on command before entering school. Parents help this learning process when they teach their child to pick up toys, catch a ball, pull up a pair of pants, or any of the numerous other learning tasks that face the preschooler.

Many educators, however, place a great emphasis upon the concepts of readiness and "maturity" in dealing with the problems that children face in school. The question is how to view the skills that signal readiness and maturity. On the one hand, they are certainly related to the age of the child, and some skills appear without any noticeable environmental input. At the same time, some of these skills are at least partly the result of learning. The most important thing to remember is that assigning a label to a problem can have some helpful implications, but the labeling process itself does not accomplish anything. Thus, if the behavior of a child is labeled *immature* or a child is deemed *not ready for school,* what are the implications for the concerned school staff member?

First, the labels *immature* and *not ready* both imply that if nothing is done, the child will eventually grow out of the problem. The implied "treatment" is to delay the child's entrance into school, retain the child in a grade, or repeat part of a grade. School personnel on the assessment team are then charged with the task of determining as best they can whether this prediction is correct. Thorough assessment that looks at many alternative explanations of the child's behavior is probably the only method of pursuing this question. Unfortunately, the existing research on the problem of retention is not very helpful in assisting the assessment team with its decision.

Generally, the research does not indicate that retention results in much benefit for the child in terms of the learning that takes place in the second year of the repeated grade. Only 20-35% of retained children learn more in the second year than they did in the first year. That is, only about one-third of retained students "blossom" during that second year (Rose, Medway, Cantrell, & Marus, 1983). Furthermore, methods of distinguishing those who might benefit from retention from those who are unlikely to benefit are not available at present.

Faced with a decision regarding retention or delayed entry into school, the assessment team has the responsibility of carefully examining both the skill level of the child and attitudes of parents and teachers toward the retention. An assessment of the child's skills is crucial to determining what skills are lacking and how they can be remediated. Teacher and parental attitudes toward the potential retention are important because of their impact upon the child's view of the situation. Every effort must be made to assure that the child's self-concept is not negatively affected by retention or delayed entry into school. Also, if a problem exists that prevents regular classroom instruction from being effective for that child, retention will not be effective. This would include behavior problems severe enough to interfere with classroom performance. Generally, retention is not recommended for handicapped children (e.g., Carstens, 1985; Germain & Merlo, 1985).

Alternately, the assessment team should consider whether some type of direct intervention might be more helpful than retention. Intervention might consist of a behavior management program, changes in the classroom environment, individual tutoring, or practice of academic skills at home. If the child's readiness skills are weak, a direct focus on improving readiness skills may be more valuable than waiting for the child to grow out of the problem.

The Place of a Developmental Perspective in Child Management

The goal of the preceding discussion was to show the differences between the cognitive skills of adults and children. It is common in our culture to see children as being very similar to adults. Television shows and movies in particular seem to put the reasoning and observation powers of adults into the mouths of children. This may be good for laughs, but it is not necessarily good for children to be viewed in this way. Children are not miniature adults. They view the world very differently from adults. Thus, it is valuable to remember the developmental sequences so that adult expectations do not exceed the child's capabilities. The three theories that were discussed are useful because they point out both the capabilities and limitations of children at various ages.

However, it is important that the parent or teacher does not become too tightly bound by the expectations elicited by each successive stage of development. Theories that use stages to describe the growth and development of children are very useful, but it must always be remembered that progression from stage to stage does not necessarily occur automatically. Active interaction with the environment is almost always a requirement for growth. A frequent tendency is to attribute child behavior to "stages" such as the "terrible twos." The problem with using a stage as an explanation is that nothing has been explained. The behavior has been labeled and nothing more. Unfortunately, attributing behavior to a stage sometimes encourages a parent or teacher to wait for the child to grow into the next stage rather than take an active role in determining the child's behavior.

Another problem with stage theories and tables of "normal" development that give "average" ages for various developmental milestones is that they can be very misleading if taken too seriously. In actuality, children develop at widely different rates and any individual child will be very unlikely to match any "normal" pattern of growth in all areas. When there is doubt concerning a child's development, the school's psychologist or a special education teacher is qualified to answer any questions about the child. As behavioral interventions are being planned for a child, it is probably wise to consider both the child's mental and chronological ages.

It is up to the parent or teacher to determine an appropriate compromise between waiting for the child to develop and challenging the child with tasks that are consistently too difficult. Many of the principles and techniques discussed in this book enable adults to maintain an appropriate compromise. First, the child is almost always sensitive to the influence of reward and punishment, so that it is generally possible to increase the frequency of desired behavior. Second, the techniques of shaping behavior and teaching chains of behavior enable the adult caretaker to teach children complicated tasks in steps that may challenge them but not cause frustration. Sound judgement reinforced by some basic knowledge of the typical child's capabilities will enable adults to foster the growth and accomplishment of their students and children. For more detailed treatments of child development see Miller (1983), Newman and Newman (1979), Thomas (1979), or any recent textbook in the area.

FOUR BASIC TECHNIQUES OF ALTERING OR MAINTAINING A BEHAVIOR

The skillful management of child behavior involves knowledge of child development, systems theory, and the principles of behavior management. The general principles of behavior management are explained in this section.

Two terms require definition before this task is undertaken. The terms are *stimulus* and *contingency*. Stimulus refers to any perceivable event in a child's environment. A stimulus can be a sound, movement, picture, verbal command, buzzing fly, itch, tap on the shoulder, word on a printed page or chalkboard, or anything else to which the child can respond in some observable way. Stimuli may be considered either appetitive or aversive. An appetitive stimulus is one that the child is likely to seek out, especially if a need for that stimulus is present. Food, especially sweets and snacks, are the best examples of appetitive stimuli. An aversive stimulus is one that the child would usually avoid. Aversive stimuli are typically painful to experience. Examples of aversive stimuli would be a spanking or the sensation that results from touching a hot stove.

Contingency refers to a rule describing the relationship between behavior and an event or consequence. For instance, if a child receives a painful burn after touching a hot stove, it could be said that the burn is contingent upon touching the stove. A contingency can be either positive or negative. A positive contingency means that a stimulus is *added* to the situation contingent upon some behavior. For example, if a child receives a sticker for producing a perfect paper in school, it could be said that the contingency was positive because the sticker was *added* to the situation contingent upon the child's behavior. On the other hand, contingencies can also be negative. A negative contingency indicates that a stimulus is *subtracted* from the situation contingent upon a behavior. For example, if a child loses dessert for misbehaving at the dinner table, it could be said that the contingency was negative because the dessert was *subtracted* from the situation contingent upon the child's behavior.

Figure 2.1 shows how the two types of stimuli and the two types of contingencies can be combined into four methods of altering or maintaining the frequency of a behavior. These four techniques are the core of behavior management techniques. All the techniques of behavior management, no matter how complex, are related to these four methods and derive their effectiveness from one of these effects on behavior. Note that it is the *relationship* between a stimulus and behavior — that is, the contingency — which determines how behavior will be affected. The effect upon behavior is indicated within each cell of the figure. These four core techniques, positive reinforcement, punishment, negative punishment, and negative reinforcement, will be discussed.

Figure 2.1.   Contingencies for Changing Behavior

| | STIMULUS | |
	Appetitive	Aversive
Positive Contingency	POSITIVE REINFORCEMENT (increases behavior)	(POSITIVE) PUNISHMENT (decreases behavior)
Negative	NEGATIVE PUNISHMENT (decreases behavior)	NEGATIVE REINFORCEMENT (increases behavior)

The four methods of modifying behavior can be summarized in a 2 × 2 table which specifies the stimulus type and contingency. The stimulus type is either appetitive (e.g., food, money, attention) or aversive (e.g., pain, a spanking) and the contingency is either positive (the stimulus is presented, that is, added to the situation) or negative (the stimulus is removed or subtracted from the situation).

Positive Reinforcement

Positive reinforcement means to *present* or add an appetitive stimulus contingent upon a child's behavior. This is the most useful of the four techniques and the one that should be used most frequently by anyone involved in planning or implementing behavior management programs for children. The effect upon behavior is to *increase* the probability that the reinforced behavior will occur in the future under the same or similar circumstances. Consider a simple example. If a child is presented with a piece of candy each time he or she raises his or her hand, one would predict that the hand raising would occur with increasing frequency until the child was stuffed with candy.

Unfortunately, it is not always possible to predict with absolute certainty that presentation of a particular appetitive stimulus will increase behavior. For this reason, it is necessary to observe the effects of a stimulus upon behavior before one can state whether that stimulus was positively reinforcing. The problem is that the effects of a particular stimulus depend upon the particular child's experiences with it. For instance, some children do not like certain types of candy. If the child does not desire the reinforcer, then behavior will not increase when the opportunity to earn that reinforcer is made available. Thus, the question of whether a particular stimulus is positively reinforcing is a question that can only be answered with certainty when its effects on behavior are known. The need for empirical verification of the effects of a stimulus and contingency upon behavior is true for all four behavior management techniques.

Punishment

To punish a behavior means to *present* an aversive stimulus when that behavior occurs. It would be appropriate to call this technique *positive punishment* because the contingency is positive, a stimulus is being *presented* when a particular behavior occurs. The predicted effect is that the behavior will *decrease* in frequency. A typical example would be use of a spanking to decrease behavior. If a spanking is effective, then the punished behavior will be less likely to occur after the spanking. However, for reasons to be discussed later, I do not recommend spankings, or any painful method, for reducing the frequency of behavior. There are effective nonpainful methods of decreasing behavior and aversive or painful events do not always decrease behavior because other contingencies may be simultaneously influencing behavior. In fact, more serious problems can be the result of using a painful aversive stimulus.

Negative Punishment

If the contingency is negative, a stimulus is *removed* when a behavior occurs. The predicted effect of negative punishment is that the behavior will *decrease*. Examples of the operation of negative punishment include all the occasions when a privilege is lost because of misbehavior. For example, if parents elect to withhold dessert because of misbehavior at the dinner table, they are using negative punishment to decrease the probability that the same behavior will occur in the future. In the school, the child who is made to stay in from recess as a consequence of misbehavior in the classroom is being negatively punished. In this case, it is presumed that the child likes and enjoys recess and that its temporary loss will serve to punish—that is, decrease—the misbehavior that occurred in the classroom.

Negative Reinforcement

Negative reinforcement occurs when an *aversive* stimulus is *removed* as a consequence of a particular behavior. The predicted effect is that the negatively reinforced behavior will *increase* in frequency under the same or similar circumstances. Consider, for example, a child who is receiving a spanking from his or her parents. If the spanking is terminated as a result of some behavior such as loud screaming or crying, that behavior is then negatively reinforced and is more likely to occur during future spankings. That is, the crying and screaming of the child can be negatively reinforced by the prompt termination of the spanking. The next time a spanking occurs, the child will be more likely to cry and scream.

Another term used to describe such a situation is *escape.* It is easy to understand how the term derives its meaning, since it is possible to view the child's behavior as a means of escaping an uncomfortable situation. Another term that is often associated with escape is *avoidance.* When an avoidance contingency is in effect, behavior *postpones* the occurrence of an aversive event. In other words, the child does something to cause the aversive event to be cancelled, at least temporarily. Consider the child who has been spanked for some misbehavior but has also learned to terminate the spankings with a good show of grief and discomfort. Now, with each successive spanking the child is likely to cry and scream in pain just a bit earlier so as to promptly terminate the spanking. Eventually, it is possible that the mere threat of being spanked will be enough to elicit crying and screaming. If the parent responds by not spanking the child, then the child can be said to have *avoided* the spanking.

Negative reinforcement is rarely used in child management and none of the techniques discussed in this book employ the technique. However, it is important to remember the term because negative reinforcement does occur in the natural environment and sometimes can explain the unexpected results of attempts to manage the behavior of children.

Summary and Discussion

To review briefly, behavior can be managed or maintained using four core techniques. They are: positive reinforcement, (positive) punishment, negative punishment, and negative reinforcement. Both positive and negative reinforcement will cause the frequency of behavior to increase, positive reinforcement by adding a stimulus and negative reinforcement by subtracting or taking away a stimulus. Both (positive) punishment and negative punishment will cause the frequency of a behavior to decline. Positive punishment means to present a stimulus that has this effect and negative punishment means to take away a stimulus.

Whether a particular procedure will have the predicted effect is always an empirical question that can only be answered by observing its effects on behavior. The important variable is how the child views the particular stimulus. For instance, most children love to pet small animals, particularly dogs and cats. One would predict that being given the opportunity to pet an animal would be positively reinforcing for most children. However, some children have a great fear of certain animals. For these children the opportunity to pet an animal may be a punishing event. Unless one has some information about the particular child, only the child's behavior in relation to the stimulus reveals what technique is actually being programmed. This is a very important principle to keep in mind while managing the behavior of children: *The only reasonable way to judge the effectiveness of a behavior management program is to observe the effects of the program upon the child's behavior.* If the program does not have the desired effects, it should be modified.

The four techniques discussed here have been a source of frustration for students in introductory psychology classes. Part of the problem of understanding how to differentiate the techniques is to recognize that, in some ways, the division is very arbitrary and depends upon what behavior is being observed and what contingency is in effect. Consider, for example, a program to reward a child for completing arithmetic worksheets by allowing him or her to go out for recess after lunch with the rest of the class. The stated rule is that all arithmetic worksheets must be completed in order for the child to "earn" recess. If completion of worksheets increased after the rule was implemented, then it would appear that completing worksheets was positively reinforced by access to recess.

Yet, this statement does not tell the entire story of what happened to the child's behavior. Indeed, completion of worksheets increased as predicted. However, if the child was busy completing worksheets other, less desirable, behaviors would then be less likely to occur. If these behaviors had been observed, it might have appeared that they were negatively punished by the loss of recess.

Note, in addition, that an appetitive (desirable) stimulus may be used to both increase and decrease the frequency of a behavior depending upon the particular contingency. If the contingency is negative, the stimulus is taken away, then the predicted effect is that the behavior will decrease. If the contingency is positive, the stimulus is presented, and the predicted effect is that the behavior will increase in frequency. Thus, the same stimulus may have different effects upon behavior depending upon the contingency that governs what will happen when the behavior occurs.

Using Versus Misusing Punishment

As noted earlier, punishment refers to the administration of an aversive stimulus immediately after a behavior has occurred which has the effect of reducing the probability that the behavior will occur in the future. Punishment is very often used in public and private schools as a means of maintaining order and discipline. When punishment is physical in nature, it is called *corporal punishment*. Corporal punishment refers to hitting with a hand or fist, hitting with an object such as a belt, paddle, cane, whip, or anything else.

Corporal punishment is used in almost every school district in the United States. Only 8 states (Maine, Massachusetts, Hawaii, New Jersey, New York, New Hampshire, Rhode Island, Vermont) legally ban the use of corporal punishment in schools and a recent U.S. Supreme Court Decision (*Ingraham v. Wright*, 1977) basically supported its use on Constitutional grounds. In the Supreme Court ruling, the judges found that corporal punishment was neither cruel and unusual punishment nor did its administration require any of the due process safeguards of the Eighth Amendment. However, widespread and frequent use, and even Constitutional support, do not mean that corporal punishment is effective or justified in schools. In fact, the weight of evidence from anecdotes and psychological research is against the use of corporal punishment in schools and indicates that even its use by parents can have unwanted negative effects.

What are some of the problems in using punishment, especially corporal punishment, in schools and in the home? The proper use of punishment is to suppress or eliminate a particular, easily identifiable, behavior. However, this is only a small portion of the goal of behavior management. In addition to eliminating or suppressing behavior, it is also important to teach the child *appropriate* behavior in the same situation. Punishment alone does not accomplish this. In fact, when punishment, alone, is used to control behavior, it can occasionally cause undesirable behavior to increase by making the child more anxious and less interested in learning, so that misbehavior may be even more likely to occur.

Corporal punishment also presents a physical danger to the child, who may be seriously hurt if the punishment is too severe or administered in dangerous ways, such as by shaking the child, which could cause a whiplash injury. Child abuse is simply not acceptable in schools, even though it occurs with a fairly high frequency under the guise of "discipline." A major danger in the administration of corporal punishment is that the punishment may not be administered in a calm and objective manner keeping in mind the goal of suppressing or eliminating undesirable behavior. Instead, the administrator of corporal punishment is frequently angry at the child. The danger is that the adult could easily lose control and administer extremely severe punishment out of this anger, causing physical and psychological damage to the child and accomplishing nothing with regard to the child's misbehavior.

When a child is hit, slapped, or spanked for a problem behavior, just what is learned? First, as noted earlier, the child may learn not to emit the behavior that was punished, but the circumstances under which such punishment is likely to be administered in school typically operates against such learning. For instance, the time between the misbehavior and the administration of punishment is typically so great that the connection between the misbehavior and the punishment is lost from the child's perspective. However, the child is likely to learn that aggression and violence are primary ways of handling problems and that those who administer punishment are to be avoided as much as possible. This is not what schools should be teaching children.

One researcher has found such a strong relationship between what he calls "severe parental punishment" and delinquency that he has proposed the "belt theory of delinquency." The theory, simply stated, proposes that one cause of delinquency is the experience of severe parental punishment (Welsh, 1976). Other research has indicated that corporal punishment administered in school has a similar impact upon the children to whom it is administered (Townsend, 1984). For additional discussion of the problem of corporal punishment in schools, see Hyman and Wise (1979).

Another reason for not using physical punishment is that the circumstances surrounding the use of punishment rarely meet the criteria needed for punishment to be maximally effective. These criteria include (a) making sure that escape from the punisher is not possible, (b) making the punisher as intense as possible, (c) punishing each occurrence of the misbehavior, (d) delivering the punisher immediately after the misbehavior, (e) introducing the punisher at maximum intensity rather than gradually increasing its intensity, (f) making sure that the punisher does not become associated with reinforcement in any way, (g) reducing the motivation to misbehave as much as possible, and (h) making an alternative response available that will allow the child to earn positive reinforcement (Azrin & Holz, 1966). Chapter 4 includes a discussion of several alternative methods of reducing undesired behavior.

In reality, children who receive corporal punishment in school can escape by running away or quitting school, are likely to misbehave without receiving punishment most of the time, are punished long after the occurrence of the misbehavior, are subjected to punishers of gradually increasing intensity, are rewarded by their peers for the punished behavior, and are probably not receiving much positive feedback from the school as a whole. Under these circumstances, it is unlikely that the punished behavior will occur less often, but it is likely that the child will be less apt to learn in school and develop an intense dislike for those who administer the punishment. In short, it is highly unlikely that corporal punishment will contribute to the education of those who are punished, and it is very likely that punishment will even interfere with the child's education.

Maintaining Discipline in the Classroom

Almost all classroom teachers are concerned with the problem of maintaining "discipline" in their classrooms. Discipline, in this context, means their freedom to teach and interact with students without interruption from misbehaving students. Although much attention is given to the topic, the wide range of methods for maintaining classroom order and administering to the task of teaching a large group of children show that no single system of classroom management has gained wide popularity and acceptance. The main reason for the heterogeneity across classrooms is that teachers, themselves, are different from each other. The management style of any individual teacher is likely to be the result of a combination of factors such as personality, knowledge imparted by coursework, and personal experience.

Despite the wide range of possible classroom management styles, a few guidelines can be specified for general classroom management that are consistent with the principles of behavior management:

Guideline 1. Specify a clear and concrete set of classroom rules. See Chapter 4 for a detailed discussion of the characteristics of good rules.

Guideline 2. Specify a clear set of consequences for rule violations and be *consistent* in the application of these consequences. Silberman and Wheelan (1980) suggest a "three-chance plan" for handling rule violations. The first time a rule is broken a warning is given, which can be as simple as stating the rule. The second time a rule is broken, the warning is repeated and the consequence (such as extra work or detention) is stated. The third time a rule is broken, the stated consequence is administered.

Guideline 3. Most of the time the most effective way to deal with a behavior that is annoying but falls outside the classroom rules is to ignore it. Remember that verbal reprimands frequently *increase* the occurrence of misbehavior.

Guideline 4. Remember that the essence of teaching is to provide an environment in which the learning of *new* skills takes place. This is most efficiently accomplished when children are receiving generous amounts of positive reinforcement for their academic achievements. Furthermore, when a student is reprimanded or punished for misbehavior, cessation of the misbehavior does not mean that the student is learning.

Guideline 5. Keep in mind the advantages of employing an assertive style of interacting with children and avoid aggressive and nonassertive behavior.

Guideline 6. When a behavior management problem becomes overwhelming or a child exhibits signs of a serious behavior problem, seek help and consultation.

Summary and Comment Regarding the Use of Punishment in Schools

In any context, the only reason for using punishment is to suppress or eliminate a behavior that is easily defined and observed. Punishment is never to be used to dissipate the anger of the offended person or as a form of revenge upon the child. In my opinion, the use of corporal punishment in schools is not justified under any circumstances. Its demonstrated harmful effects far outweigh any benefits that might be obtained. Childhood is a period in the life of human beings that should be devoted to the acquisition of skills needed for success as an adult. The most efficient way to learn a new skill is through practice and positive reinforcement. Thus, a child's life should be full of opportunities to earn praise, respect, and even material rewards from caretakers as they learn the skills needed for adult life.

The exceptional child, who constantly seems to require punishment in various forms to survive in the classroom and even tempts the most caring and thoughtful educator to consider corporal punishment, is probably the least likely child to benefit from it. Instead, such a child probably needs a caring adult to take an interest in him or her and make an appropriate referral to a school psychologist, social worker, or counselor. More likely than not, the resulting assessment will reveal that the child has needs that go far beyond the school environment.

While most behavior problems are defined in terms of the *presence* of certain behaviors, it is more appropriate and logical to conceptualize of behavior problems as representing the *absence* of crucial skills in certain contexts. Thus, even in those cases characterized by the presence of a highly annoying, disruptive, or dangerous behavior, a major part of the behavior management plan is to determine what skills are appropriate and arrange the environment so these skills will be learned.

Although it is recognized that children will occasionally exhibit undesired behavior in a given situation, only nonpainful methods of punishment, such as timeout and response cost, will be discussed as methods of reducing such behavior. Furthermore, the goal in any discussion of the use of punishment is to clear the way for teaching needed skills to the child. That is, a behavior management program will rarely end when a particular behavior is successfully suppressed because it is the rare child who will replace the annoying behavior with an appropriate focus on learning once the annoying behavior is suppressed. The rule is that the child will need to learn skills that will allow him or her to behave appropriately in that environment.

chapter 3

STEP-BY-STEP PROCEDURES FOR ASSESSMENT AND MANAGEMENT OF BEHAVIOR PROBLEMS

Behavior management techniques are an extremely powerful set of tools for influencing behavior. Because children are dependent upon adults for most of their material needs, their behavior is very flexible and can be easily managed. The behavior of children in early and middle childhood (ages 1 to about 12) is particularly vulnerable to the influence of behavior management techniques. In contrast, adolescents are likely to be relatively independent of adult influence and more difficult to change with behavior management programs.

An interesting paradox is that the youngest children, who are most easily influenced by behavior management techniques, are the least able to express their feelings and discuss those events that may be contributing to behavior problems they manifest in school. For instance, a 6-year-old boy whose parents are in the midst of marital conflict surrounding a divorce will not be capable of articulating the turmoil he is experiencing. Yet, it is likely that his learning and general behavior will be adversely affected. Sexually abused children are also subjected to stresses that have profound effects upon their emotional and academic lives, but they can simultaneously be under extreme pressure to keep the source of the distress hidden.

A behavior management program could focus on a narrow behavioral objective, such as decreasing disruptive behavior or increasing time-on-task. However, what if the child is the subject of severe physical abuse or an antagonistic custody battle? In cases where environmental stresses underlie behavior problems in school, only the *school's* problem is solved by a successful behavior management program. The child may be in need of additional services, a need that may become hidden by successful management of the child's behavior in school. Often, the more severe the behavior problem shown by a child in school, the more likely it is that the problem does not exist in isolation, but, instead, is part of a system of problems involving both the school and the child's home. Although problems within the family are sometimes beyond the reach of school personnel, it is certainly a disservice to the child to ignore the possibility that interventions going beyond the school setting might be needed.

One purpose of this chapter is to outline a general method for assessment of problem behaviors. By answering the assessment questions discussed in this chapter, a clear picture of the problem behavior can be obtained. After the assessment procedure has been described, the steps in conducting a behavior management program will be outlined.

A GENERAL METHOD FOR ASSESSMENT OF PROBLEM BEHAVIORS

The assessment and management of children's behavior can be approached either formally or informally. An informal assessment or management approach is warranted when it is believed that the problem behavior is not very serious and is restricted in scope. For example the kindergarten child who frequently calls out in class and interrupts other students may present a minor problem, limited in scope, that can be resolved without resorting to detailed assessment and complicated behavior management procedures. Because of the limited time available in any educator's day and the unavoidable fact that the most serious problems tend to demand the greatest attention, much of the behavior management efforts of school personnel are conducted informally. The characteristics of informal assessment or behavior management are (a) little in the way of written documentation, with the exception of brief notes, is involved, (b) the assessment process is restricted to the frequency of the target behavior, (c) parental involvement is minimal, (d) such programs are typically conducted by the classroom teacher, perhaps with some consultative assistance, (e) the success of the program is often judged subjectively, and (f) the program typically involves a relatively small time commitment.

By way of contrast, a formal assessment or a formal behavior management program involves great attention to detail and addresses all of the steps outlined in this chapter. Of course, the division between formal and informal procedures is really arbitrary. In point of fact, most behavior management efforts, which are subject to the very real restrictions imposed by the sometimes limited resources available in a school, are likely to represent a compromise between the formal and informal approaches. Occasionally, it is even necessary to attempt to resolve a problem without the support of the child's parents. An assessment may reveal that a child's home is far from ideal and the interventions attempted by those at school may be unsuccessful. Whatever the restrictions, one is obligated to do one's best for the child, while maintaining a reasonable perspective on what can be accomplished.

The problem with informal methods is that something important may be overlooked. One possibility that all educators must consider is that a child is being subjected to some form of abuse. Educators are legally mandated to report their suspicions to appropriate child-protection agencies. It is also possible that an exclusive focus upon *problem* behaviors could cause the real problem to be overlooked. For example, a child may occasionally show violently aggressive behavior in the classroom. However, a thorough assessment may reveal that the child lacks social skills, such as making requests and cooperative play, and consequently behaves aggressively to gain attention. Furthermore, it may turn out that the child is socially isolated and neglected at home, having no opportunity to learn appropriate behavior.

Unfortunately, regardless of the thoroughness of an assessment, there is always the possibility that some important fact has not been obtained or a hypothesis about the child was not tested. The goal of assessment and problem management, then, is to gain an understanding of the child and the target problem while reducing the probability that important characteristics or potential problems have been overlooked. When informal procedures are used, the probability of overlooking something is greatest. Formal procedures decrease the probability of overlooking something important. In the final analysis, it is often professional judgement rather than objective facts that plays an important role in determining how a problem will be approached.

Any analysis of a problem situation, including the management program proposed to remediate it, only has the status of an hypothesis that is subject to verification via an empirical test. That is, both the conclusions supported by the assessment results and the resulting behavior management program are subject to change as new facts become available. For instance, after many weeks of a moderately successful formal behavior management program, a child's mother could reveal to the assessment team that the child's father is an active alcoholic and that she has just filed for divorce. Such a revelation would shed an entirely different light on the problem. While the behavior management program may be continued with only minor modifications, supplementary services may be sought to help the child cope with the family situation. Flexibility at all stages of the assessment and behavior management processes is an extremely valuable asset for all school personnel who undertake to conduct behavior management programs.

The following description of the formal assessment process has been adapted from Kanfer and Phillips (1970) with modifications to make it more applicable to the school environment and school-related problems. The eight steps involved in the assessment process are listed below and then followed by a detailed explanation of each step.

Step 1 General analysis of the problem and its impact upon academic learning and performance.

Step 2 Clarification of the problem.

Step 3 Motivational and reinforcement analysis.

Step 4 Developmental analysis of the problem.

Step 5 Analysis of the child's self-control.

Step 6 Analysis of the child's social relationships in school.

Step 7 Analysis of the child's sensory capacity.

Step 8 Analysis of the child's behavior at home.

Step 9 Analysis of interpersonal relationships at home.

Step 10 Initial identification of the problem and targets for the behavior management program.

Step 1: General Analysis of the Problem and Its Impact upon Academic Learning and Performance

What is the thing to do when a behavior problem appears? The first step is to state the problem in general terms and reconstruct, as much as possible, its history. Documentation of any informal attempts to correct the problem will prove very helpful if a formal behavior management program is necessary. The earliest attempts to remediate a problem may include strategies such as placing the child in a different location, a conference with the child, communicating with the child's parents, conferring with a colleague, or using "assertive discipline." It is when these efforts fail that a more structured approach can prove helpful.

At this point, a number of different personnel may become involved along with the classroom teacher who initially identified the problem. For instance, a school psychologist or special education teacher may be given permission to assess the child by his or her parent. In other school systems, the teacher may consult formally with colleagues, the school principal, or any other person with expertise in the problem area. Finally, the classroom teacher may find that help is unavailable or unnecessary and proceed to deal with the problem alone. Regardless of who is involved, the basic structure of the assessment process remains the same.

Once a problem has been tentatively identified, some initial questions about it should be answered. The most obvious question is: What is the problem? The answer should be stated in whatever terms seem appropriate at the time. It is also helpful to classify the problem as either a skill deficit (the child fails to emit a desired behavior) or a behavior excess (the child is doing too much of something undesirable).

Once the problem has been tentatively identified, its relation to academic performance can be considered. Early in the assessment process, one can tentatively determine whether and how the behavior problem affects academic performance. Eventually, a complete assessment of the child's academic skills (ability, achievement, and motivation) may be needed. The assessment may reveal that the child apparently has the academic skills to succeed in school but the behavior problem is interfering with classroom performance.

It is also appropriate to analyze the problem behavior, as initially defined, in terms of its frequency, intensity, and duration. It is important to gain information regarding stimulus conditions that tend to surround occurrences of the problem behavior. This includes both conditions that precede the behavior and those that follow it, that is, when and where the behavior occurs, what, if anything, seems to "set it off," and how adults and the child's peers react to it.

When Step 1 is complete, the assessor should have a general impression of the problem behavior which includes a tentative definition, a brief history of the problem and previous intervention efforts, and stimulus conditions that tend to surround the problem's occurrence. Interestingly, the activity of looking closely at problem behavior sometimes resolves the problem without any overt attempts at remediation. This can occur for different reasons, such as subtle shifts in patterns of attending to the child's behavior. Or, the "problem" might simply be a temporary occurrence that does not require any intervention, or responds immediately to the standard management techniques used in the classroom. Should this happen, it can be documented for future reference.

Step 2: Clarification of the Problem

This step is an extension of the first step. The goal is to consider the causal relations that might exist among the observations made up to this point and define the problem behavior in more detail. Evidence that the problem behavior is maintained by circumstances in the environment is likely to be sought during this stage of assessment. Also, it is useful to determine the impact of the problem behavior upon others in the school such as the child's peers, the classroom teacher, administrators, playground monitors, and anyone else who comes in contact with the child. This analysis should provide answers to three important questions: First, does the initially identified problem behavior occur in a wide range of situations or is it generally restricted to a single situation? Second, what does the child gain from the behavior that tends to maintain it over a long period of time? And, third, what is the impact of the behavior upon others in the child's environment?

Step 3: Motivational and Reinforcement Analysis

Although behavior assessment and management focuses upon problem behavior, it is also important to gain some perspective on the child's strengths. Such information can be used in planning rewards and incentives to offer the child in the behavior management program. Two questions should be answered: First, what does the child do well? And, second, what does the child like in terms of activities, toys, or whatever else might be relevant to a behavior management program?

Step 4: Developmental Analysis of the Problem

Several questions related to the problem behavior can be pursued from a developmental perspective. The most important question concerns the child's developmental status relative to age. It is desirable to know whether the child's social, academic, self-help, and physical skills are age-appropriate. This can be most easily ascertained by formally or informally ranking the child with respect to his or her classroom peers in each of these areas. This analysis should establish expectations about the child's behavior and indicate at least to some extent whether the problem behavior really represents a deviation from behavior expected of a child at that stage of development. In addition, the assessor should be aware of the possibility that a more in-depth assessment of intellectual, physical, social, and adaptive skills may be necessary.

In addition to ascertaining the developmental status of the child, it can be helpful to obtain a detailed history of the behavior problem. This may require interviewing both the child's parents and previous teachers, but it can prove extremely helpful. Although it may reveal that the problem is long standing and becoming worse, it may also indicate that the problem has developed recently or that someone in the child's past has already devised an effective means of coping with it. Another interesting possibility is that adults who previously had contact with the child may not have regarded the behavior as a problem.

Finally, a brief medical history of the child and a detailed look at his or her school attendance record, along with any other pertinent data that may be in the child's cumulative file, can add to one's understanding of a problem behavior. The presence of a major medical problem or frequent absences from school may both be important in planning a formal behavior management program.

Step 5: Analysis of the Child's Self-Control

This analysis is directed at both the methods and degree of self-control shown by the child in daily life. It includes an evaluation of both deficits and excesses in self-control, either of which could become the focus of a behavior management program. With respect to the originally identified problem behavior, it is important to determine whether that behavior is apparently within the control of the child, which allows one to decide whether the problem can be conceptualized as the result of not performing a known skill, or as a need to learn the skill. The behavior management program required to teach a new skill is naturally somewhat more complicated than a program to increase the frequency of a previously mastered skill.

To determine whether the problem behavior is under the control of the child, one seeks information about it across different environments. If the child is able to control a behavior excess (such as aggressive behavior) or perform a skill that appears to be a deficit at other times, then one has evidence that the problem behavior is, indeed, at least partially under the control of the child.

Step 6: Analysis of the Child's Social Relationships in School

Many behaviors are maintained by the attention they bring from adults and peers and this is one aspect of the child's social relationships that should not be overlooked. In addition, it may also be useful to observe whether the child has friends and how many. Take note, also, of whether the child is welcomed into group activities or rejected. In general, the goal of this analysis is to obtain a picture of how the child functions socially with peers and significant adults.

Step 7: Analysis of the Child's Sensory Capacity

Sight and vision are crucial to any child's survival in school and deficits in either of these senses can lead to both academic and behavioral problems. Therefore, when a behavior management program is being contemplated, it is important to at least informally assess the child's hearing and vision. A child could appear to be ignoring or even defying adult requests when, in fact, they are not being heard. Likewise, the child who is disruptive when lessons are being presented on the board may be unable to see clearly what is being presented or may be asking neighbors for clarification. In any case, it is important to consider the possibility that sensory deficits are related to the child's problem. If any such deficits are suspected, a thorough assessment should be undertaken immediately.

Step 8: Analysis of the Child's Behavior at Home

An analysis of any child's behavior at home greatly depends upon the willingness of the child's parents to share information with school personnel. Often, it takes great diplomacy to elicit information from parents, who may feel somewhat threatened by any contact with their child's school. On the other hand, there are also parents who are willing to talk in great detail and with little inhibition about their homelife and how they see the behavior of their child. Basically, three questions should have priority: First, does the behavior problem identified in school also appear at home? Second, how are behavior problems handled at home? And, third, what problems are seen at home in addition to those identified at school?

It is very important to avoid negative and judgmental comments about either the child or the child's parents when seeking information from them. Any involvement of the family system in maintaining or even exacerbating the problems identified in school is likely to be revealed very slowly, if at all. In initial meetings with parents, the primary goals should be accurate communication and maintaining a positive relationship. It may take several meetings before school personnel have an accurate picture of the relationship between the home environment and behavior in school. In some cases, parents are blatantly uncooperative and it is necessary to work around them as much as possible. Chapter 5 is devoted to the issue of cultivating good relationships with parents and understanding the impact of the family upon behavior in school.

Step 9: Analysis of Interpersonal Relationships at Home

At this level of assessment, it is desirable to know the composition of the family living with the child, whether the child is living with natural or stepparents, how many siblings live at home, and whether any other people are living in the household such as stepsisters or stepbrothers. Once the composition of the child's household is understood, information about the relationships among the people living at home should be obtained. It is particularly important to learn how each person living in the household gets along with the child. Of equal interest is whether conflict exists in the family, particularly between the mother and father. It is also interesting to ascertain whether the parents and/or other significant adults in the family see the child's behavior in the same way and whether parents and other responsible family members respond consistently to the child's behavior. A divorce, either accomplished or impending, would also be a significant factor. If the parents are, indeed, divorced, the degree of involvement of the noncustodial parent in the child's upbringing may also prove to be helpful.

Step 10: Initial Identification of the Problem Behavior and Potential Targets for a Behavior Management Program

Once the initial assessment has been completed, it is necessary to integrate the information and decide, first, whether intervention is necessary. If intervention is deemed necessary, then the target of intervention must be determined. A frequent outcome of a thorough assessment is that the original problem behavior is discovered to be secondary to another problem identified by the assessment. Furthermore, the primary problem may not be the initial target of intervention.

How does one get from the mass of data generated by the assessment process to a consistent, integrated view of the child that points to an intervention plan? First, it helps to realize that the process leading up to the intervention can be as simple or as complicated as one makes it. The complexity of an intervention plan is largely determined by two variables. First is the level of the intervention; that is, whether it is an initial intervention conducted by a classroom teacher working independently or an intervention that involves a special education staffing team. As one proceeds to higher and higher levels of intervention (i.e., from teacher to administrator to school psychologist consultation to special education staff) the assessment is likely to be more detailed, since higher levels imply that the problem is of a more serious nature and that earlier intervention efforts have failed.

The complexity of an assessment is also influenced by the nature of the initial data which may indicate an immediate need for more information. As soon as a behavior is observed, it may immediately be apparent that the problem is serious and requires immediate attention. High magnitude aggressive behavior resulting in injury to other children or threats of self-harm would fall in this category. Signs of physical or sexual abuse, or a variety of problems in several different environments can also indicate the need for additional and detailed assessment.

As one struggles to integrate the data obtained from a problem assessment, it also helps to realize that assessment is a continuous process. Furthermore, any conclusions implied by an assessment should not be regarded as final. Instead, they are best regarded as hypotheses, which are subject to revision at any time. One can never eliminate the possibility that some new bit of data will completely change one's view of a problem behavior, and the intervention that once seemed completely reasonable may suddenly appear inadequate or incomplete. Fortunately, the principles of behavior management are quite forgiving, and it is rare that harm would arise from such a circumstance.

Finally, in my experience, the more one knows about a child, the more confusion and contradictions are generated. With respect to the confusion, remember that the data may be confusing, but the child is behaving consistently with respect to his or her perception of the environment. The assessor's task is to identify that consistency and determine what, if any, interventions are implicated. With respect to the contradictions, remember that only *one* child is being assessed and the contradictions exist from *your* perspective, not from the child's. I have often found that resolving the contradictions that an assessment inevitably produces can make the greatest contribution to my understanding of a child's behavior.

Figure 3.1 provides a summary of the general assessment procedure just presented. This figure can serve as a guide during the planning of behavioral interventions. In the sections that follow, the steps involved in actually conducting a behavior management program are described.

Figure 3.1. Summary of the General Assessment Procedure

> *Step 1: General Analysis of the Problem and Its Impact upon Academic Learning and Performance*
>   A. State the problem in general terms, including its history.
>   B. Is it a behavior excess or a skill deficit?
>   C. What is the impact of the problem behavior upon academic performance?
>   D. Describe the problem's frequency, intensity, and duration.
>   E. What conditions precede and follow the behavior?
>   *(continued)*

Step 2: Clarification of the Problem
  A. Consider causal relations that might exist among observations.
  B. Define the problem behavior in more detail.
  C. What evidence suggests that the problem behavior is maintained by circumstances in the environment?
  D. Determine the impact of the problem behavior upon others.
  E. Does the behavior occur in a number of different situations or is it generally restricted to a single situation?
  F. What does the child gain from the behavior that tends to maintain it over a long period of time?

Step 3: Motivational and Reinforcement Analysis
  A. What are the child's strengths?
  B. What does the child like in terms of activities, toys, or whatever else might be relevant to the behavior management program?

Step 4: Development Analysis of the Problem
  A. Are child's skills age-appropriate?
  B. What is the history of the problem behavior's development.
  C. Obtain a brief medical history of the child.
  D. Obtain a detailed school attendance history and review the child's cumulative file.

Step 5: Analysis of the Child's Self-Control
  A. Evaluate the child's deficits and excesses in self-control.
  B. Does appropriate behavior appear in other environments?

Step 6: Analysis of the Child's Social Relationships in School
  A. What role does attention play in maintaining the problem behavior?
  B. Does the child have friends?
  C. Does the child participate in group activities?

Step 7: Analysis of the Child's Sensory Capacity
  A. Are the child's hearing and vision okay?

Step 8: Analysis of the Child's Behavior at Home
  A. Does the behavior problem appear at home?
  B. How are behavior problems handled at home?
  C. What other problems are seen at home?

Step 9: Analysis of Interpersonal Relationships at Home
  A. What is the composition of the child's household?
  B. How do others in the family get along with the child?
  C. Do responsible adults respond consistently to child's behavior?
  D. Is family conflict present?
  E. Are the child's biological parents divorced? Is the noncustodial parent involved with child? To what extent?

Step 10: Initial Identification of the Problem Behavior and Potential Targets for a Behavior Management Program
  A. Integrate the information. Is intervention necessary?
  B. What will be the target of intervention?
  C. Is additional data needed?
  D. Reminders:
    1. Assessment is a continuous process.
    2. All conclusions remain subject to revision.
    3. Children behave consistently with respect to their perception of the environment.
    4. Resolving contradictions can help in understanding the child.

STEPS IN CONDUCTING A FORMAL BEHAVIOR MANAGEMENT PROGRAM

A formal behavior management program is a continuation of the assessment process. Not only does the intervention follow from the assessment, but continued assessment is also a key element of formal behavior management programs. When informal behavior programs are used, it is helpful to keep in mind that the central characteristic of behavior management programs is that they should be sensitive to the information they generate. That is, the behavior targeted for intervention is carefully observed throughout the program and the program itself is changed to accommodate the feedback that is generated. If the program is unsuccessful, it is modified. When informal behavior management programs are used, it is important to have some basis, even if undocumented, for judging the success or failure of the program.

A formal behavior management program consists of eight steps:

Step 1 Identify the problem.
Step 2 Refine the definition of the problem.
Step 3 Assess the baseline rate.
Step 4 Identify the reinforcer and contingency.
Step 5 Begin the program.
Step 6 Observe the effects of the program and initiate steps to strengthen generalization beyond the training environment.
Step 7 Modify the program if necessary.
Step 8 Fade out the program.

These steps overlap somewhat with the formal assessment process. Assuming that a formal assessment has been conducted, it might be possible to move directly to Step 3 and begin gathering the baseline data. This would require that a suitable definition of the target behavior had already been established. On the other hand, even a complete and formal assessment may result in an intervention plan that targets a broadly defined area of behavior, such as deficits in social skills, which requires further refinement before it is sufficiently concrete to be the target of a formal behavior management program. Each step in a formal behavior management program will be described.

Step 1: Identify the Problem

Typically, when a behavior management program is contemplated, a problem has already been identified. The initial statement of the problem is likely to be rather broad. The student may be labeled a poor student, hostile, aggressive, hyperactive, lazy, disobedient, disruptive, anxious, or anything else that might motivate school personnel to intervene. Once the problem has been identified in general terms, it is necessary to determine the nature of the assessment that will be undertaken prior to beginning a behavior management program.

Numerous paths may eventually lead to a formal behavior management program. These paths may or may not include a formal assessment, so the essential steps leading to a satisfactory definition of the problem behavior are included in both the assessment and intervention processes. Thus, whether or not a formal and detailed assessment has been conducted, it would be possible to follow the steps in a formal behavior management program and successfully resolve the problem. However, important factors could be overlooked. Another strategy is to begin a formal behavior management and a formal assessment at the same time. Indeed, some behavior problems require an immediate response. It is also possible that a formal behavior management program could be the next logical step in a long series of attempts to resolve a problem behavior. Regardless of the path that leads to a formal behavior management program, the process remains the same.

Step 2: Refine the Definition of the Problem

To refine the definition of the problem behavior, one must state the problem in a manner appropriate for a behavior management program. Since the primary feature of all behavior management programs is the delivery of rewards, the event that determines when a reward will be delivered must be clearly recognizable. If it is not, the person conducting the behavior management program will not have a clear idea of when to administer the prescribed contingency. The likely result is that responses to the child's behavior will be inconsistent and the behavior management program will be in danger of failing. The child will also be faced with unpredictable reward, making it difficult to develop an idea of what is expected of him or her.

Personality traits and global behavioral labels (such as *aggressive, disruptive, depressed, hyperactive, anxious*) are not appropriate targets for a behavior management program because they do not specify *what* behavior occurring under *what* circumstances will be rewarded or punished. Instead, the problem behavior needs to be specified in concrete, measurable terms. A good definition of a behavior to be managed or modified has three basic characteristics. First, the target behavior should not require any interpretation on the part of the observer. In other words, it should be possible to easily determine when the target behavior has occurred without reference to whether the behavior was provoked by someone else or what was the intention of the child. Second, the behavior must be countable or measurable; that is, it must occur in discrete units that can be counted or it must be possible to determine what percent of a particular time interval the child was performing the target behavior.

Finally, the third characteristic of a good definition of a behavior is that one should be able to explain the definition to another person. Then, once the definition of the behavior has been agreed upon by two people, they should be able to observe the child for a period of time and independently (i.e., without consulting with each other) arrive at nearly identical results when recording their observations of the child's behavior. Psychologists who study the behavior of children employ several different techniques to ensure that their observational methods are reliable; that is, they can be repeated across time and with different observers without changing the outcome. Although such stringent tests would be beyond the needs of an applied behavior management program conducted in school, it is helpful to consider whether a particular behavior management program has a reliable measure of the target behavior. Involvement of a second observer is one method to increase reliability of the observations.

In addition to defining behavior in terms that are concrete, countable or measurable, and reliable, it is important to specify the problem in terms of a behavior to be increased. This should almost always be possible. The exceptions are those few cases where the child's behavior presents a danger (usually in terms of injuring another child) to self or others. For instance, if the initial definition of the problem behavior was disruptive classroom behavior, the problem could be redefined as a deficit in work behaviors. Then, instead of punishing disruptive behavior with timeout or keeping the child in from recess, the child could be earning rewards for completing assigned classroom work. A good general principle to remember is that the child who is engaged in desirable behavior does not have time to cause trouble.

Step 3: Assess the Baseline Rate

The baseline rate of a behavior refers to its frequency or rate of occurrence during a period of time when a behavior management program is not in effect. In applied behavior management programs conducted in school, baseline data is obtained prior to the beginning of a program. Once the program is begun, observational data continues to be collected using the *same* technique. Collection of baseline data provides the standard against which the success of the behavior management program is judged. If the frequency or rate of the target behavior changes sufficiently in the desired direction, the program is regarded as successful.

When the goal is to establish scientifically whether a behavior management program is effective for remediating a particular type of problem behavior, researchers often return to baseline conditions after a program has begun and later reinstitute the behavior management program. The purpose is to establish that the behavior management program caused the observed changes in behavior. However, successful behavior management programs conducted in school do not require demonstrations of their validity. In other words, it is not necessary to change a winning strategy.

Techniques for collecting baseline observations are determined by the frequency and nature of the target behavior. The simplest technique is to count each occurrence of the target behavior. This technique is appropriate for behaviors that do not occur very often and are likely to occur at irregular times. When this technique is used, observations must be totaled over some time interval such as an hour, day, week, or month. For example, the number of times per week that a child cries, the number of times per day that a child hits another student in class, or the number of times per week that a child completes arithmetic worksheets could constitute the baseline data for a behavior management program.

Sometimes the absolute number of times a behavior occurs is not an appropriate baseline measure because the number of *opportunities* for the behavior is either limited or varies from week to week. In such cases it is a good idea to determine a *percentage* for the behavior. For example, if the number of arithmetic worksheets assigned per week varies between five and fifteen, the baseline measure could then be the percent of assigned worksheets completed each week. The goal of the behavior management program would be to increase this percent to near 100. Similarly, if the goal of a behavior management program was to encourage a child to arrive at school on time, a suitable baseline measure might be the percent of days per week that the child arrives on time. Using a percent gives the flexibility of dropping from the baseline data holidays and days when the child is legitimately absent or late.

The method of actually recording baseline observations can vary from very simple to quite complex. One of the simpler techniques is simply to make a mark on a piece of paper, a card, or in a gradebook each time the target behavior occurs. The advantage of simply counting a behavior is that recording observations should not take too much of the observer's time, an important consideration for most classroom teachers. For some behaviors, it would be desirable to record each instance of the behavior along with a few comments about the situation, such as what led to the incident and how others responded to it.

Some of the behaviors that become the subject of behavior management programs are so pervasive in the school that it is impractical to count each occurrence, either because the behavior occurs too often or it is typically an ongoing behavior that cannot be accurately divided into discrete units for counting. Time-on-task, being out-of-seat, inattention, and tics or strange mannerisms are examples of such behaviors. Time sampling procedures are the usual way of handling such situations.

When a time sampling procedure is used, observations are recorded during a particular period of time, which may occur everyday, once a week, or anything in between. Observations may be recorded during art period, for example, when another teacher takes over the class and the regular classroom teacher is free to observe. Alternately, observations could be conducted during a certain hour each week when the school psychologist is available. An important consideration in using time sampling is to carefully specify when observations will be recorded. The goal should be to keep the conditions as constant as possible from observation period to observation period. As much as possible observations should be recorded at the same time each day and under the same relative conditions such as right after lunch, during an afternoon reading lesson, or during an independent work period.

Once a suitable time period has been designated, a number of recording techniques can be used. If the target behavior occurs in discrete units, then the behavior need only be counted during the observation period. Some behaviors do not occur in discrete units; for example, time-on-task or being out-of-seat. These behaviors do not occur in countable units, but it is possible to determine what percent of time a student is engaged in either of these behaviors. This is accomplished by dividing the observation period into discrete intervals and employing some rule to determine whether the child will be counted as being engaged in the target behavior during the time period or some portion of it. A number of different methods for determining a baseline rate under these conditions can be used. At the end of the observation period the number of intervals during which the student was engaged in the target behavior is divided by the total number of intervals in the observation period. The result is a decimal value, which can be multiplied by 100 to give the percent of time that the child was engaged in the target behavior.

Consider some examples of observation methods. The most precise method of determining a baseline rate is to determine the total amount of time the child was engaged in the target behavior during a particular period of time. The technique requires use of the classroom clock and a stopwatch. To begin the procedure, the observer determines the amount of time that the child will be observed after formulating an operational definition of the target behavior (e.g., "on-task"). A 10- or 20-minute interval should be sufficient. When the time interval begins, the observer uses the stopwatch to keep a cumulative record of the amount of time the child was engaged in the target behavior. That is, the stopwatch is allowed to run only when the child is engaged in the target behavior so that the total amount of time engaged in the target behavior is obtained at the end of the observation period. The percent of time engaged in the target behavior can be calculated on a daily basis along with data from a control child observed under the same conditions. To keep the conditions as equal as possible for the control and target child, they could be observed on alternate days or during alternate 5-minute periods.

Another, less precise, method is to estimate the rate of the target behavior by making observations at designated intervals during the observation period. At each designated point in the observation period, the child is observed and scored for the presence or absence of the target behavior. The advantages of this method are that it is easier to use and accurate observations of a control child can be obtained by alternating observations of the target child and a control child. The method begins with the selection of an appropriate observation period and recording method. A prepared sheet divided into squares and having separate areas for recording data from the target child and control child would work well. An observation is made at designated intervals ranging from 10-60 seconds depending upon the complexity of the coding system and the number of children being observed. The child's behavior during the interval is ignored. The observer records only what is occurring at the end of each interval.

For instance, using 10-second intervals, the observer looks at one of the children being observed every 10 seconds, recording that child's activity on the record sheet. If three children (one target, two controls) were observed every 10 seconds, each child would be observed three times per minute. A 30-minute observation period would result in 90 observations per child. A percent could be determined by dividing the number of times a particular behavior was observed by 90 and multiplying by 100.

A method of observing on-task versus off-task behavior is to observe each student in a classroom for a short interval such as 4 seconds each. A plus is recorded if the child is on-task during the 4-second interval and a minus recorded if the child is off-task for any part of the 4-second interval. Then, the percentage of intervals on-task can be computed for the target child and the remainder of the class. It takes a little practice to coordinate recording and observation, but the technique avoids the biases that could result from choosing a particular control child to observe.

The sophistication of any observation technique can be increased by comparing data from two observers. If the definition of the target behaviors is sufficiently concrete, substantial agreement should be found. If agreement is not substantial (80-100%), the definition of the target behavior probably needs clarification and revision.

By using one of these procedures, it should be possible to obtain baseline data for just about any behavior. There are a few additional points to keep in mind while obtaining the baseline data. First, it is very important to specify very clearly what procedures were used to gather the baseline data so these procedures can be continued *without change* when the behavior management program begins. If the conditions of baseline observation are not held constant, then any changes that occur in the target behavior may not be attributable to the effects of the behavior management program.

Another point to remember is that baseline observations need not be restricted to a single behavior. By making up a simple coding system, it is possible to obtain information about several behaviors. This can be very handy when the problem is an undesirable behavior, such as being out-of-seat but it has been decided that the management program will focus on rewarding time on task. By observing both behaviors, it is possible to obtain a clear picture of the impact of the behavior management program.

Finally, it may be helpful to point out a very interesting phenomenon that could occur when baseline observations are begun. It is possible that the act of obtaining the baseline data may, all by itself, cause the observed behavior to change. The change may or may not be in the desired direction. For instance, if a teacher stops what he or she is doing, walks over to his or her desk, and makes a mark in the gradebook, every time a child emits or fails to emit a problem behavior, the child's attention may be drawn to the problem behavior and it could improve spontaneously.

Step 4: Identify the Reinforcer and Contingency

During the collection of the baseline observations is a convenient time to decide upon the reward and contingency to be used in the behavior management program. Finding a reward that can be easily delivered at school can be a major problem under some circumstances. Often a token reward program in which points or tokens are earned in school and exchanged for rewards at home represents the best solution. This technique is described in Chapter 4. Whether delivered at home or at school, it is still necessary to select some reward.

Christian (1983) suggested that rewards used in behavior management programs conducted in school be placed on a hierarchy ranging from the most concrete rewards to the most abstract rewards. The categories or levels of consequences, along with a few examples of each, include

- Infantile Physical Contact: hugs, pats, physical closeness
- Food: milk, cookies, raisins, banana chips, candy, gum
- Toys: marble, kite, clay, car, truck, doll
- School Implements: eraser, ruler, pencil, notepad
- Privileges: free time, computer access, errands, collect/distribute papers
- Praise: verbal comments, grades, certificate, attention of special adult (e.g., principal)
- Internal Self-Reinforcement: "I did well!," "I got all the problems right!," "My work is done!"

Christian points out that most children in a regular classroom are operating at the two highest levels of reinforcement, praise and internal self-reinforcement, most of the time. Thus, when dealing with a child's problem behavior the goal should be to start at the highest level possible on the hierarchy and advance toward the even higher levels. Making the advance to higher levels of reinforcement and complete independence from the behavior management program is the goal in Step 6.

Once a reward has been selected, it is necessary to state the contingency or rule for administering that reward. As explained in Chapter 2, the contingency defines the relationship between behavior and the reward (or punishment). A contingency can specify either that a stimulus is presented or removed when a behavior occurs or fails to occur. A contingency can be very simple, specifying that a simple reward such as food or positive attention be delivered when the child engages in a particular behavior. On the other hand, contingencies can be very complicated, specifying complicated relationships among a variety of behaviors, a point system, and rewards to be delivered by the child's parents at home. It is a good idea to put the contingency in writing and have someone else look at it before it is announced to the child. The statement should be clear, objective, and consistent with earlier statements of the problem and the refined definition of the target behavior.

Step 5: Begin the Program

Beginning a behavior management program is very simple and consists of simply announcing the rules of the program to the child. Children should not be given more details regarding the program than they are capable of understanding. For preschoolers and kindergarteners, it is probably best to keep the explanation as simple as possible and merely tell them that they have an opportunity to earn something if they can pay attention or get their work done. Older children would usually be capable of understanding a more detailed explanation.

Once the program is begun, it is very important that it be objectively administered. The rules of the program should provide most of the necessary guidance as to when rewards are delivered or taken away. If the administrator of the program finds himself or herself in the position of making subjective judgements regarding what should be done, the program should be revised to eliminate the subjectivity. Keep in mind, however, that this is not an uncommon occurrence, since children often will be curious about the limits of a particular program and attempt to establish limits that are in their favor.

It is also important to avoid lengthy discussions with the child as to whether a particular behavior meets the criteria for a reward, since one could inadvertently reward the child for ingenuity in explaining why he or she hit someone, failed to turn in an assignment, or otherwise met or failed to meet a rule of the behavior management program. However, when the child behaves in such a way as to merit a timeout period or loss of a reward, a brief explanation is in order. The explanation should focus on the child's behavior and not contain any aggressive comments about the child. When a reward is delivered it should always be accompanied by a positive comment.

Finally, it is important to be patient and remember that the behavior management program, and not the child, is subject to evaluation if things do not work out as expected.

Step 6: Observe the Effects of the Program and Initiate Steps to Strengthen Generalization Beyond the Training Environment

This step is a continuation of what was begun in Steps 4 and 5. The baseline observations are continued throughout the program and, once the program is begun, become the indicator of the program's success or need for modification. If behavior changes in the desired direction, the program should be continued without modification until the appropriate behaviors are well established. At the point where desirable behavior is strong, steps to strengthen generalization beyond the training environment may be begun. The purpose of these steps is to bring the child's behavior under the control of the natural environment without the structure and rules of the behavior management program. Strengthening generalization beyond the training environment becomes an issue when the child is in a special education class or the initial steps in the behavior management program have been conducted outside the regular classroom. In either case, it is desirable that behaviors learned in one setting also occur in others, including the regular classroom.

Strengthening generalization from a training setting to the classroom can be accomplished by either bringing elements of the classroom into the training environment or taking elements from the training environment to the classroom. For instance, having the child's regular classroom teacher visit a program that takes place away from the classroom can give the teacher a chance to evaluate elements that could be employed in the classroom. Then, by fading out those elements with which the teacher is not comfortable or cannot implement for practical reasons (see Step 8), it is possible to construct a program that is similar to the classroom.

Stokes and Baer (1977) reviewed the literature on the technology of promoting generalization and derived nine categories of techniques. They defined generalization as the occurrence of a trained behavior across different, nontraining conditions. They call the first category of methods "train and hope," which is to effect a behavior change without any explicit attention to promoting generalization and then note any generalization that happens. The second category of techniques, "sequential modification," means to assess generalization of a newly learned behavior and then, if generalization has failed to occur, initiate modifications designed to accomplish it. "Sequential" modifications consist of instituting the successful environmental manipulations in other settings.

The third category of techniques is to introduce natural contingencies for maintaining the behavior. This is the most reliable method of promoting generalization and means to transfer control of behavior from the original behavior management program to stable, natural contingencies within the environment to which the child returns. One of the requirements of promoting generalization via this route is that behaviors must be carefully selected so that their occurrence will be rewarded by natural contingencies outside the training environment. This type of generalization is particularly important in training social skills, because the acceptance of the child's peers and significant adults determines success of the training.

A fourth category is the training of sufficient examples to obtain generalization across a number of untrained conditions. Stokes and Baer cited an example of their own work, in which retarded children were trained to greet adults. When a child was trained to greet one experimenter, generalization to other adults did not occur. However, when training was conducted with only two experimenters, the greeting response generalized to over 20 members of the institution staff, and newcomers as well. Thus, while generalization to numerous settings may be desirable, it may not be necessary to conduct explicit training within each of these settings to obtain generalization.

Another category of technique is to "train loosely." This means to be somewhat irregular in the conditions of training and in the definition of acceptable responses. Variations in the setting and in the exact stimuli presented to the child would also fall in this category. The point is that the more liberal are the training conditions, the less likely is behavior change to be restricted to the exact training conditions.

Stokes and Baer also discuss the use of "indiscriminable contingencies," which means that, to some extent, contingencies (i.e., the rules for delivery of rewards) that are at least somewhat unpredictable are most likely to lead to generalization. This includes both the schedule of reinforcement and the conditions under which it is delivered. An essential component of many behavior management programs is to gradually change from continuous reinforcement (reinforcing each example of a correct response) to intermittent reinforcement (allowing some responses to go unreinforced). This concept is explained more thoroughly in Chapter 4.

"Programming of common stimuli" means to include elements from environments targeted for generalization in the original training. For instance, if training in some academic skill is given in a particular setting, generalization to other settings is most likely to occur when elements from these settings are included in the original training. This could be done, for example, by including regular classroom worksheets in training that takes place in a psychologist's office or a resource room. Another technique would be to have the child's classroom teacher participate in training once behavior change has occurred in the original training environment. A related technique is to promote "mediated" generalization by training verbal labels to appropriate behavior in both the original environment and settings to which the behavior is to be generalized.

Finally, Stokes and Baer suggest that generalization, itself, may be a trainable response that should be reinforced, at least intermittently, when it occurs.

Each of the behavior management programs discussed in Part 2 includes specific recommendations for promoting appropriate generalization of newly learned behavior to other environments.

Step 7: Modify the Program, if Necessary

Behavior management programs frequently do not work the first time. This is a very common experience. The best thing to do when this occurs is take a look at the child, the situation at home and school, and modify the program in a reasonable way, if necessary. More specifically, several aspects of a behavior management program can be examined when it is ineffective.

First of all, the program may simply need more time to take effect. Unfortunately, there are really no concrete guidelines regarding the length of time required for a program to "take hold." However, the frequency of the target behavior and the frequency of the reward or punishment should be determining factors. For a behavior management program involving a behavior occurring several times per day and punished by timeout, one would expect to see effects of the program within several days to a couple of weeks. For a program involving an infrequent behavior, such as completing homework, that is rewarded by points which can be used to "buy" other rewards each Saturday, improvement may not be noted for 2 to 4 weeks.

A second reason for the apparent ineffectiveness of a behavior management program is that something important may have been overlooked when the original assessment was performed. My own experience has been that behavior management programs can sometimes be frustratingly ineffective when the child's home is unstable. An impending divorce, disagreement between the parents regarding rules and discipline, or alcoholism are examples of situations at home that can spill over into the school and complicate management of the child's behavior. When such situations arise, there is sometimes little that can be accomplished at school. However, a behavior management program that uses highly desirable rewards and does not involve any input from the parents may be successful. Then, after allowing much more than the usual time for the program to take effect, slowly involve the parents in its administration. Alternately, the school psychologist or social worker could become involved in assessing and working with the family, making a referral to other professionals, if appropriate.

Another potential reason for the ineffectiveness of a program is that it is either too simple or too complicated. A program could be too simple when a behavior targeted for change does not really capture the essence of the child's problem. For instance, an older child could be regularly failing examinations and in-class assignments. A reasonable strategy for dealing with such a problem might be to place the child on a behavioral contract that rewards academic success with privileges at home. However, this approach might not work if the child's problem was debilitating test anxiety. A program emphasizing relaxation and imagery techniques, study skills, and academic success might be more effective.

On the other hand, a program could be too complicated. Too many behaviors may be specified at once, the child may not have sufficient understanding of the program, or too many adults may be involved. In such cases, the solution is to simplify the program.

It is always possible that the program design is sound, but the reward is insufficient to promote behavior change. Observation of and negotiation with the child are probably the best ways of determining more desirable consequences for behavior. Even timeout can be ineffective if the child has access to something rewarding. For example, the child could gain reinforcing peer attention by making faces, could play with something in his or her pocket, or amuse himself or herself in other ways. Any of these activities would tend to decrease the effectiveness of the timeout. In such cases, a response cost procedure or improved isolation of the child (within reasonable limits) may have the desired effects.

Other problems that could possibly interfere with the success of a program include inconsistent administration of contingencies, the target behavior was not specified clearly enough, or the program was faded out too quickly. If these problems are noted, the behavior management program should be adjusted accordingly.

Step 8: Fade Out the Program

The truly successful behavior management program eventually puts itself out of business, so to speak. That is, elements of the program are slowly faded out so the target behavior occurs at a normal rate without the necessity of a formal management program. Fading of the program is accomplished by reducing the amount and frequency of reward. At the same time, praise and other rewards from significant adults (good grades from the teacher and positive attention from the parents, for example) take the place of the structure of the behavior management program.

Thus, in order to fade out a program, two things are necessary. First, the amount of behavior between rewards must be *slowly* increased, and second, abstract rewards must be *slowly* substituted for the concrete, material rewards with which most programs begin. The most likely problem to be encountered while fading out the program is that behavior deteriorates from previous levels. When this occurs, merely go back to an earlier step in the fading process and try again at a later time. Numerous examples of this process are provided in Part 2.

CONCLUSION

In order to simplify the presentation, both the assessment and behavior management processes have been presented in a stepwise manner. However, neither process is linear. Both are driven by the information that they generate. Thus, at any time the logical next step could be to return to an earlier step in the process in order to try something else or gather more information about the child. An important characteristic that I believe administrators of behavior management programs must possess is flexibility. Children are always communicating with adults and the wise adult listens and acts upon the messages that are received. This means being willing to revise hypotheses and change intervention strategies as necessary.

chapter 4

ADDITIONAL PRINCIPLES AND TECHNIQUES

This chapter covers additional principles and techniques that are frequently relevant in behavior management programs. Some knowledge of these concepts is necessary for the well-rounded behavior manager. The topics covered in this chapter are discrimination, schedules of reward, modeling, shaping, behavior chains, token reward, the Premack principle, behavioral contracting, and methods for reducing the frequency of behavior.

DISCRIMINATION

Reinforcement or punishment does not *always* follow a behavior. Certain conditions must often be met before reinforcement or punishment will be available. At school, for instance, behavior considered appropriate on the playground (e.g., playing football or running) may meet with disapproval if emitted in the classroom. Likewise, the child who voluntarily studies and completes worksheets during recess is likely to be regarded as "different" by his or her peers. The typical child learns to discriminate recess from the classroom by being rewarded for the behaviors considered appropriate in each setting.

When a behavior is not rewarded (or punished) unless a particular stimulus or set of stimuli is present, that stimulus is known as a discriminative stimulus, which "sets the occasion" for or signals the availability of reward or punishment. When a child responds appropriately to a discriminative stimulus, it is said that the child has learned the discrimination or learned to discriminate the stimuli that signal the appropriateness of behavior. Discrimination is also the name for the process by which a child learns to respond appropriately to stimuli that are similar. Examples would be learning to name colors or recognize the letters of the alphabet. Discriminations are learned because the discriminative stimuli signal what behavior is appropriate and likely to be rewarded.

A classroom teacher is teaching children to discriminate when she or he designates certain times (e.g., work periods) when talking is not allowed, and other times (e.g., free time) when talking is okay. The labels are used as discriminative stimuli when they are announced at the beginning of a particular period of time and the teacher responds appropriately to behavior during those periods. The teacher who makes the stimuli as obvious and different from each other as possible will be the most successful at maintaining the desired conditions. For example, a reversible sign with *don't talk* in red letters on one side and *free time* in green letters on the other side would be more effective than just an announcement from the teacher at the beginning of one period or the other.

A much more difficult discrimination for a child to learn would be illustrated by those situations where conflict and inconsistent discipline at home result in a child who behaves unacceptably at school. Although the ideal approach to remediation in such a situation would be to involve the child's parents in a behavior management program with the dual goals of improving the child's behavior in school and helping the parents improve their own child management skills, eliciting parental cooperation is not always possible. This would result in an unfortunate, but not hopeless, situation. The child would tend to respond much more slowly to behavior management programs conducted in school, because of the need to discriminate between the characteristics of the home and school environments. However, with patient and consistent administration of the behavior management program, the child could learn to behave appropriately in the school even if behavior at home remained a problem.

Most behavior management programs involve explicit or implicit discriminative stimuli. The individual planning a behavior management program needs to take note of such stimuli and design the program to enhance their effectiveness. This involves, first, making the discriminative stimuli as distinctively different as possible. The more obvious and different the stimuli are, the more likely the child is to attend to them and learn to behave appropriately in their presence. Second, ensure that the consequences for behavior (either appetitive or aversive) are as consistent as possible with respect to the discriminative stimuli. If consequences for behavior occur inconsistently across the discriminative stimuli, the child will not acquire the discrimination. Another method that may enhance the acquisition of the discrimination is to provide different rewards in the presence of the discriminative stimuli (e.g., Carlson & Wielkiewicz, 1976).

EXTINCTION AND SCHEDULES OF REINFORCEMENT

Extinction refers to the gradual decrease in the frequency of a behavior that occurs when reinforcement is discontinued. The fact that extinction occurs is the reason that the initial advice to a teacher seeking consultation about a disruptive pupil is often "ignore the behavior and maybe it will go away." The accuracy of this advice depends upon whether all sources of reinforcement can be eliminated. If the child receives no other reinforcement for the behavior, then extinction is likely to take place.

An interesting relationship exists between extinction and the proportion of responses that are reinforced. If every single response (of a certain class or type) is reinforced, then reinforcement is said to be *continuous*. When some responses are not reinforced, reinforcement is then said to be partial or *intermittent*. It is possible to deliver intermittent reinforcement on four different schedules: fixed interval, fixed ratio, variable interval, and variable ratio. In a fixed ratio schedule of reinforcement, reinforcement follows every Nth response, where N may be any number greater than 2. (If $N = 1$, reinforcement is continuous.) When a variable ratio schedule is in effect, reinforcement still depends upon the *number* of responses, but the number of responses required between reinforcement varies unpredictably around some average value. In fixed and variable *interval* schedules, reinforcement is delivered for the next response following passage of either a fixed or variable amount of time.

It is not really important to remember the definitions of the four schedules of reinforcement, but it is important to understand the effect of continuous versus partial or intermittent reinforcement. The effect is simple. When reinforcement is discontinued, it will take much longer for an intermittently reinforced response to disappear than for a continuously reinforced response. That is, intermittently reinforced responses are said to be more *resistant to extinction* than continuously reinforced responses.

This well-established fact is important in planning behavior management programs for two reasons. First, if an assessment reveals that an undesirable behavior is being reinforced on an intermittent schedule, it will be much more resistant to change than a continuously reinforced response. In such a case the program will work best if extended beyond normal time limits and if an alternative, incompatible response is strengthened as part of the management program. Second, when a new or previously weak skill is being modified via a behavior management program, it is important to move from continuous to intermittent reinforcement before the program is terminated, so the the new behavior will exist at a maximum strength. Recall that this is the goal of Step 8 of a formal behavior management program.

SHAPING AND BEHAVIOR CHAINS

Many of the skills that children need must be learned in a stepwise manner, either because they are complicated or involve a large number of steps. Long division, tying a shoe, getting dressed, walking, and printing letters of the alphabet are examples of such skills. If these skills were taught by rewarding only perfect performance, both trainer and trainee would be very frustrated. Instead, such complicated skills are usually taught in small steps. The methods typically used are shaping and treating the skill as a behavior chain.

Shaping

Shaping a behavior means to reward successive approximations of the target behavior. That is, one begins by rewarding less accurate or expert responses than are acceptable later in the learning process. The criterion for reward is raised in small steps until only a polished performance is rewarded. That is, a performance that was acceptable and rewarded early in the training is not rewarded at a later time, because the criteria have been raised so that the child must emit a performance that is closer to the goal.

A parent teaching a child to hit a ball with a bat is one example of the shaping process. The parent begins by prompting the child (giving verbal directions, guiding the child in correct motions, and modeling for the child) to assume a proper batting stance. The first few times the ball is thrown to the child, the parent rewards any swing at the ball no matter how close it comes to the ball. As the child gains skill, the criteria for reinforcement (attention and praise) are changed. Slowly but surely, the child is required to come closer and closer to hitting the ball in order to receive positive feedback. Eventually, only physical contact with the ball is rewarded. Later, only good contact that propels the ball a fair distance is rewarded. In this manner the parent shapes or sculptures the behavior by changing the criteria for a reward until the goal of firmly hitting the ball is reached.

A teacher might use a similar technique to teach a child to write a letter of the alphabet. The teacher would begin by rewarding an attempt that is shaped somewhat like the target letter. As the child practices the letter, the teacher would raise the criteria for reinforcement until only a near perfect attempt, which clearly has all the major features of the letter and does not look like any other letter, is rewarded. In point of fact, it would be unusual for a teacher to sit down with individual children and shape their letter writing and copying skills. Instead, the usual technique is to have each child trace letters to learn their basic shape, then slowly reducing the amount of the letter that is traced while the amount to be formed by the child is increased. However, as the children's skill increases the teacher must still judge which copies are acceptable and which copies indicate a need for more practice. In this manner, the children's letter copying is shaped by the feedback from the teacher.

Shaping and rewarding successive approximations may be necessary in any behavior management program in which the child learns a new skill. It is most helpful if the steps in the shaping process can be stated as part of the behavior management program. For instance, a fourth grader who does not show appropriate work behaviors in the classroom could initially be rewarded for being on task for 2 minutes. Then, over the course of the behavior management program, the amount of time spent on task and the amount of work required in a time period could be raised in successive steps until the child's behavior resembled that of other students in the classroom. Unfortunately, it is not very often that a behavior to be shaped has such obvious steps toward acceptable performance. Typically, shaping a behavior more closely resembles an "art" than a technique of science.

The most troublesome aspect of shaping a behavior is deciding when to raise the criteria for reinforcement. In my own experience, more reinforced trials are necessary for a given level of performance at the beginning of the shaping process than in the middle or end. Also, the process seems to go most smoothly when a fairly constant rate of reinforcement can be maintained. Thus, it would be desirable to raise the criteria for reinforcement at a slow enough pace that the rate of reinforcement does not drop suddenly, otherwise the child may become frustrated over the loss of reinforcement and become uncooperative.

Behavior Chains

A behavior chain is a series of discrete behaviors learned in a particular sequence. The steps in making a bed or long division are examples of behavior chains. Typically, behavior chains are taught by beginning with the first step and taking the child through the chain in sequence until the entire chain of behaviors is mastered. This is appropriate when the child has the ability to memorize the sequence and is able to prompt herself or himself verbally while performing the chain. However, there is an alternate method of teaching behavior chains, rooted in animal learning experiments, which also is effective.

In this method, the *last* behavior in the sequence is taught first and then behaviors are added to the chain in *reverse* order. Consider bed-making as an example. In order to teach this skill to a young child the parent would first perform all the steps in the process except the last, leaving it to the child to complete. Successful completion would be followed by generous social reinforcement and praise. Then, after the child had mastered the last step in the process, the parent would begin to complete the task except for the last two steps, rewarding the child only if these were completed. As the child continued to learn, the parent would perform less and less of the sequence while the child would be required to do more and more in order to receive praise. Technically, what is happening is that each step in the sequence becomes a signal or discriminative stimulus for the next step in the sequence.

It would be possible to teach a variety of academic and nonacademic behavior sequences in the manner described above, but in both the classroom and the home several different teaching and learning processes are likely to be taking place at once. Behavior is being modeled by adults, who may be both shaping behavior and rewarding partial or complete performance of behavior chains. The point to remember is that various methods are available for teaching complex behaviors to children and when remediation of a behavior problem requires teaching a complex new skill to the child, these methods should be used.

CLASSICAL VERSUS OPERANT CONDITIONING

The majority of behavior management techniques, including those discussed up to this point, involve what is called *operant* or *instrumental* conditioning. What these techniques have in common is a reward or punishment that is delivered as a *consequence* of a predefined *response*. The criterion as to whether operant conditioning has occurred is whether or not the probability of the target response changes across time.

Classical conditioning involves the same stimuli as operant conditioning but the relationship of the stimuli is different. In classical conditioning, an appetitive or aversive stimulus is presented after a *stimulus*. When classical conditioning is being conducted in a laboratory, behavior is measured but it has no influence upon whether an aversive or appetitive stimulus is delivered. Classical conditioning, then, involves *pairing* of stimuli, independent of behavior. The outcome of classical conditioning is that the stimulus presented first takes on characteristics of the aversive or appetitive stimulus, in terms of its ability to elicit certain responses from the organism. Classical conditioning is believed to play a role in the acquisition of fear, anxiety, and phobias. In addition, some of the ways of managing phobias, anxiety, and fears involve techniques derived from classical conditioning. These issues are discussed further in Chapters 6 and 9.

OBSERVATIONAL LEARNING

It is not always necessary that children learn new skills through trial and error. In fact, this type of learning can be very inefficient and even dangerous. The natural environment is full of lethal consequences that would strike any adult or child who chose an incorrect response. Crossing the street at the wrong time, failing to heed obvious signs of impending danger, learning to swim, or learning to drive a car are only a few examples of learning situations with hazardous consequences. Instead of learning by trial and error it is also possible to acquire new behavior via vicarious processes. Vicarious processes involve observation as opposed to direct participation.

Observation of a model engaging in some behavior can, according to Bandura (1969), result in three different effects. First, it is possible for the observing child to acquire new behaviors that were not previously in his or her repertoire. This might include virtually any behavior that could be the target of a behavior management program. The second potential effect of observing a model is that already learned responses could become either inhibited or disinhibited. This effect results from observing the consequences of the others' behavior. For example, a child's disruptive behavior could be inhibited by seeing another child experience punishment for similar behavior. The third effect that observing a model can produce is to set the occasion for performing some previously learned behavior.

An example might be when a classroom teacher and a child go to a window to watch an event taking place outside, and the other students in the class follow suit.

In addition to the simple presentation of an observable stimulus, several variables have an impact upon the effectiveness of observational learning. Primary among these variables are attentional factors, since a child who is not attending to the relevant aspects of the model's performance will not learn enough about the event to reproduce the behavior. Variables that influence attention include the attractiveness and rewarding qualities of the model, the vividness and novelty of the modeling stimuli, and motivational conditions.

If a child is going to acquire behavior via observation at one point in time for performance at some later time, the information gained during the observation must be retained in memory. Repetition of the behavior sequence to be acquired and rehearsal of the material by the observer would be two variables generally conceded to have the greatest influence upon retention. While the first is under the control of adults, the second is not, except by indirect means. Again, motivational factors in the observational learning situation may greatly influence retention. Another factor, largely beyond the control of adults, is whether the child's motor skills are sufficient to allow the child to reproduce the observed behavior. If remediation of behavior via observational learning is attempted and either motor or memory processes appear to prevent acquisition of the new behavior, then additional assessment may be needed. Either a complete assessment of academic skills or assessment by an occupational or physical therapist may be in order.

Incentive and motivational processes also play a key role in observational learning. That is, a behavior management program can be designed to reward a child for copying the behavior of another. Beginning such a program is likely to have a positive effect upon attention, motor performance, and retention as well. A behavior management program that does not directly involve observational learning can be enhanced by employing some of its principles. For instance, if one child in a class is exhibiting excessive disruptive behavior, rewarding another child in the class for appropriate behavior may enhance the probability that the first child's behavior will improve and may speed the progress of a behavior management program. In cases where a child lacks important skills, observational learning using a peer model could prove more efficient than shaping the behavior. In sum, observational learning can serve as a useful adjunct to a behavior management program or it can be its central feature.

TOKEN REWARD

Token reward programs are among the most useful procedures available for behavior management programs. Token rewards can be delivered without interfering with ongoing projects or behavior and their effectiveness is not tied to a single reward. Because the implementation of a token reward program is very similar to being paid for work, the concept is easy to communicate to consultees and parents, who are likely to view such programs positively.

A token reward is almost anything of little or no value that can be exchanged by the child for something desirable. A token reward is analogous to money. Money, itself, cannot be eaten or keep a person warm but it can be used to purchase food and shelter. Likewise, tokens, by themselves, have no inherent value, but they can be used to "purchase" rewards that are valued. Gold stars, points, marbles, specially marked pieces of paper, various chips (e.g., poker), or anything else that can be conveniently delivered and saved by the child can be used as a token. Concrete objects that can be handled are best for younger children, while points will usually work well with older children. The simplest token reward programs can be implemented by telling the child, "If you can earn five of these, then you can trade them in for anything in this box!" The success of the program will depend upon the child's understanding of the instructions, and the value of the rewards contained in the box.

It may be helpful, when a token program is begun, to be somewhat loose with the definition of the target behavior (an excellent opportunity to practice shaping behavior) and be generous with tokens, until the child has earned enough to turn them in for a reward. Then, by showing the child what has been accomplished and how to exchange the tokens for a reward, the likelihood that he or she understands the system is increased. Numerous examples of formal behavior management programs involving token reward are described in Part 2.

THE PREMACK PRINCIPLE

David Premack (cited in Ross, 1981) observed that a response of higher probability can be used to reinforce a response of lower probability. Teachers and parents who say, "Before you can go outside, you must finish your work," are applying this principle. More than anything else this principle serves as a reminder that by watching children one can learn what they like to do. Then, if one has or can gain control over the preferred activity, it can be used to reward less likely but desirable behavior. Furthermore, even the child who is most resistant to a behavior management program must be gaining some reinforcement from some source. By watching and learning what activities a child prefers, it can be possible to construct an effective behavior management program.

BEHAVIORAL CONTRACTING

A behavioral contract is a written and signed agreement between two parties, who agree to engage in a mutual interchange of privileges and responsibilities. Each privilege specified in the contract is earned by fulfilling a specific responsibility. Like any other behavior management program, a behavioral contract should be in force only after baseline observations of the specified behaviors have

been obtained. A behavioral contract is different from other behavior management techniques in that behavioral contracts specify privileges and responsibilities
for *both* of the involved parties, while parents or teachers are administrators of
contingencies, which they dictate in most other methods. Consequently, a behavioral contract represents the formal outcome of a mutually satisfactory negotiation
between two parties who desire behavior change from each other.

Behavioral contracts are useful under a variety of circumstances. Any behavior
management program can be improved by involving the child in its design and
putting its provisions into writing so that all who are involved can refer to it. This
is particularly true of programs that involve the child's parents, because communication is made more concrete and the rules may be looked at and discussed at any
time. This could save the child's teacher a few phone calls.

Another application of behavioral contracts is in both self-contained and
resource special education classes. In these settings, a standard behavioral contract that outlines the teacher's expectations, rules of conduct, academic expectations, consequences of both desirable and undesirable behavior, and any other
aspect of the program relevant to the student's success can be signed by both the
teacher and student. The student's contribution to the contract can be to set personal goals for academic accomplishment and behavior. Although student input
into these contracts is limited, by signing such a contract, the student indicates an
understanding of the rules governing behavior in the room and a commitment to
following those rules.

At the most sophisticated level, behavioral contracts can be used as a negotiating tool for resolving conflicts between children and adults. Successful conflict
resolution would normally require a series of several behavioral contracts,
because the first draft will rarely capture the essential needs of those signing it.
Instead, several drafts may be needed before the parties feel comfortable enough
to reveal their most important needs within the context of the negotiating process.

Good behavioral contracts are like good behavior management programs.
They state the specific responsibilities to be performed by each party and the specific privileges earned by each party as a consequence of performing those
responsibilities. Of course, the more concrete and specific the definitions of the
behaviors are, the more effective the contract is likely to be. However, the definitions of behaviors can require repeated negotiation. Careful attention to baseline
observations before the contract is in force and continued measurement of these
behaviors after the contract takes effect are provisions that should be included in a
contract. Also, behaviors of *both* parties who sign the contract are monitored.

Clauses that specify a bonus for complying with the contract and sanctions for
failure to comply may also be included in a behavioral contract. Finally, a monitoring and feedback system, which informs each party when responsibilities have
been fulfilled, should be written into the contract. The last clause in a contract
should specify when the contract will be reviewed and renegotiated, if necessary.
A sample behavioral contract is presented in Figure 4.1.

Figure 4.1. A Sample Behavioral Contract

1. Mike agrees to come home before 9:00 P.M., Sunday through Thursday nights, and before 12:00 midnight Friday and Saturday nights. For each night he is on time, Mike receives $1.00 from his parents. Mike also receives a bonus of $5.00 for seven consecutive nights of being on time.

2. If Mike accumulates a total of more than 2 hours of tardiness from Saturday through Friday nights, he will wash the car and mow the lawn on Saturday.

3. Mike's parents agree to question Mike regarding his whereabouts and activities for no more than 2 minutes on nights when he is late and not at all when he is on time. In exchange for a perfect week of not exceeding these time limits, Mike agrees to attend church and eat dinner with the family on Sunday.

4. Mike's parents will maintain a record of Mike's evening arrival times and Mike will keep a record of the amount of time his parents question him regarding his whereabouts and activities.

5. This contract remains in force for 2 weeks. At the end of 2 weeks, the contract may be extended or renegotiated.

6. Signatures:
   Mike:

   Mother:

   Father:

TIMEOUT AND OTHER METHODS OF DECREASING UNDESIRABLE BEHAVIOR

Almost all children emit undesirable behavior at some time in their development. What is considered unacceptable behavior varies from parent to parent, teacher to teacher, situation to situation, and from time to time. All school personnel are faced with deciding what constitutes acceptable boundaries for children's behavior. Once boundaries have been established, how to deal with unacceptable behavior becomes the important issue. Since spanking or any other form of corporal punishment are not given consideration in this book, other methods of decreasing or eliminating undesirable behavior are needed. Fortunately, several effective methods exist.

Ignoring Behavior

The least troublesome method of eliminating behavior is to ignore it. This is particularly true for the classroom teacher whose primary means of behavior control is verbal reprimand. Frequently, verbal reprimands have been found to have reinforcing rather than punishing, properties; that is, reprimands often increase or maintain the strength of the behavior they follow. Similarly, embarrassed or exasperated parents who allow a child's temper tantrum to be followed by some desirable event are increasing the likelihood of a future tantrum in similar situations. By ignoring such behavior, the positive consequences that might follow it can be eliminated, thereby decreasing the chances that the child will behave unacceptably in the future.

There are two potential difficulties in attempting to eliminate behavior by ignoring it. The first is that it may be a relatively long time before the behavior is finally extinguished. This is especially true if the behavior has been followed by positive consequences under similar circumstances in the past. A behavior that has recently appeared will be easier to eliminate. The second difficulty is that ignoring a behavior may lead to a temporary increase in its frequency before it begins to decline. This increase is typically attributed to the frustration that results from the unfulfilled expectation of reward. Furthermore, if the behavior is attended to (i.e., rewarded) after it has been ignored on several previous occasions, it will be even more difficult to eliminate the behavior due to the effects of intermittent reinforcement. Thus, the key to eliminating a behavior by ignoring it is to be patient and consistent.

Timeout

Timeout has already been mentioned several times as a technique of nonviolent punishment. The essence of timeout is that a child is placed in a boring location, where nothing of interest is available, immediately after some undesirable behavior occurs. The timeout location should not be frightening or lacking in light or air (i.e., do not use a closet). In school, an isolated chair, the hallway, an office, a coatroom, or a specially constructed area might be used for timeout. Some schools use a portable timeout area consisting of a U-shaped wall about 5 feet tall, which can be placed around a desk located in the rear of the classroom. Timeout is a very simple procedure that can also be used at home where the kitchen, guestroom, a stairwell, laundry room, or chair could become timeout areas.

The length of a timeout period can vary considerably. Some authors suggest 1 minute of timeout for each year of age. Thus, a typical range might be between 5 and 10 minutes. Timeout should be administered *immediately* after the undesirable behavior. The person administering the timeout should be calm but firm. The timeout may be accompanied by some brief explanation such as, "You can't stay here if you (hit the teacher)." If the child continues to display undesirable behavior, such as a tantrum, during the timeout period, the timeout should be extended until the child is behaving appropriately. The purpose of such an extension is to avoid rewarding undesirable behavior by releasing the child from the timeout. Some states and school districts have guidelines regarding the length and location of timeout periods and these should be consulted to be sure they are not violated. Once the child has been released from timeout, it may be useful to briefly discuss why timeout was administered and have the child think of alternative ways that the situation leading to timeout could have been handled.

If a timeout location is selected in advance, timeout has the advantage of being a simple and effective way of eliminating undesirable behavior, which can be applied as necessary causing minimal disturbance for the adult or the child. The most important point about timeout is that the timeout area must be boring and timeout must be administered immediately after the undesirable behavior. Timeout can be applied "as needed" or as part of an organized behavior management program.

Wherry (1983) cautions that the use of timeout involves the potential for violations of the individual rights of the student. He advises that informed consent be obtained from the child's parents prior to the use of timeout, response cost, and overcorrection (a method used to suppress undesirable behavior). In addition, Wherry suggests the following guidelines for the use of timeout based upon judicial proceedings: First, timeout should be employed in situations where the student's behavior creates "substantive" disruption. Second, the length of timeout should not exceed fifty minutes to one hour. Third, the child should be provided with books or lesson materials during timeout. Fourth, the student should be closely and directly supervised. In general, it seems that the practitioner can avoid problems if timeout is employed only to decrease very disruptive behavior and concurrent programs to increase desirable behavior are implemented.

It is also important to monitor the effect of timeout upon the target behavior. Solnick, Rincover, and Peterson (1977) cite two attempts to use timeout that failed. In one instance, timeout was actually reinforcing to a girl who engaged in self-stimulating behavior during the timeout period. The opportunity to engage in such behavior during the timeout actually caused the target behavior to increase. Thus, in applying timeout, it is important to establish that it actually causes the target behavior to decrease. Within a classroom, this might fail to occur if the timeout allowed the child to escape from an unpleasant situation, such as doing seatwork, or if the child managed to obtain social reinforcement from peers during the timeout period. Observation of the child's behavior during the timeout period can provide some information about how the timeout period is functioning.

Solnick et al. also studied the effectiveness of timeout with a 16-year-old retarded boy. It was found that timeout was ineffective in reducing undesirable behavior until the nontimeout environment was enriched so that it included more reinforcing stimuli. Similarly, it should be the case that timeout results in the loss of at least some reinforcement when it is applied in the regular school environment. If the timeout and nontimeout environments are not distinctively different, timeout can not be expected to be effective.

Foxx and Shapiro (1978) described a unique form of timeout which may be appropriate under some circumstances. For their procedure, each child was required to wear an object such as a ribbon that could be established as a discriminative stimulus for positive reinforcement. Whenever a student misbehaved, the ribbon was removed and the child excluded from all forms of teacher-dispensed reinforcement and participation in rewarding activities. In this procedure, the child is in timeout but remains in the classroom. Foxx and Shapiro demonstrated that a 3-minute timeout (extended if misbehavior continued) was effective in reducing misbehavior. They suggested that the procedure would be effective and convenient with lower-functioning special education classes. An advantage of the procedure was that classroom visitors knew with which students they could interact and which students were to be ignored.

In order to effectively implement such a procedure, it would be necessary to establish the ribbons as discriminative stimuli for positive reinforcement. Foxx and Shapiro accomplished this by providing teacher praise and edibles to the students for good behavior and wearing their ribbon. The procedure could also be faded out by substituting a less obvious discriminative stimulus such as a wrist band.

Removing a Privilege

Another method of decreasing undesirable behavior is to remove a privilege, reward, or access to a desirable activity when a child behaves in an unacceptable manner. This would represent an application of negative punishment, since a positive stimulus is removed (subtracted) from the situation. For instance, the child who misbehaves in class or fails to complete work (assuming this is a reasonable expectation), could be forbidden from going outside for recess. Parents and teachers typically control numerous rewarding activities that can be withdrawn when a child's behavior is unacceptable. However, this method will not work well if the child ends up losing all or most privileges, since the child then has "nothing to lose" by misbehaving. In such cases, a concurrent program to reward appropriate behavior will be necessary.

Logical Consequences

When the consequence for an undesirable behavior is logically related to the behavior itself, one is employing a behavior change technique known as *logical consequences*. The technique involves letting the natural and logical consequences of behavior affect the child (Dreikurs & Grey, 1970). For example, if a child has spent the morning in off-task behavior and fails to complete seatwork, then a logical consequence might be that the child must miss a desired activity (i.e., recess) in order to complete the unfinished work. In the home, the parents of a child who refuses to pick up his or her dirty clothes might respond by refusing to pick up or wash the clothes. Dirty, unwashed clothes are made the logical consequence of not picking clothes up. A child who carelessly or purposefully breaks an object could be required to pay for replacing the item. When logical consequences for misbehavior can be identified, they can be very effective in reducing the problem behavior.

Saying "No!"

One of the most universal methods of eliminating undesirable behavior is simply to say the word, "No!," in a strong, firm voice when undesirable behavior occurs. However, for some teachers and parents this technique is very effective, while for others it is almost totally useless. Why? The difference lies in the consistency with which a repeat occurrence of the undesired behavior after the word, "No!," has been followed by some action, such as timeout or loss of a privilege. If the child knows that the word, "No!," carries some weight and that repetition of the undesired behavior will consistently lead to timeout or loss of a privilege, then the child is likely to heed the warning. On the other hand, if "No!" is an empty threat only occasionally backed up by action, then the child is not likely to respond.

Rewarding Other Behavior

Probably the most important aspect of decreasing undesirable behavior is to provide fewer opportunities for such behavior to occur by rewarding the behavior that is desirable in the same situation. When desirable behavior occurs at a high rate, undesirable behavior is less likely in that situation. For example, if a child frequently behaves aggressively, the amount of aggression will decrease as the amount of cooperative play increases. In all cases where one is trying to decrease the frequency of an undesirable behavior, a concurrent program should be in effect to increase preferable behavior in that situation .

MAKING RULES FOR THE CLASSROOM AND HOME

Rules are one of the most basic elements of classroom and home discipline. A few simple rules, fairly and consistently enforced, can be the basis for a productive and happy classroom. On the other hand, when rules are complicated, unfair, and inconsistently enforced, much of the teacher's time will be spent in nonteaching tasks, productivity may be low, and the students may suffer from the insecurity that can result from an unpredictable environment.

Silberman and Wheelan (1980) suggested a few guidelines for good rules that are consistent with the general principles discussed throughout the present book. First of all, they suggest that rules must be clear to both children and the adults who set them. Conflict may arise when children and adults have different ideas concerning whether the requirements of a rule have been met. For instance, if a classroom rule states that students should prepare for their reading lesson right after lunch, what does this mean? Should all books and materials be out before the bell rings? Or, should the students be discussing the story they read most recently? Both students and adults should know ahead of time just what the requirements are of any particular rule.

The second guideline suggested by Silberman and Wheelan is that rules should be enforceable. If a rule is to be enforceable, they suggest that it should represent a realistic value which the child is capable of obeying, and that the responsible adult should be in a position to determine whether it is obeyed. From a teacher's perspective a rule specifying that fighting is not allowed in class would appear realistic and enforceable. However, if the rule stated that students are not allowed to fight while in school, then the teacher is placed in a position of monitoring behavior that may occur in places and at times when she or he is incapable of ascertaining the facts.

Silberman and Wheelan also suggest that holding a discussion about a rule before enforcement begins can be helpful to both the children and adults involved. A discussion provides an opportunity for ambiguities and misunderstandings to be cleared up and allows the adults to present the rationale for the rule. Children may also have ideas about how the rule can be improved and made less aversive from their perspective.

The final guideline for good rules is that the adult should have some plan for dealing with violations of the rule. If a contingency plan is devised beforehand, the teacher or parent can avoid reacting unfairly or angrily. When the consequence is specified as part of the rule, then it becomes the student's job to behave appropriately and the teacher's job to administer rules fairly and consistently. Generally, if the limits on their behavior are stated clearly students will occupy their time with the task of learning and few students will require formal behavior management programs to remediate unacceptable behavior.

SOURCES OF ADDITIONAL INFORMATION

Chapters 1 through 4 have been designed to provide a reasonably thorough introduction to the techniques of behavior management. However, many readers may wish to pursue the topics that have been discussed in more detail. Numerous sources are available and a few will be mentioned here.

The most basic principles of learning and behavior modification may be found in any introductory psychology textbook such as Morris (1982) or Darley, Glucksberg, Kamin, and Kinchla (1981). More advanced books on basic learning and the theories built up around it would include Bolles (1975), Bower and Hilgard (1981), Maser and Seligman (1977) and, for a historical perspective, Hearst (1979) or Dollard and Miller (1950). Books that describe the application of learning principles to human behavior include Staats (1963, 1975), Bandura (1969, 1977), and Turner, Calhoun, and Adams (1981). Books devoted to the topic of managing the behavior of children include Alberto and Troutman (1986), Morris and Kratochwill (1983a), Ollendick and Cerny (1981), and Ross (1981). The latter three books are compared by Prout (1984). Benson (1979), Millman, Schaefer, and Cohen (1980) and Bellack and Hersen (1985) briefly describe therapies for a wide variety of behavior problems. The handbook edited by Walker and Roberts (1983) provides a more general overview of childhood problems and their treatment. These works would provide a fairly current knowledge base for the school practitioner.

To maintain currency with the most recent developments in learning theory and behavior management, professional journals provide the best source of information. Among those I have found valuable are *Journal of Consulting and Clinical Psychology, School Psychology Review, Psychological Bulletin, Child and Youth Services, Annual Review of Psychology, Journal of Applied Behavior Analysis, Behavior Research and Therapy, Child Development, Psychology in the Schools*, and the *Journal of School Psychology*. Every practitioner must develop his or her own library and journal reading preferences. The books and journals just cited represent only a sample of what is available to the professional.

chapter 5

THE MUTUAL EFFECTS OF THE HOME AND SCHOOL UPON CHILD BEHAVIOR

When a problem in either behavior or academic achievement appears within the school, the tendency is to conduct interventions that include the child's parents as passive participants in the process. However, parents, and the environment they create at home, have a profound influence upon a child's behavior in school. Furthermore, the way a child behaves in school can also influence the home environment. The two environments, home and school, both contribute to the way a child behaves.

The purposes of this chapter are to closely examine how child behavior is influenced by both the home and school and to provide some ideas that encourage parents to take an active role in remediating behavior problems in school. The chapter begins with an introduction to the family as a system and proceeds to a discussion of the impact of family conflict upon child behavior in school. The remainder of the chapter deals with assessing the child's family system, communicating with the child's family, and actively involving parents in the remediation process.

THE FAMILY SYSTEM

Behavior problems arising in school can be examined from many perspectives. The simplest and most efficient perspective is to define the problem behavior and attempt to remediate it without considering the possible contribution of factors outside the school. For a large number of behavior problems arising in school, this straightforward approach will eventually solve the problem. However, only part of the child's time is spent in school and events outside of school often have a major impact upon school behavior. Parental divorce and child abuse are two examples of family problems that can have a great impact upon school behavior. A broader perspective views the child as behaving within a *system* consisting mainly of both the home and school and intervening with this entire system. Developing a successful behavior management program requires the cooperation of home and school. In some cases, cooperation can be very difficult to obtain because both parties are directly involved, to some degree, in maintaining the problem.

Consider, for example, the dynamics of school phobia. A child with severe school phobia shows signs of extreme distress and resistance when it is time to attend school. The child may cry, fight, or exhibit signs of illness in association with school attendance. If the child is allowed to miss several days of school, attendance can become extremely problematic because resistance can be so strong or the appearance of illness so realistic, that the child's parents are not able to cope. Consequently, parents then are in the position of actively or passively supporting nonattendance.

The school's point of view is, of course, very different from that of the parents. Attendance is typically the primary concern and, not being familiar with the parents' problem, the initial response is to simply state a need to have the child return to school. The parents may then respond with hostility, since they have been doing their best to cope with an extremely difficult situation. The only way regular attendance will be reestablished is if the parents *and* the school staff cooperate with each other to formulate a program.

The general goal of a systems approach to child behavior is to assist the home and school to disengage emotionally from the problem so they can cooperate in a helpful manner to "normalize" the child's role in each system (Fine & Holt, 1983a). If the problem is school phobia, the child's parents will need to stop supporting nonattendance and set the stage for reentering school. The school staff must also be prepared to support the child's return to regular attendance by providing positive consequences and professional expertise to ensure a positive outcome. Unless a coordinated, cooperative effort is made, the goal of reestablishing school attendance may not be met.

It can be difficult to bring the family and school to a cooperative relationship because the child's problem behavior may play an essential role in maintaining the equilibrium of the family system. For instance, a single parent may support nonattendance out of neglect, excessive dependance, or fear that the noncustodial parent may kidnap the child. In such cases, the efforts of school personnel to change the child's behavior may be fruitless, unless some form of family intervention is undertaken. Family stresses such as conflict, separation, divorce, abuse, or alcoholism may also be adversely affecting school performance. If these or similar problems are not remediated, the child can be expected to continue having difficulty in school. When family intervention is not immediately feasible or is beyond the expertise of available personnel, a systems view helps the school practitioner understand the extent of family involvement in the child's problem behavior and make the appropriate referrals while adjusting the behavior management program as needed.

When approaching problem behavior from a systems perspective, Zimmerman and Sims (1983) suggest that one investigate whether the problem behavior is, at some level, reinforcing to the child's parents. They suggest that problem behavior many times has a primary function in the marital relationship where attention is directed *toward* the child, and *away* from the marital relationship. In such cases the child's behavior can reinforce the parents via alliances with the child against the other parent or via misbehavior on the child's part that hurts one of the parents. Thus, while the problem behavior is troubling to the parents, the cost of *not* maintaining the problem is even greater because the stability of the marital relationship will be threatened.

In order to understand exactly how a child's problem behavior relates to the system as a whole, it is necessary to view the behavior within the system out of which it arises. One of the basic tenets of family systems theory is that an exclusive focus upon the child will miss the interrelationships that may be contributing to the behavior. If the individual child's behavior is changed without a complementary change in the *system*, the system as a whole is likely to resist the change so that the original problem behavior will be likely to reappear, perhaps in a different form or in a sibling.

The logic of systems theory is that the system is composed of interrelated parts, and a change in one part will affect all the parts. The system as a whole will maintain a homeostatic balance; that is, a change in one part of the system will result in pressure from other parts of the system to restore the original balance. The balance is typified by the roles played by individuals in relation to each other. These roles are maintained by the rules, both implicit and explicit, that govern the system. If the behavior of one individual in the system is changed without changing the rules of the system, pressure from other parts of the system will operate to restore the original homeostatic balance. This process is described by systems theorists as a negative feedback loop.

The complementary process, positive feedback loops, allow the system to change. Zimmerman and Sims point out that a healthy system possesses a balance of positive and negative feedback loops. This allows the system to respond flexibly to internal and external stresses. Families that are typified by a high level of either positive or negative feedback loops are likely to be threatened by any sort of change, even normally occurring changes such as a child leaving home.

Some of the rules that govern a system may be rules about rules (metarules). In a healthy system, there are metarules that allow for changes in rules. However, according to Zimmerman and Sims, families having a child with a behavior problem often lack metarules that allow for change. This is sometimes called *pathological equilibrium*, which is a form of homeostasis within the system that is maintained at the expense of one of its members. If a successful behavior management program were to be focused upon such an individual, then the system would readjust in some way to maintain the original balance. This could result in the appearance of new behavior problems in the same individual or in a sibling. Thus, some behavior management programs are not likely to be successful unless intervention is aimed at the system as a whole to help the members arrive at new rules that can accommodate the changes.

The most important point to make in regard to family systems is that they are resistant to change. That is, any intervention on behalf of the child is likely to be resisted by the system as a whole which will readjust to maintain its original balance. The implication is that soundly designed behavior management programs could either fail entirely or lead to additional problems as the family system resists the changes brought about by the child's improved behavior.

Thus, what family systems theory says to the school staff member planning a behavior management program is to beware of the characteristics of the child's family system. If the target behavior is part of that child's role in the family, or is somehow reinforcing to family members, a behavior management program may be unsuccessful unless the entire system is changed. To provide a more concrete orientation to these principles, the following section presents a brief summary of how problems that may arise within a family system can affect the academic and social behavior of a child in school.

THE RELATIONSHIP BETWEEN THE FAMILY SYSTEM AND SCHOOL BEHAVIOR

An almost infinite number of family problems can affect the behavior of a child in school. Instead of attempting to provide a list of such problems, two problems that affect a large number of children will be examined: divorce and child abuse.

Divorce

Divorce affects a great number of schoolchildren. Hetherington (1979) projected, given the rates of divorce in the 1970s, that 40-50% of children born in the 1970s would spend some time living in a single-parent family. Bane (1979) estimated that 30% of children born in the 1980s would experience a parental divorce before they reached the age of 18. Drake (1981) cited data indicating that one out of every six children in this country lives with one parent and that one-third of the children referred to child study teams in one school district were from divorced or separated families. Regardless of the source of the estimate, it is clear that divorce affects a substantial number of children.

Effects of Parental Divorce and Conflict upon Children. There are numerous reasons for expecting parental divorce to have negative effects upon children. Hetherington (1979) provides one perspective. She views divorce as a process that typically begins with a shift in the family situation involving disequilibrium, and perhaps conflict, prior to and during the divorce. Following the separation and divorce is a period of adjustment to living in a single-parent family, which continues for about 5 years. Most children then reenter a two-parent family, which then requires additional adjustment.

Over the short term, parental divorce can be viewed as a stress-inducing crisis for all involved. According to Hetherington, stresses associated with conflict, loss, change, and uncertainty may all be critical factors. Over the long term, the availability of important adults, discipline styles, economic circumstances, and support systems are all likely to be changed by divorce. All of the environmental changes and events surrounding a divorce can be expected to have at least some impact on a child's behavior.

The range of potential behavioral effects of parental divorce upon children is considerable. The loss of a primary attachment figure and role model might be expected to cause depression and difficulty in mastering the tasks of development. If dissolution of the marriage involves open conflict between the parents, one might expect numerous negative sequelae, such as inconsistency in discipline practices, exposure to poor models of social behavior, feelings of abandonment, emotional neglect, and self-blame (Pfeffer, 1981).

Any of these consequences could affect a child's academic performance or social behavior in school. The relevant empirical literature on this issue is so extensive that a thorough review is impossible in the present context. Thus, the present discussion will be restricted to two questions: First, what general effects of divorce upon children have been empirically documented and what are the most salient parameters of these effects? Second, what specific effects does divorce have upon the academic performance and social behavior of children within the school?

The General Impact of Divorce upon Children. Children show a variety of responses to the divorce of their parents, including depression, irritability, aggression, poor self-concept, academic problems, anger, and shame (e.g., Drake, 1981). The particular impact of parental divorce upon a particular child has been shown to vary with the age of the child, the time since the divorce, the characteristics of the child, and the degree of conflict within the marital relationship.

Emery (1982) reviewed much of the recent literature on the effects of divorce on children. He concluded that parental conflict was more important than whether or not a divorce was obtained. Children living in homes characterized by interparental conflict had the greatest risk of showing behavioral problems and their risk was greater than that of children from broken or intact homes that were relatively harmonious. Such conflict in both broken and intact families appears to lead to problems characterized by "undercontrol" (e.g., aggression, acting-out, etc.). Finally, boys are more likely than girls to exhibit "obviously maladaptive" behavior and girls are likely to respond to marital turmoil in more subtle ways such as by becoming anxious or withdrawn or experiencing problems in relationships with the opposite sex.

Slater and Haber (1984) compared the adjustment of adolescents as a function of family background, sex, and degree of conflict in the home. The presence of family conflict was associated with higher levels of anxiety, lower self-esteem, lower self-concept, and a tendency to view events as being outside their control. Furthermore, adjustment was not related to whether their parents were divorced or separated.

Parental divorce has also been shown to have different effects as a function of the age of the child. Preschool children have been observed to exhibit diffuse anger and grief, aggression, regression, self-blame, rejection of strangers, anxiety, moodiness, and irritability. Latency-aged children apparently exhibit a somewhat better understanding of the divorce process responding with grieving, fear, fantasies of responsibility and reconciliation, depression, displaced aggression, anger toward parents, and loyalty conflicts. Adolescents reportedly show sadness, shame, embarrassment, anxiety about the future and marriage, premature or promiscuous sexual behavior, deidealization of their parents, and withdrawal (Drake, 1981; Guidubaldi, Cleminshaw, Perry, & Mcloughlin, 1983; King & Kleemeier, 1983).

In a study of variables predicting treatment outcome, Webster-Stratton (1985) found that single-parent families of conduct-disordered children were most likely to fail to respond to therapy. The authors attributed this to the associated economic difficulties encountered by single-parent families along with the lack of social support systems. Thus, in addition to the stresses generated by divorce and separation, such families seem to have the greatest difficulty in dealing with the problems of their children. It seems likely that these findings would also apply to attempts of school personnel to implement behavior management programs with children. Children whose parents are separated, divorced, or experiencing marital conflict may not respond to behavior management programs as well as children from stable homes.

The Impact of Divorce upon Academic Achievement and Social Behavior. A study by John Guidubaldi et al. (1983) was an attempt to develop a nationwide sample of children from divorced families. Their technique was to solicit the participation of members of the National Association of School Psychologists (NASP). Those members who responded to the original request were asked to randomly select two children each from the first, third, and fifth grades. One child from each pair was to be from an intact family and the other from a currently divorced single-parent family. The resulting sample contained children from 38 states and was reasonably well distributed with respect to sex of the child and marital status of parents. The dependent measures included intelligence test scores, achievement test scores, social competence measures, and characteristics of the school and family environment.

Guidubaldi et al. most thoroughly examined the effects of parental divorce upon academic achievement. The general pattern found for reading, spelling, and mathematics achievement scores was as follows: Boys from single-parent families performed most poorly on these measures at each grade level with the exception of third-grade mathematics scores. Furthermore, these boys' achievement scores dropped across the three grade levels. First-grade girls from divorced families, on the other hand, performed worse than their intact-family controls on all three measures of achievement, but, with the exception of fifth-grade reading, and third- and fifth-grade spelling, achieved at the same level as their controls in the third and fifth grades. Only in mathematics did achievement levels of girls of single-parent families fall below first grade levels, and an equivalent drop was obtained for girls of intact families.

Other analyses indicated that children from divorced families were more likely than their counterparts from intact families to be referred to a school psychologist (confirming my personal impression and congruent with Beattie and Maniscalo, 1985, who found that children enrolled in special education classes were significantly less likely to be living with both biological parents than students exclusively in regular education classes), to be in programs for reading difficulties, and to have repeated a grade in school. The divorced-family child's relationship with the noncustodial parent was related to academic and social adjustment. A more positive relationship was associated with better adjustment. As noted by the authors, many important relationships remain to be teased out of this impressive data base. However, the analyses reported so far confirm that divorce has a negative impact upon children's academic achievement.

Guidubaldi et al. were not as thorough in their analysis of the impact of parental divorce upon social behavior as they were in their analysis of its impact upon achievement. They found statistically significant differences between children of single-parent and divorced families but the differences were not analyzed in detail. Not even the means of the dependent variables were presented. Significant differences related to social behavior were found for failure anxiety, unreflectiveness, social involvement, negative feelings, withdrawal, blaming, socialization, grade in conduct, peer rejection (teacher rating), peer popularity (parent rating), and locus of control. Analyses of covariance controlling for WISC-R full scale IQ score and family income level did not significantly alter this pattern.

Two additional generalizations derived from these analyses were that girls and younger children showed the fewest adverse effects of being in a divorced family. Also, fewer adverse effects were shown by children of divorced parents who had positive relationships with their noncustodial parent. This latter finding is important because it points to a potentially serious omission in the Guidubaldi et al. study that deserves some discussion. This omission concerns the influence of the degree of parental conflict, pre- and post-divorce, upon children's adjustment. Those children able to have a positive relationship with the noncustodial parent are likely to be from families where conflict surrounding the divorce and separation was minimal or handled well. This implies that parental conflict plays an important role in the adjustment of children from divorced families as found in the Emery (1982) review. Hopefully, future reports of the Guidubaldi et al. data base will include some reference to the effects of parental conflict upon the adjustment to divorce.

In a study not related to the NASP data base, Guidubaldi and Perry (1984) studied the entire entering kindergarten class in a suburban school district. They found that children living in single-parent families entered kindergarten with significantly less social and academic competence than children from intact families. This finding persisted across a wide variety of measures of social and academic competence and when the analysis controlled for the impact of socioeconomic status. In general, there is little doubt that parental divorce influences a child's adjustment in school. Hopefully, future reports will lend additional insight into the causal structure of such effects and lead to effective interventions for remediating them.

Intervention with Children of Divorced Families. It should be clear that parental divorce may represent a major change in a child's life that may lead to disturbances in academic and social behavior. Yet, even given the plethora of data regarding the effects of parental divorce upon children, no theory has been advanced to provide a base from which to formulate intervention strategies. However, one possibility that may merit some consideration is whether Kübler-Ross's (1969) "stages" of adaptation to death in adults might also describe the grieving process of a child whose parents divorce. Her list of potential reactions to death includes denial, rage and anger, bargaining, depression, and acceptance. It seems that all of these reactions are present in the findings reported above.

Given that one accepts the potential validity of using Kübler-Ross's potential reactions as a way of categorizing the effects of parental divorce upon children, two intervention goals are implicated. First, one might hope to avoid the grieving process altogether by assisting the child to see that neither parent is "lost" from the child's perspective. Second, in cases where the noncustodial parent does more or less disappear from the domestic scene, a reasonable intervention goal would be to assist the child toward realistic acceptance of the inevitable (cf. King & Kleemeier, 1983).

These two general goals can be translated into more specific strategies. Drake (1981) points out that a child's school can be an important source of stability and support at a time when the home is unstable. Any adult in the school may become a source of support and teachers can ease the transition to a single-parent family by showing sensitivity to the child. For example, the teacher can include examples of working mothers and single-parent families in examples used in class. In addition, a school staff member can provide support and positive feedback at a time when the parents are too preoccupied by other issues to fulfill this role.

Guidubaldi et al. (1983) point out that school psychologists and others in the school can advise divorcing and divorced parents of the need to maintain contact with their children. This is particularly important in the case of boys from mother-custody households. The school can be particularly important in providing opportunities and encouragement to the noncustodial parent to remain involved with the child's school by including them in conferences and providing them with copies of the child's progress reports. These authors also state that individual and group counseling for children of divorced families should be given priority in schools. The rationale and outline for such an intervention is described by Kalter, Pickar, and Lesowitz (1984).

With respect to specific issues surrounding behavior management programs in cases where marital conflict has an impact upon the child's behavior, several suggestions can be made. First, school staff members must be alert to the possibility that marital conflict underlies a child's behavior or academic problems. Frequently, this is not difficult to determine because marital partners in conflict often volunteer negative information about their spouses. Such information may include reports that the other partner is often absent, has a drinking problem, is unemployed, or "doesn't care." This type of information can also be elicited by asking simple questions, such as whether the two parents agree that a problem exists, how the other spouse reacts to problem behavior, or how consistent the parents are when it comes to discipline issues.

If the outcome of an interview with a child's parents indicates that school problems may be related to marital conflict, it may be helpful to tell them about the negative impact that such conflict may have upon school behavior and performance. While it is important to state that parental decisions are the responsibility of the parents, it is possible to lessen the impact of such decisions upon children. Family therapy, participation in group therapy, parenting skill classes, allowing children to attend support groups for children of divorced parents, and other locally available community services may be helpful to all involved in the situation. Behavior management programs can also assist in remediating problems in the school and home, but some cautions are necessary.

Parents experiencing the emotional turmoil surrounding separation and divorce may not be capable of administering or conducting behavior management programs involving their children. They may experience difficulty setting limits, enforcing rules, administering contingencies, and following through with promised rewards or punishments. In the worst cases, undesirable behavior is rewarded by one parent as a way of "getting" the other parent, making behavior management efforts extremely difficult. It is important for school personnel to avoid entering the conflict between parents, focusing instead on the needs of the child. Programs that involve the child's parents in key roles may be destined to fail. The optimal strategy may be to centralize the program within the school environment and keep parental involvement to a minimum. Programs that involve points or tokens should be administered by school personnel, who should also dispense the contingencies using, if possible, material back-up reinforcers provided by the parents.

As a behavior management program becomes established and effective, it would be desirable to include one or both parents but their participation should be carefully monitored. Important roles should be given to the parent or parents only when an ability to carry out its responsibilities has been demonstrated by previous behavior. An extra effort may be necessary to ensure that rules and contingencies are well understood by the responsible parent.

Parental divorce is an event that will be experienced by a large portion of school-aged children. In many cases parental divorce will be associated with problems in school that will require referral to professionals outside the school and/or behavior management programs based in school. However, sad as it may be, divorce is a fact of life for many children and, regardless of the negative impact, it is possible for school personnel to manage the resulting behavioral problems. However, conducting behavior management programs with this group may require special attention to their unique needs.

Child Abuse

Child abuse, both the use of excessive corporal punishment and sexual abuse, has attracted a great deal of attention in recent years. It is a rare week that goes by without some mention of either specific cases of abuse being processed in the courts or some general article about child abuse appearing in the various news media. In fact, educators in most states are now obligated to report suspected cases of child abuse to appropriate social agencies (Guyer, 1982).

Many parents who abuse their children have a history of abuse in their own childhood and/or are likely to be ignorant of the basic facts of child development. Characteristics of abused children themselves, such as premature birth, temperament, and handicapping conditions, are also associated with a high probability of abuse. Wolfe (1985) reviewed studies comparing abusive and nonabusive parents. He found that abusive parents generally display symptoms of depression and health problems and are likely to be involved in stress-inducing family situations that impair their competence as parents. Their children come to reflect the qualities of this environment, behaving so as to present the parent with a high number of problem situations, which helps maintain a relatively high level of conflict. The general pattern within an abusive family, then, is one of disharmony, conflict, frustration, stress, and the relatively infrequent use of positive rewards. Generally, abusive parents are impaired in the skills needed to function as competent parents and become involved in a continuing cycle of reciprocal coercive interactions with their children. Thus, any view of the origins of abusive parenting must consider the entire context of the family system (cf. Belsky, 1980).

To say that child abuse is an interactive process does not imply in any way that it is a healthy process. From the viewpoint of school personnel, the effects upon the child are of the greatest concern. Chapter 6 includes a detailed discussion of the indicators of child abuse, since recognizing its occurrence is an important function of the school. Among the behavioral characteristics associated with child abuse, both sexual abuse and excessive corporal punishment, are depression, withdrawal, crying, fear, frequent absenteeism or tardiness, precocious sexual behavior or language, poor academic performance, running away from home, and hyperactivity.

Williams (1983) noted that a consistent finding in research on the effects of child abuse is that abused children are significantly more aggressive that non-abused children. Other behaviors that she found to be associated with physical or sexual abuse included hyperactivity, withdrawal, passivity, sexual malfunctioning, guilt, shame, anxiety, running away from home, and suicide attempts. Recall that the "belt theory" of delinquency, discussed in Chapter 2, attributes delinquent behavior to overly harsh parental punishment. Finally, moderate to severe physical injury, and even death, are possible outcomes of the most severe parental abuse of children. If a child shows one or all of these characteristics in excess, it is very likely to attract the attention of the school staff and precipitate a conference with the parents.

Barahal, Waterman, and Martin (1981) studied the social/cognitive development of a sample of abused children who were not showing signs of behavioral problems. They found IQs of the abused children to be about 10 points lower than those of a well-matched group of control children. In addition, the abused children showed less confidence in their ability to influence events in their environment than the nonabused children. This difference was strongest for negative events. In addition, the abused children were lowest in sensitivity to socioemotional contexts and highest in egocentricity. Barahal et al. concluded that remediating the social skill deficits of abused youngsters may be necessary if the generation-to-generation cycle of child abuse is to be broken.

As noted earlier, the school's role in helping abused children begins with knowledge of what constitutes abuse, what behavioral indicators accompany it, and the obligations of school personnel under state laws governing reporting of child abuse. Thus, the main role of school personnel is to recognize abusive situations and take appropriate action to end them. If behavior management of problem behavior is needed in the school, parental involvement may need to be minimal because their ability to cope with their child's behavior is demonstrably poor. However, successful behavior management programs conducted in the school may be valuable tools for helping the parents improve their own skills.

THE ROLE OF THE SCHOOL
IN SYSTEMS-BASED PROBLEMS

This chapter focuses upon the role of the family in problems that come to the attention of educators in school. Both parental divorce and child abuse are examples of family system disturbances that may have a great effect upon a child's

behavior and academic performance in school. Of course, many other characteristics of the family environment may affect behavior in school, such as a death or
serious illness, loss of a job by either parent, birth of a new sibling, a move to
another school, alcoholism, the value the parents place upon education and learning, and an infinite number of other characteristics. Now, if the child's behavior
plays some role in the family system, efforts to modify the child's behavior based
solely in the school may not be effective. Fine and Holt (1983b) point out that even
excessive corporal punishment may serve some function within a family system.

It is helpful to approach problems from the perspective that the entire system
sometimes needs help, not just the child. Otherwise, any behavior management
program conducted exclusively in the school could be doomed to failure because
the entire family system would be threatened by a change in the child's behavior.
How, then, should the personnel in the school system who desire to remediate a
child's behavior approach the problem in such a way as to make the changes as
compatible with the family system as would be necessary to assure success? I
believe that two components are involved in the process. First, a trusting, nonthreatening relationship must be established with the parents. Second, the school
staff must be prepared to conduct some assessment of the family system dynamics
in order to determine what roles the child's behavior may play in that system.

Communication with the Child's Family

Under normal circumstances, schools routinely communicate a great deal with
parents. Regular communications include report cards and scheduled conferences, meetings of the parent-teacher organization, and various notes that are
sent home with students. However, when a special conference with the parent or
parents is requested by the school, the proposed topic is usually "bad news" from
the perspective of the parent(s). For instance, it might be necessary to elicit parental permission to conduct a detailed assessment of the child's academic and emotional status, inform the parents that a formal behavior management program is
required to remediate a behavioral problem, present the results of an assessment,
or discuss some other problem related to the child's academic and/or social
adjustment.

Even if the news turns out to be positive, the initial reactions of parents to a
request for a school conference is likely to be negative. Since the school represents
a source of public authority, they are likely to feel threatened by the prospect of
having their competence as parents scrutinized. Those who represent the school
should be sensitive to this possibility and gear their communication to the needs of
the parents. If the early interactions with the parents are conducted in a nonthreatening manner, it may be possible to elicit their cooperation and help when
more sensitive topics are dealt with at a later time.

Although it is impossible to present guidelines and techniques that are appropriate for every situation, the following paragraphs will discuss some techniques
and ideas that may prove useful in parent conferences.

Attribution Theory. Psychological research in the area of attribution is concerned with trying to understand what is involved in how people infer causal relationships. The relevance of attribution research to school-parent relationships is based upon a very simple premise: *Parents do not like to be regarded as responsible for their children's problems.* In fact, if parents are blamed or accused by school staff of being responsible for the problems of their children, they are likely to take a defensive stance that is almost certain to impede progress toward remediating the child's behavioral or academic problems.

Research into the issue of how people attribute causes indicates that people tend to take credit for positive outcomes and deny responsibility for negative outcomes (Harvey & Weary, 1984). Thus, one goal of a school conference should be to communicate at least something positive to the parents and to present negative information (i.e., the description of the problem) in a way that totally avoids pinning the responsibility upon the parents. It is particularly important to avoid forcing the parents into making what would be called "internal and stable" attributions. An internal attribution ascribes the cause of an event to some internal characteristic of the individual; a stable attribution is one that cannot be changed. Research into the origins of depression indicates that people who tend to make internal and stable attributions regarding the cause of negative events are good candidates to become depressed (Seligman, Abramson, Semmel, & Von Baeyer, 1979).

On a more practical level, a parent conference should not be an opportunity for the school to express its frustrations toward a child's parents. If parents come away from a conference with the idea that they are bad or incompetent parents, they are likely to become angry, depressed, or upset with the school. In addition, they may even deny most of the information presented at the meeting and will be either overtly or covertly uncooperative with any program proposed by school personnel. Although information must be communicated at a parent conference, it should not be presented in such a way as to place blame on anybody.

Listening Skills. One of the most important things to do in a parent conference is to listen. Despite the fact that certain people within the school may be experts on a certain, narrow area of a child's functioning, the child's parents know more than anyone else about the child. Acknowledging the parents' expertness and giving them the opportunity to share information about the child should be one of the goals of a parent conference. Often the child's parents and the school share common concerns about the child's academic progress and behavior. On the other hand, it may be discovered that the parents do not place the same value on success in school as teachers, school administrators, and special education staff.

Listening to parents (or anyone else) is not just a matter of being polite and quiet. It also means that the listener must truly gain some understanding of the ideas and feelings being communicated. One technique of gaining understanding of another's ideas is to rephrase what has been said and repeat it back to the parents with particular emphasis upon acknowledging the feelings that were expressed. By saying things back to the parents in different words, one is able to check on the accuracy of their own interpretation of what has been said.

Sometimes, of course, important thoughts and feelings are left unsaid. For this reason it is also important to attend to the body language of the parents. If the parents appear uncomfortable or hostile, it may be fruitful to inquire whether they are satisfied with the conclusions or direction of the conference. This can often be most easily accomplished by making an indirect inquiry rather than approaching the potential problem head on. For instance, asking parents how they have been coping with a particular behavior may reveal that many things have been tried unsuccessfully or that they feel helpless and have given up trying to cope with the problem. In either case, it is up to the school staff to come up with fresh approaches, instill confidence in the plan developed by the team, and ensure that the parents have input into the final plan.

Grieving. Previously, it was noted that children tend to show behaviors that correspond to the stages of the grieving process when their parents divorce. These stages—denial, anger, bargaining, depression, and acceptance—can be used to describe the categories of behavior that are likely to appear whenever a person suffers a major loss. When parents receive news that their child in some way is not "normal," they may tend to react to the news as though they, too, have suffered a major loss. Indeed, they have suffered a loss, namely, of a "normal" child (Waterman, 1982). The identification or birth of a handicapped child is also likely to have an impact upon the entire family system, which may need outside help in coping with the handicapped child (Harris & Fong, 1985).

Many factors contribute to the ease with which parents move toward accepting the reality of a child's problem behavior and the need to do something about it. These factors include the severity of the problem, the degree to which the problem is a part of the family system, the personalities of the parents, and the manner in which the parents are informed of the problem. Waterman recommends that parents be informed in a direct manner that accurately, realistically, and completely describes the problem without any false reassurances that the child will "grow out of it." In addition, she suggests that both sensitivity to the emotional needs of the parents and dealing with them as rational, mature persons eager to learn more about their child may be helpful to the majority of parents.

School personnel should recognize that parents are likely to express a wide range of emotions when they are confronted with the facts about their child's behavior and academic performance. Some of these emotions may be directed against the school and the people who work there. It is probably wasted effort for school personnel to defend themselves against these emotions, particularly anger. Instead, it would be most helpful to redirect the energies of the parents toward contributing to the resolution of the child's problem behavior. In many ways a meeting with a child's parents is similar to a counseling or therapy session. In their review of family therapy, Zimmerman and Sims (1983) note that some families undergoing therapy do not improve but deteriorate instead. Two therapist characteristics were consistently associated with deterioration: first, therapists who had "poor relationship skills" and directly attacked "loaded issues" and family members' defenses very early in treatment; and second, therapists who did little to support family members.

It seems reasonable to assume that similar effects could be expected in parent meetings conducted in the school. Thus, the suggestion is that school personnel should be aware of the emotional issues likely to be revealed in a parent conference and avoid attacking the parents on sensitive issues. In addition, the parents should leave the meeting feeling supported by the school rather than in conflict with the school. After all, all parties involved in the conference are really trying to help the child succeed in school and prepare him or her for life. With this common goal in mind, it should be possible to focus upon helping the child.

However, as noted earlier, a child's behavior does not exist independently of the systems in which the child lives. This includes the family system, which may in some overt or covert manner support the problem behavior of the child. Two questions need to be addressed. How do school personnel determine the role of the family system in the child's behavior? And, what can be done once the family system is understood? These questions are addressed in the following sections. The first section addresses the problem of what questions to ask regarding the family system. The remaining sections deal more specifically with the question of how to involve the family in a positive way with remediation of the child's behavior.

ASSESSING THE FAMILY SYSTEM

A complete assessment of a child's family system is not likely to be performed by personnel in a school system because of time constraints and the lack of people trained in family assessment and therapy. Nevertheless, a lot can be learned during a family conference, hypotheses can be generated about the family system, and the relationship between the child's behavior and the family system can be studied. Frequently, it may be possible to involve the family in helping the child in a healthy way. In other cases the family system may be in such bad shape that referral to a family therapist, social agencies, or the legal system may be the only recourse for the school. Many cases will fall somewhere in between, and it will be up to the school to do the best it can for both the child and family under circumstances that may be far from ideal.

Assessing the family system consists of posing questions, forming hypotheses, and seeking confirmatory data, just as in conducting a behavioral assessment of the child. Techniques of assessment include administration of standardized assessment instruments to the parents, asking questions of the parents, and observing the reactions and interaction of the parents during the conference and other times as opportunities are available.

Four areas are of interest in gathering information about the family. First, it is desirable to obtain as objective a picture as possible of the child's behavior at home. Second, it is valuable to learn something about the marital relationship and how the child gets along with siblings. Third, it would be valuable to learn as much as possible about how the parents cope with the child's behavior at home. Finally, it can be useful to gather some general information about how the parents have been coping with problem behavior and developmental milestones such as toilet training. (See Azrin & Foxx, 1974, for a behavioral approach to toilet training.)

While it sounds easy to gain an objective picture of the child's behavior at home, the only truly reliable way to do so is to conduct a home observation, and even this technique has its own unique problems. Several behavior checklists and child personality measures are available for those who are trained in their use. These measures can be valuable because of their objective nature and the feedback that they provide to parents. On the other hand, confusion can result from trying to assess the child's behavior at home. This is especially likely if the parents have different views of the child's behavior. An acceptable method of obtaining a picture of the child's behavior at home is to ask the parents directly. This might be done after both parents have completed an objective measure of the child's home behavior.

Once a picture of the child's behavior and the parental perception of it are obtained, it may be relevant to move on to a discussion of how the child interacts with his or her siblings. In addition, a comparison of the siblings may reveal what different roles are played by each child in the family system. A common pattern in family assessment is that one child plays the role of "problem child" in the family system. If this is noted it is possible that the child's behavior has a role in maintaining the family system and could be quite resistant to change in both the home and the school.

Assessment of the marital relationship is valuable because the existence of conflict is almost certain to be reflected in the behavior of the child. Conflict may be revealed in a number of ways. First, if only one parent is able to attend the conference, despite the best efforts of the school to have both parents attend, this may suggest conflict in dealing with the children or that one parent is more or less the source of power. Typical parent conferences involve only the mother, but this does not provide the school with a picture of how both parents interact. If only one parent attends because the marriage has dissolved in a divorce, it may be prudent to inquire gently as to the nature of the relationship prior to the divorce. Single parents are often quite candid about the behavior of the former spouse and much can be learned by just listening.

When parents have undergone a divorce, the impact upon the child is likely to be long standing, particularly if the marriage was full of conflict, one or both parents is or was alcoholic, or if the child was or is physically abused. A line of inquiry can be begun by asking the parent how the child was affected by the divorce and whether the child remains in regular contact with the noncustodial parent. Sometimes, the conflict that led to the divorce is continued after the divorce by involving the child. Visits to the home of the noncustodial parent can be particularly trying for all involved and may turn out to be associated with misbehavior at home or in school.

As yet, the literature on child behavior therapy does not suggest any particular strategy for helping children cope with the divorce of their parents. However, when a family systems assessment suggests that divorce and/or marital conflict are affecting a child's behavior, it may be prudent to examine the child's level of social skills and consider whether a focus upon social skills training (see Chapter 11) may remediate problem behavior.

The last two areas to assess are the parents' skills at coping with the identified problem behavior and the general problem-solving skills of the parents. Questions about the child's behavior at home can be extremely valuable. First, the parents may be lacking some basic skills in behavior management, which can be addressed in a nonthreatening manner, if possible. If the topic elicits a defensive response, it may be best to drop the issue until a later time or approach it from a different perspective. A second possibility is that the parents have been inconsistent in their approach to the problem or they simply do not recognize that a problem is present. Another possibility is that parents may reveal abusive tendencies by misattributing negative motivation to the behavior of their child. Bauer and Twentyman (1985) found that physically abusive mothers tended to agree that their children were attempting to annoy them, even when the available information was insufficient to justify such a conclusion. Thus, it may be useful to determine the attributional style of parents with respect to the behavior of their children. A tendency to attribute negative motivation to their children's behavior may suggest a potential for abusive behavior.

A more indirect approach to finding out about the coping skills of the parents is to question them regarding how developmental milestones and more mundane daily routines are or have been approached. Toilet training is one developmental milestone about which it can be useful to question the parents. Parental convenience, peer and societal pressure, and entry into school all make most parents highly motivated to accomplish toilet training smoothly and "on time." In addition, toilet training is one of the earliest efforts of the parents to bring their child into conformity with set standards. Thus, the experience is important to both child and parents because it sets the stage for the teaching style of the parents. The successful techniques and parental attitudes that develop during this period are likely to receive continued use and reinforcement as the child grows.

If the parents complain that toilet training was a difficult or problematic period, it may be helpful to obtain more detail. Toilet training should never be accompanied by harsh punishment since this will tend to worsen performance. If the parents report that harsh punishment was necessary to accomplish training, it is possible that punishment is overused by the parents in other discipline situations.

Another issue of interest is when toilet training was begun. Overly punitive parents are often ignorant of the normal stages in child development and might be expected to begin toilet training unreasonably early.

Techniques of handling daily routines can also reveal how skillful the parents are. Getting to bed on time in the evening is the beginning of a sequence of events that includes getting up the next morning, eating breakfast, getting dressed, and, quite often, leaving for work and the local day-care center or school. Several decades ago, a child's behavior in the morning and evening was not extremely important because the majority of families were composed of a working husband and a housewife/mother. However, in today's world many families are composed of either single parents or a pair of working parents. In these cases, it is important that the child's behavior not interfere with the parent's routine for arriving at work on time. A complication in these situations is that the child's attention-seeking behavior is likely to be very high. Questioning the parents about daily routines can contribute to an understanding of how potential conflict is handled, how rigid or flexible the family system is, and whether the behavior observed in school is a part of a larger, systemwide pattern.

A final area that can provide a perspective on the family system is how rules, disobedience, and consequences are handled in the family. A discussion of rules, which can be used to guide the assessment, was included in Chapter 4. Some significant indicators would include whether the parents can specify rules and consequences clearly, the consistency of enforcement, and whether the focus is upon reward or punishment.

As the school staff and parents become more comfortable with each other, the place of the child in the family system should become more apparent. This process may extend over several meetings and is likely to involve special education staff, the principal, and/or the school's psychologist. In addition to discussing the practical issues of child management with the parents, those who participate should be aware of other issues. Fine and Holt (1983a) suggest that an assessment of the family system should seek answers to a variety of questions. Among these questions are the following: (a) Who holds the power at home and school? (b) What roles does the child play in each setting? (c) What triangulation of relationships exists in each setting? (d) How rigid are the home and school systems? (e) How are different family members affected by the child's behavior? (f) How is the family system maintained? (g) What is lost and gained by family members if the child changes?

As the assessment data is obtained and noted, the family can then be placed on an imaginary continuum with respect to the degree of involvement in supporting the child's problem behavior in the school. At one end of the continuum is the family system that has little to do with the child's school behavior, where the parents are deeply concerned about the child's success in school and are willing to cooperate as fully as possible with attempts to remediate the problem. At the other end of the continuum are those families where the child's problem behavior in school is minor compared to problems within the family system. This would include families with one or more actively alcoholic parents or where one or both parents are abusive or neglectful.

As in all behavioral assessments, the results are *hypotheses*, subject to revision as more data is obtained. The action taken by the school will depend, of course, upon the nature and severity of the problem. In some cases, legal action may be mandated. In other cases, the school, with the assistance of appropriately trained personnel such as a school psychologist or social worker, can attempt to remediate the problem behavior of the child with the assistance of the family. The possibility that family systems problems will require referral to either private or public assistance agencies or professional therapists should always remain an option for those who work within the school system.

A TECHNIQUE FOR PLACING A POSITIVE PERSPECTIVE ON FAMILY SYSTEMS PROBLEMS

When a family system assessment leads to the hypothesis that the child's misbehavior plays an important role in the maintenance of the entire system, how can the school bring about a change in behavior via a parent conference? Bowman and Goldberg (1983) have suggested that "reframing" is a technique that can be of some value.

The essence of the technique is that an attempt is made to alter the current patterns by dealing with them in an indirect manner that avoids eliciting defensive behavior from the parents. As pointed out at the start of this chapter, most parents are motivated to maintain a positive self-image of their parenting skills and will respond defensively to suggestions that they are at fault or need to change in order to improve the child's behavior. The mechanism of change in the reframing technique lies in placing the behavior in a frame that emphasizes the positive motivations of all concerned. The goal is to bring to the surface previously unrecognized positive and caring feelings, which are frequently masked by angry and apparently uncaring ones. By reframing the problem in this manner, new options for change are opened up for the family.

Consider a hypothetical example of the application of the technique. Assume that a child has been referred for evaluation showing poor academic performance and unacceptable outbursts of aggressive behavior. An assessment of the family reveals that the child's behavior is similar at home where the child lives with his divorced mother and two sisters. Further analysis of the behavior reveals that the most troublesome time for the child are the Mondays that follow visits to the noncustodial father, which take place on alternate weekends. Furthermore, independent interviews of both the mother and father indicate that they are frequently in continued conflict over financial and parenting matters.

In order to frame this hypothetical situation in a positive way that presents some options for change, it is first necessary to avoid blaming any of the family members. Then, in the presence of both parents, one might note how both are having difficulty coping with the new living arrangement, which may be even more confusing to the child. The child, in turn, is motivated to please both parents and may even be blaming himself or herself for the breakup of the marriage. By bringing these underlying feelings to light, it may be possible to encourage the parents to be more consistent with each other and try to communicate that the divorce is their own problem and does not belong to the child. Alternately, one could explain the difficulty that children experience in such situations and encourage the parents to seek counseling for the child.

The key, then, is to emphasize the positive motivation of each individual in the family and then frame the situation around these "hidden" motivations.

BEHAVIOR MANAGEMENT OF PARENTING BEHAVIOR

Although the major focus of this book is upon managing the behavior of children in school, it seems reasonable to conclude this chapter with some notes on how the behavior of parents can be managed to the benefit of their children. Basically, two approaches are available. One can either work directly with parents via a workshop or training format or one can indirectly involve parents in the management of their children's behavior via programs that are conducted in the school.

Numerous curriculums for training parents in child management skills are available. The books, *Taking a Look at Discipline* by Garman (1983), *How to Help Children with Common Problems* by Schaefer and Millman (1981), and *Effective Parents/Responsible Children* by Eimers and Aitchison (1977) are excellent examples of such resources. One of the most popular is the S.T.E.P. program (Systematic Training for Effective Parenting). Most communities will have such programs regularly available. Parents can be referred to these programs by those in school. School systems can also arrange to offer such programs through their adult educations departments. One problem with such programs is that parents who are already competent tend to enroll in these programs to improve their skills, while those parents who truly need improved parenting skills do not recognize the need and are unlikely to enroll.

Within the school, it is possible to involve parents in behavior management programs and provide instruction in the theory of behavior management via workshop formats. This not only contributes to remediating the problem behavior of the child but can also give the parents supervised training in the use of behavior management principles. Two good places to begin such training are discussed in Chapter 10. One of these programs is the program for rewarding mastery of basic facts. This program is very simple and can be described easily in a handout.

When it is decided to train parents in such a program, it is probably best to have the parents practice a few times under supervision of someone who has experienced success with the program in the past.

An alternative method of encouraging parental involvement in behavior management programs is to use a home note system. The details of this program are also described in Chapter 10. Its essence is that the teacher provides feedback to the parents regarding the acceptability of the child's behavior and academic performance in school. The parents then award points for good or improved behavior. The points can be used by the child to "purchase" rewards previously agreed upon by both the parents and child. Research suggests that training in behavior management skills accompanied by instruction in the principles of behavior management is an effective technique for helping parents cope effectively with the problem behavior of their children and that the instruction in general principles enhances the effect of the training in behavior techniques (McMahon, Forehand, & Griest, 1981).

Any of these techniques may, if circumstances are right, allow a child's parents to become involved in a positive way with the management of their child's behavior. This could begin the process of replacing previously unhealthy patterns of interaction with more healthy ones.

WHAT IF NOTHING SEEMS TO WORK?

It is an unfortunate fact of life that sometimes a person's best efforts are not enough. This can happen in child behavior management just as often as in any other setting. Sometimes family systems will not respond to efforts to change long-standing patterns of interaction. One example of such a family would be one in which any member has an unrecognized drinking problem.

The first thing I would advise is that all involved with such a family recognize that some things can not be changed, at least not as quickly as one would hope. Second, behavior management programs may continue in the school even without real cooperation from the child's parents. Such programs may not be as effective as they could be but, with persistence, they can improve the classroom situation. Programs that provide increasing structure can restrict the child's options of misbehavior. Special education services, such as programs for the emotionally or behaviorally disturbed (ED/BD), may be one route for increasing structure.

Even when the messages and contingencies effective in the home and school are not consistent with each other, the child can learn to conform to the expectations of either environment. The learning process will be slower under these circumstances. Another potentially helpful strategy is to assess the child's level of social skills. Learning to recognize and respond appropriately to feelings and learning appropriate styles of interacting with peers are often problematic for children who live in disturbed family systems. Clear limits upon behavior and clear, consistently enforced consequences for misbehavior should be effective in decreasing disruptive behavior of children, regardless of the nature of their home environment. It may be a problem to find ways of effectively rewarding appropriate and desired behavior if the child is enmeshed in an unhealthy family system. Persistence, ingenuity, and a sincerely caring attitude on the part of those working with such a child can have a positive long-term effect.

PART 2
APPLICATIONS

chapter 6

OVERVIEW OF SPECIFIC PROBLEM AREAS

One of the primary functions of professionals who work in school systems is identifying children with behavior and learning problems. An appropriately thorough assessment produces a large amount of data, which must be organized in order to provide a coherent picture of the child and how he or she functions at home and school. One method of summarizing the data is to determine whether the child's behavior matches a particular diagnostic category such as *hyperactive* or *learning disabled*.

There are both advantages and disadvantages to labeling a particular behavior problem. One advantage is that a label or diagnosis is often necessary for access to special education services or having medical insurance pay for treatment. Another advantage is that one often gains additional information about a particular child when a diagnosis is judiciously used. For instance, a diagnostic label can suggest treatment strategies that might be helpful or other areas of behavior that should be investigated. An accurate diagnosis can provide a concise summary of a particular behavior problem and suggest approaches for dealing with it.

Diagnostic labels also have several disadvantages. The most serious problem is that a diagnostic label, itself, may be considered the problem instead of the behavior of the child. This sometimes happens when medication is used to control hyperactivity. Medication may work to change some aspects of the behavior, but it will not provide a child with needed social or academic skills. The problem comes about when these other aspects of the problem are neglected, once relief has been provided for the major problem. That is, hyperactivity may appear to be "cured" when the child remains still and seated, yet, academic functioning may still be poor or the child may be without friends. Both problems require additional intervention.

A second problem with diagnostic labels is that they may become permanently attached to children and work to their disadvantage. Labels can create expectations below the child's capabilities, interfering with academic progress and personal achievement. For this reason the procedures for labeling a child in order to provide special education services are quite strict and designed to protect the child's rights, as noted in Chapter 1.

Diagnostic labels should be employed cautiously. At best a diagnostic label is an hypothesis about the child's behavior that is subject to revision at any time. With this attitude, one can lessen the possibility that the label will become a reified part of the individual child. The label is only a shorthand description of *some* aspects of the child's behavior. As new information is obtained, the label, and the approach to dealing with the child, could change. For instance, a child could initially be labeled as *hyperactive*, but as information is obtained about self-concept, mood, and sleeping patterns, the label could change to *depression*. Finally, information provided by the child and others about the home environment could suggest that *abused child* is the most appropriate label. With each revision of the label, the most appropriate strategy for managing the problem may also change. The primary focus should remain upon the child, with the label serving as a shorthand description of the child's behavior as currently understood.

CATEGORIES OF BEHAVIOR PROBLEMS

The remainder of this chapter presents an overview of diagnostic categories that are most often used to describe the behavior problems of children. These categories will then form chapter headings for the remaining chapters in Part 2. The goal is to first take a detailed look at the most common behavior problems of children and then, in the following chapters, to provide some suggestions for managing these problems in the school. Reading this chapter will not transform the reader from a novice to an expert in behavioral assessment and clinical diagnosis, but it will provide the practical knowledge for identifying behavioral problems and formulating reasonable strategies for managing them.

Keep in mind, however, that children are unique individuals. A child's particular pattern of behavior may not always precisely fit a diagnostic category and a behavior management strategy that has been shown to be effective in studies of groups of similar children may not work when it is applied to a particular child. Furthermore, patterns of interaction within the family system may work against behavior management programs conducted in the school. The implication is that those who wish to apply behavior management techniques must remain flexible. A particular behavior management strategy should be used when the behavior characteristics displayed by the child match those for which the program was designed. When a particular management strategy does not work, new strategies and additional data about the child and her or his family are needed.

Some of the following descriptions are based upon *DSM-III*, the *Diagnostic and Statistical Manual of Mental Disorders* (3rd edition), published by the American Psychiatric Association. This manual contains diagnostic criteria for all recognized mental disorders. Its use is not without controversy (e.g., Schacht, 1985; Smith & Kraft, 1983; Spitzer, 1985), but it is used by a majority of mental health practitioners. One of the main reasons for its usage is that a *DSM-III* diagnosis is required by most medical insurance companies for reimbursement of psychological or psychiatric treatment costs. On the other hand, despite its widespread use it has been criticized for lack of reliability, for emphasis on a disease-based model, for having a low capability of indicating appropriate treatment or prognosis, and for the lack of scientific evidence to support its categories.

Nevertheless, *DSM-III* is very likely to be encountered by school personnel especially when they review clinical records generated by psychologists and psychiatrists. Ready access to a copy of the *Quick Reference to the Diagnostic Criteria from DSM-III* (American Psychiatric Association, 1980) is very useful for school personnel who need to examine clinical records generated by sources outside the school system. In the present context, *DSM-III* will be used as a general guide to some of the behavior categories that are discussed. However, the primary emphasis should always remain upon the behavior of the child and not upon the diagnostic category. The use of diagnostic categories is primarily an organizational method for grouping together similar behaviors and pointing out behavior management techniques that may be of value in dealing with them.

Hyperactivity

Hyper is a prefix meaning excessive. To say that a hyperactive child exhibits too much activity is really an understatement. In the regular classroom, a hyperactive child is likely to be noticed first, because he or she (but most likely he) is typically engaged in activities other than assigned classroom work. The child's time is occupied by a variety of irrelevant activities, such as running around the classroom, annoying other students, playing with objects in or around his desk, fidgeting, talking, and other behaviors in opposition to the goals of the classroom. Such students are likely to experience great difficulty in properly organizing a task and are also likely to switch from an assigned task to some irrelevant, off-task activity, even when they are closely supervised. From the classroom teacher's point of view, these children are likely to be noted for their inability to pay attention or follow directions.

Hyperactivity is one of the most commonly identified behavioral problems of children, with estimates of the incidence ranging from about 3% to as high as 20%. Boys are three to ten times more likely to be labeled hyperactive than girls. Studies that follow children diagnosed as hyperactive into later life indicate that hyperactivity declines somewhat but associated problems may be present even in adulthood (Schwartz & Johnson, 1985). Explanations of the cause of hyperactiv-ity range from claims that it is a constitutional trait to the notion that hyperactivity is caused exclusively by environmental factors.

The criteria for diagnosing hyperactivity and the terminology employed in *DSM-III* are frequently seen by school personnel. The cluster of behaviors which most of us would refer to as hyperactivity, is called *attention deficit disorder with hyperactivity* (*DSM-III*, 314.01) by physicians and psychiatrists. To meet the cri-teria for this category, the child must show onset of hyperactivity before age 7 and the behavior must be of at least 6 months' duration. The child also must show problem behaviors in three areas: inattention, impulsivity, and hyperactivity.

Inattention is indicated by the presence of three of the following behaviors: often fails to finish things he or she starts, often does not seem to listen, is easily distracted, has difficulty concentrating on schoolwork or other tasks requiring sustained attention, and has difficulty sticking to a play activity. *Impulsivity* is indicated by the presence of three of the following behaviors: often acts before thinking, shifts excessively from task to task, experiences difficulty organizing work, needs a lot of supervision, frequently calls out in class, and has difficulty awaiting turn in games or group situations. Finally, *hyperactivity* is indicated by the presence of two of the following: runs about excessively or climbs on things, fidgets excessively or has difficulty sitting still, has difficulty staying seated, exces-sive movement during sleep, and is always "on the go" or acts as if "driven by a motor."

Although the *DSM-III* criteria provide a reasonably complete listing of the behaviors associated with hyperactivity, in practice the use of these criteria presents several problems. First, and probably most obvious, though the criteria are reasonably detailed, they lack specificity. For instance, what do the words *excessive* and *often* mean in this context, and how would one *ever* know whether or not a child had acted without thinking? Another problem is that many of the behaviors in the above lists are quite normal, particularly in boys. Thus, there is more to the identification of hyperactivity than simply determining whether a given cluster of behaviors is present. One must also determine the impact of such behavior on the child's life. For instance, one would want to know whether the child is failing to accomplish academic work while hyperactive. One would also be wise to consider the age of the child and to look carefully at the behavior of the child's peers. Younger children are typically more active and restless than older children. It is important, then, to observe the child's peers in order to determine whether the target child's behavior is really different and interfering with success in school. Consideration of all the contextual variables such as peer relations, home environment, and classroom environment will provide valuable data that can contribute to understanding the source and effects of the child's behavior. Chapter 7 is devoted to a description of behavior management strategies that have proven useful with hyperactivity and associated behaviors.

Childhood Depression

The word *depression* can indicate a variety of conditions ranging from a temporarily depressed mood to a serious and chronic state marked by statements regarding self-destruction and death. The research literature on childhood depression has been rather sparse up to the 1970s, and comparatively little is known about it. Schwartz and Johnson (1985) estimated that depression occurs in about 28% of children referred to clinics and in about 2% of the general population.

The characteristics associated with depression can be divided in two categories: physical and behavioral. The physical signs are poor appetite or loss of weight, increased appetite or significant weight gain, loss of energy, fatigue, tiredness, difficulty in concentration or thinking, and sleep irregularities. Sleep irregularities are characterized by difficulty getting to sleep or staying asleep, too much sleep, or awakening unusually early.

The behavioral signs of depression include first and most important, a distinctively depressed mood characterized as sad, blue, hopeless, down in the dumps, low, or irritable. According to *DSM-III*, a disturbance in mood must be prominent and persistent but not necessarily the most dominant sign. In children, a persistently sad facial expression can be used to infer a depressed mood. Other behavioral signs of depression include apathy, lack of interest in activities formerly regarded as fun or enjoyable, excessive or frequent crying, statements indicating lack of self-worth or self-reproach, apprehension, poor school performance, excessive or inappropriate guilt, low self-esteem, statements about death or suicide, a suicide attempt, social isolation, nonreactivity, and psychomotor disturbance (Cantor, 1983; *DSM-III*).

A few of these behavioral signs require additional explanation. Nonreactivity means that nothing (a joke, story, trip to the zoo, for example) seems to improve the child's mood. Psychomotor disturbance refers to two opposite types of behavior, psychomotor retardation and psychomotor agitation. Psychomotor retardation is manifested in a marked slowing of behavior and thought processes as indicated by long delays in answering questions, a slow rate of speech, little movement or motor activity, and a general slowing down of motor and psychological activity. On the other hand, psychomotor agitation is characterized by restlessness, agitation, and high rates of activity.

Depression is also associated with plans or thoughts about suicide. Even children as young as 5 can behave in ways that would purposefully lead to death (Cantor, 1983). The practitioner must not ignore suicidal tendencies in individuals showing signs of depression. Any statements regarding thoughts or plans of suicide *must* be taken seriously and professional consultation immediately sought. Most cities will have a crisis line, hotline, or similar telephone counseling service that can help in identifying the seriousness of a suicidal threat and provide access to additional sources of help. Not every child (or even most children) who appears "depressed" will be suicidal, but any overt indications of suicidal tendencies *must* be taken seriously. Considering such a possibility is one of the hypotheses suggested by the presence of depressive signs.

When a significant number of behaviors associated with depression are observed, the child may be labeled *depressed*. Kazdin, Esveldt-Dawson, Sherick, and Colbus (1985) assessed a group of children in a psychiatric facility who had been diagnosed as depressed using *DSM-III* criteria. After admission and diagnosis, several paper and pencil measures of depression were administered to the children and their mothers, and the children were directly observed for several days. It was found that depressed children engaged in significantly less social activity and less affect-related expression (smiling, frowning, arguing, or complaining) than nondepressed children. This relationship held with respect to parent-reports and the initial diagnosis but not for the children's self-reports.

Thus, while a *DSM-III* diagnosis does relate to overt behavior, children's self-reports of depressive symptoms do not necessarily correspond with other sources of information (e.g., Kazdin, French, & Unis, 1983). Generally, identification of depression in children needs to be done using multiple sources of information. Furthermore, children's reports may contain much information of value such as suicidal tendencies, negative expectations about the future, and other characteristics of depression (Kazdin et al., 1983).

Within the school environment, several circumstances might bring behaviors associated with depression to the attention of school practitioners. Academic problems, manifested in poor work habits, and an inability to concentrate are likely to initiate concern. Another cause of concern is that a child may show signs of a low self-concept manifested in frequent self-directed negative statements. Finally, a child may be performing at or near the average level, academically, but nevertheless attract attention because of persistent sadness, social isolation, crying, expression of suicidal intent, or other signs of depressed mood.

Hyperactivity versus Depression. Schwartz and Johnson (1985) discuss a category of childhood depressive reactions they call masked, in the sense that the child's depression is overshadowed by other characteristics. That is, the reason for referral may be hyperactivity, psychosomatic symptoms, or delinquency, but the underlying problem is depression, which is only later identified via interviews and behavioral observations. Consistent with this notion, Leon, Kendall, and Garber (1980) found that depressed children tended to be rated as significantly more hyperactive/impulsive than nondepressed children. Yet, the conclusions from this study were that childhood depression and hyperactivity do not have a generalized behavioral disturbance in common. Instead, it seems that while hyperactive or impulsive behavior may be common to both syndromes, childhood depression has unique characteristics that distinguish it from other pathological conditions.

Leon, Kendall, and Garber's study involved normal third- to sixth-grade youngsters. They found that parent ratings of hyperactivity and depression on the Personality Inventory for Children (Wirt, Lachar, Klinedinst, & Seat, 1977) were not systematically related. Furthermore, anxiety, psychosomatic complaints, perfectionism, and learning problems differentiated depressed from nondepressed children irrespective of the presence of hyperactivity. Studies by Schwartz, Friedman, Lindsay, and Narrol (1982) and Homatidis and Konstantareas (1981) provide additional empirical confirmation of this finding.

Depressed and hyperactive children are likely to have somewhat different styles of behaving in the academic environment. The hyperactive child is likely to be engaging in a variety of high magnitude behaviors that interfere with accomplishing school work. On the other hand, the depressed child is most likely to be more passive but equally unproductive. At home, depressed mood and behavioral features — such as somatic complaints, perfectionism, and anxiety — are likely to be the distinguishing features of depression. Apparently, hyperactivity and depression have hyperactive/impulsive behavior, inattention, conduct problems and learning problems in common. In addition to these signs the depressed child is likely to manifest passivity, somatic complaints (e.g., sleep and appetite disturbances), clearly depressed mood, passive-inattention, anxiety, tension, and perfectionism. At present, a need exists for more research on the differences between hyperactive and depressed children, but these studies suggest that despite some similarities in diagnostic criteria, in practice it is clearly possible to differentiate hyperactivity and depression in children.

With respect to behavior management for depressed or hyperactive children, a reasonable way to begin a program might be to focus directly upon academic performance using the strategies described in Chapter 10 without regard to whether the child is depressed, hyperactive, or neither. Alternately, it may be reasonable to consider the strategies discussed in Chapters 7 and 8 which relate specifically to hyperactivity and depression. If acting out behaviors — such as crying, pouting, being out of seat, tantrums, or fighting — are occurring with such frequency that the child spends little time in academic activity and perhaps interferes with other students, these "hyperactive" behaviors may logically be the initial focus of behavior management. Later, the focus may shift to behaviors regarded as more uniquely characteristic of depression, such as depressed mood, low self-esteem, excessive or inappropriate guilt, social isolation, anxiety, psychosomatic complaints, perfectionism, passive-inattention, or failure to engage in activities usually regarded as fun or enjoyable. It is important to recall that a diagnostic label is really just an hypothesis about behavior. As circumstances change and new information is obtained, one's conceptualization of a problem and the most appropriate management strategy are also likely to change.

Typically, hyperactivity and depression are also approached differently from a medical perspective. Frequently, the manifestations of either hyperactivity or depression are severe enough to warrant assembling a special education team and/or obtaining consultation from outside the school district. If a psychiatrist or other medical doctor is consulted, hyperactivity is often treated with stimulant medication and depression is often treated with a tricyclic antidepressant. If such treatment is undertaken, continued behavioral assessment of problem areas is necessary since many aspects of the child's problem behaviors may not be alleviated by medication.

In sum, childhood depression is indicated by a cluster of behaviors that overlap somewhat with the characteristics of hyperactivity. Where hyperactivity is characterized by inattentive, impulsive, and hyperactive behavior accompanied by learning problems, depression can have these or similar characteristics plus a disturbed mood, anxiety, psychosomatic complaints, perfectionism, anxiety, and passive-inattention. Flexibility is called for, since the line separating hyperactivity and depression can be very indistinct. Both hyperactivity and depression may be effectively treated with prescribed drugs, although continued behavioral assessment of problem areas is necessary even if drug therapy is undertaken. A wide range of formal behavior management programs may be useful for children who manifest signs of hyperactivity or depression. These are discussed in Chapters 7, 8, 10, and 11.

Childhood Anxiety and Related Problems

Everyone becomes anxious or fearful on certain occasions. For children, the first day of school, a trip to the dentist or doctor, or a surprise confrontation with a large dog would normally elicit fear. Although some fear of many situations is reasonable, fear of a situation may become irrational and maladaptive causing the child to avoid the situation completely. If the unreasonably feared situation is important to the individual's adaptation or survival, such as a job interview for an adult or going to school for a child, then the fear may become a focus for intervention. When this occurs, the fear may be called a *phobia* emphasizing the irrational nature of the problem.

In order to understand phobias it is helpful to introduce a concept which has not been touched upon so far, namely, classical conditioning. Classical conditioning involves the same basic elements as reinforcement and punishment, but the relationship among the elements is viewed differently. In reinforcement and punishment, the appetitive or aversive stimulus is programmed to follow a specific behavior. In classical conditioning, the appetitive or aversive stimulus is programmed to follow the presentation of another *stimulus*, which is called the *conditioned stimulus* (CS). The essence of classical conditioning is embodied in what happens to the CS. Before conditioning begins, the CS has no effect upon the individual to whom it is presented. During conditioning the CS is presented immediately followed by an appetitive or aversive stimulus for several conditioning trials. After completion of a sufficient number of conditioning trials, the CS demonstrates properties similar to the appetitive or aversive stimulus. That is, if the aversive stimulus elicits fear, then after a sufficient number of conditioning trials the CS will also elicit fear.

Two examples of human experiments involving the classical conditioning paradigm (both cited in Ross, 1981) illustrate the nature of the process. In 1920, Watson and Rayner classically conditioned fear to a white rat in an 11-month-old boy. Prior to conditioning, the boy would approach the rat and showed no evidence of fearing it. During conditioning a loud noise, which caused the boy to cry and withdraw from the rat, was presented each time he approached the rat (the CS). After several trials, the boy showed signs of fear and withdrawal from the previously neutral white rat. Via classical conditioning, then, the boy came to fear the rat. Should the boy have continued into adulthood with an irrational fear of rats that was strong enough to interfere with normal functioning, he might have come to the attention of a mental health professional who would have diagnosed a phobia.

A second classic demonstration was conducted by Mary Cover Jones in 1924. In this demonstration a child with a *preexisting* fear of rabbits was conditioned not to fear them. This was accomplished by conducting all conditioning trials while the boy was eating. The procedure was to bring the rabbit into the same room with the boy while he was eating but keeping the rabbit at a great enough distance that no obvious fear response was evoked. Then, as the child continued eating, the rabbit was brought closer and closer to him. At the end of a couple of months of such training the boy was able to touch and fondle the rabbit without any signs of fear. Apparently, the fear originally produced by the rabbit was replaced by approach responses as a consequence of pairing the rabbit with eating. In theory at least this experiment provides an example of how the classical conditioning process might be useful in eliminating a phobia.

Childhood phobias may develop in several ways, one of which includes the process of classical conditioning. According to the classical conditioning view, any time a painful or fear-eliciting stimulus occurs, there is the potential for classical conditioning of fear to the neutral stimuli (CSs) associated with that event. For instance, the procedure used by Watson and Rayner could describe how a phobia of rats was acquired by the boy. Alternately, a child bitten by a dog could acquire an unreasonable phobia of all dogs. Thus, when loud noises, painful stimuli, or fear-eliciting events occur in the environment of a child, the potential exists for conditioning which could cause a phobia to develop.

Another way that phobias might develop is through cognitive processes such as by imagination or actual observation of frightening events. For instance, one family member might learn a fear by observing another family member's response to a feared object. A younger sibling could observe the behavior of an older sibling who has a phobia of snakes and could acquire the phobia through hearing the sibling describe the supposedly frightening results of meeting a snake, watching the sibling react fearfully to certain situations, and being reinforced with praise and attention for behaving in a way that is similar to that of the sibling.

Another mechanism in the development and maintenance of phobias is the rewarding properties of avoiding the feared situation or object. Fear is an unpleasant emotion, which most of us seek to avoid. Whenever a child approaches a feared object or situation the build-up of fear or anxiety is aversive. As pointed out in Chapter 2, any behavior that results in a reduction or removal of an aversive stimulus will be likely to *increase* in frequency. Thus, the feared situation is likely to be escaped or avoided with increasing frequency. This behavior would tend to strengthen, or at least maintain, the phobia.

Regardless of how a phobia developed, adult and peer behavior in relation to the phobia is also likely to be a factor in its continuation. For example, as a child exhibits signs of anxiety and fear, adults and peers are likely to respond in a sympathetic manner. Furthermore, adults may cooperate in helping the child to avoid the fear-evoking situation. These events strengthen the phobic behavior.

It is normal for a growing child to have some fears. Most childhood fears are outgrown without becoming the focus of adult attention. Such fears might include loud noises, strangers, and separation in the first year of life; various imaginary creatures or dogs in the second and third years; the dark in the fourth year; or school and social situations when the child reaches school age (cf. Ollendick, Matson, & Helsel, 1985). What divides a common age-appropriate fear from an unreasonable fear or phobia, which might be a target for behavior management, is its appropriateness and the extent to which it interferes with normal activity. For instance, it is reasonable for a 3- or 4-year-old to fear the German shepherd that lives down the street and avoid the yard in which the dog roams. It is not reasonable if the child avoids going outside to play or refuses to go to school for fear of a dog.

Other indicators of anxiety that may suggest a problem include unrealistic worry about future events, excessive need for reassurance, somatic complaints (headaches, stomachaches) for which no physical basis can be established, marked tension or inability to relax, persistent and excessive avoidance of contact with strangers, and avoidance behavior that interferes significantly with normal activity. These behaviors may become associated with a wide variety of feared situations and can be exhibited over a wide range of severity. Table 6.1 provides a more complete list of behaviors associated with anxiety. Most of these behaviors are listed in various categories of *DSM-III*. For present purposes, three specific examples of childhood fears will be discussed: exaggerated childhood fears, school phobia, and test anxiety. These three general categories should cover the majority of cases school personnel are likely to encounter.

Table 6.1.   Behavioral Indicators of Anxiety

Unrealistic worry	Difficulty with breathing
Fear that major attachment will leave and not return	Trembling or shaking
	Motor tension
Reluctance or refusal to go to sleep	Jitteriness or jumpiness
Avoidance of being alone	Restlessness
Nightmares	Persistence of anxiety
Physical symptoms of stomachaches, headaches, nausea, vomiting	Rapid breathing
Temper tantrums or crying to avoid contact with feared situation	Rapid heart rate
	Overconcern about competence in a variety of areas
Inability to relax	
Excessive need for reassurance	Sweating
Restrictions in normal activity	Diarrhea

Exaggerated Childhood Fears. In the present context, an exaggerated childhood fear refers to an age-appropriate, common fear that has gotten out of hand. The key to this category is to carefully consider what out of hand means. If a fear of the dark prevented children from enjoying a movie or sleeping in their own beds, the fear may be regarded as out of hand and a potential focus of professional attention. The primary criterion is the impact of the fear and avoidance upon the child and his or her daily functioning in school and at home. It is a subjective judgement on the part of those in contact with the child as to when a childhood fear may be considered exaggerated. The indicators of anxiety discussed earlier and listed in Table 6.1 may serve as a source of behavioral indicators as to when a fear may require formal intervention.

School Phobia. School phobia is the childhood fear that most often receives attention in the research literature. It is characterized by avoidance of school. Since frequent or continuous absence from school creates problems for the school, the parents, and the child, it is not surprising that this is one of the most common phobias treated by clinical and school psychologists. A distinction is often made between school phobia, which is a persistent and compelling desire to avoid school, and separation anxiety, where the fear is of separation from one or both parents. If the child refuses to enter school even if accompanied by a parent, the problem can be labeled simple school phobia. On the other hand, a child showing characteristics of separation anxiety will accompany a parent to school with no problem but show fear when it comes time to separate from the parent. In addition, fear of separation would be a predominant theme in the child's life when separation occurs for any purpose, school being only one instance.

Whether the focus of the problem is separation or school itself, the child's responses to the parents' attempts to get the child to go to school will be similar. These may include complaints, on school days, of physical symptoms such as headaches, nausea, vomiting, and stomachaches. It is also likely that the child will show unrealistic fear revolving around an attachment theme such as fear that harm will befall the parents or that the child will become lost and permanently separated from home and family. It is a common pattern that school avoidance begins on a Monday following an episode of sickness that occurred the previous Thursday or Friday.

Although treatment will be given a thorough discussion in Chapter 9, it is important for both treatment and assessment purposes for the school staff member who is dealing with a case of school phobia to make some effort to determine the role of the parents. That is, how do the parents influence and perhaps support the child's absence from school? It is very possible that the parents have inadvertently or overtly contributed to the child's phobia. This is most likely to happen when parents reinforce the child's early efforts to avoid school with their attention and sympathy. Then, as the situation escalates with absences reaching an unacceptably high frequency, the child may show *extreme* resistance to attempts at forcing school attendance. Such resistance may greatly exceed the parents' ability to cope, even to the extent that their best and most persistent efforts to get the child to school may fail due to the intensity of the child's resistance. It is at the point where the situation has gotten out of control that school personnel are often requested to intervene. School personnel who may become involved in such a case should be forewarned that the basic treatment issue is getting the child back into school. While easy to say, it may require extreme effort to accomplish.

Test Anxiety. Tests and examinations are the sine qua non of education. In fact, so much importance can become attached to certain tests that taking them becomes as much an exercise in coping skills as a test of knowledge. When attempts to cope with a test situation begin to dominate the test itself to the extent that performance is seriously impaired, then the cause might be test anxiety. The signs of test anxiety consist either of complete avoidance of tests or reports of physical complaints while taking a test. The physical complaints might consist of any of the signs of anxiety listed in Table 6.1.

As with all of the behavioral problems discussed in this book, it is necessary to make a distinction between behavior that may become the focus of a behavior management program versus normal behavior that might be expected under the circumstances. Low to moderate amounts of anxiety would be expected in most test situations, and, in fact, are typically associated with optimum performance. How does one differentiate normal anxiety, which boosts performance, from excessive anxiety, which interferes with test performance? In addition to reports of physical discomfort during and preceding the test situation, one would also seek evidence that test performance was lowered. A typical report under such circumstances would be the inability to recall information that they felt they knew very well. It would be especially noteworthy if the information were recalled immediately or soon after the individual left the test. This, and general reports of being preoccupied with anxiety and worry rather than coping with the task of taking the test (i.e., studying appropriately), would indicate that test anxiety was interfering with performance to the extent that some behavior management programs may prove beneficial.

Conclusion

Exaggerated childhood fears, school phobia, and test anxiety are three different manifestations of the same problem, namely, excessive fear. Within limits each problem can occur under normal circumstances and be resolved without external help or a need for behavior management. Chapter 9 will address techniques shown to be beneficial in cases where anxiety or fear has become a focus of attention because normal school performance was consistently disrupted.

ACADEMIC PROBLEMS

Academic performance is the major concern of almost every teacher, parent, and school professional. Chapter 10 describes programs, which can be applied by both teachers and parents, to improve or maintain acceptable school performance. The purpose of this section is to outline the circumstances under which such programs might be successful and to caution against those circumstances where additional adjustments may also be necessary.

General Considerations

Four basic areas must be assessed when a behavior management program is considered for a child experiencing academic difficulties: ability, achievement, motivation, and sensory capacity. The importance of such an assessment is twofold. First, a behavior management program may be unnecessary, or even harmful, under some circumstances such as when the child has developed a hearing problem. In such a case, rewards for academic achievement will not be nearly as helpful as a trip to the doctor. Second, academic programming must take place at a level that is appropriate to the child's academic skills. For instance, a child of average ability who shows a large deficit in reading achievement may need individual tutoring or special education in order to be successful. Again, behavior management strategies that ignore the need for additional help may cause great frustration for the child. Thus, the importance of a complete assessment of the child's functioning in school cannot be underestimated. What follows is a brief description of the four areas which must be assessed.

Ability. Ability is measured using an individually administered intelligence test such as the Stanford-Binet Intelligence Scale, the Wechsler Intelligence Scale for Children—Revised, the Wechsler Preschool and Primary Scale of Intelligence, the Wechsler Adult Intelligence Scale—Revised, or the Kaufman Assessment Battery for Children. Although debate over exactly what these tests measure continues, the fact is that they do very well at predicting academic achievement.

One way to view intelligence testing is that it provides a sample of the child's academic skills in a context that greatly restricts the operation of many extraneous variables that can influence academic performance. Testing is conducted by an experienced examiner with only the one child present. The one-on-one nature of intelligence testing ensures that a sample of the child's best performance is obtained. Furthermore, the examiner is in a position to know when performance is not optimal by observing and noting the child's behavior. The classroom environment, by contrast, is structured so that the child may fail to demonstrate his or her best performance even under the supervision of the most skillful teacher. It is easily possible for an individual child to engage in nonproductive behavior, such as not attending, talking, or not working on assigned tasks, when 20 to 30 other students are also in the classroom. Thus, when contrasted with achievement in the classroom, the results of an individual intellectual assessment can provide useful information about the child.

Achievement. Achievement refers to the mastery of the skills and facts taught in school. Theoretically, achievement and ability are concepts that can be measured independently, but in reality, tests of ability use many tasks that involve past learning. There are a number of individually administered achievement tests, such as the Woodcock-Johnson Psychoeducational Battery—Part II, the Wide Range Achievement Test, the Peabody Individual Achievement Test, the achievement portion of the Kaufman Assessment Battery for Children, and the Kaufman Test of Educational Achievement. Individually administered achievement tests have some of the same advantages as individually administered tests of intelligence. That is, testing is conducted under conditions that provide an opportunity for the child to display his or her best performance away from the relatively unstructured environment of the classroom. The practical difference between tests of achievement and intelligence is that intelligence tests generally provide a sample of intellectual, reasoning, and problem-solving ability by presenting the child with a series of tasks that are a mixture of the familiar and unfamiliar. Achievement tests focus exclusively upon achievement in familiar subject areas, such as oral and written language, reading, and arithmetic. When intelligence and achievement testing are both conducted, valuable information, which can be used in educational programming, is obtained.

Motivation. Motivation refers to the underlying drive to behave appropriately or, in the present context, to achieve academically. An analogy is that humans must be motivated by hunger in order to seek out and consume food. In a practical sense, it is impossible to measure the motivation that underlies academic performance. Instead, the concern is whether or not the child's environment supports efforts in academics. Support may take the form of attention, praise, material rewards, or any other events that contribute to reinforcing and maintaining academic accomplishment. When environmental support for academic accomplishment does not exist, is inconsistent, is overshadowed by individual behavior problems, or is overshadowed by family problems, one may find that academic achievement is unacceptably low. Formal behavior management programs may be necessary in these cases.

Sensory Capacity. Whenever a child's academic accomplishment is not meeting expectations, it is possible that his or her sensory capacity has fallen below optimal levels. This can occur even in a child who has previously passed a hearing or vision test. Since vision and hearing are essential to academic performance, it is absolutely imperative that a problem in these areas be ruled out when a child experiences academic difficulties. Tables 6.2 and 6.3 list behaviors associated with hearing and vision problems, respectively. A screening test for vision or hearing problems takes so little time and effort that the presence of any of these signs should be cause to contact the appropriate specialist. Obviously, if the screening indicates a potential problem, medical consultation should be sought as soon as possible.

Table 6.2.   Behavioral Indicators of Hearing Difficulty

1. A history of frequent middle ear infections
2. Difficulty in comprehending directions or understanding conversation
3. Asks frequently for repetitions of things said
4. Confuses similar sounding words
5. Difficulty gaining the child's attention unless visual contact is made with the child

Table 6.3.   Behavioral Indicators of Visual Difficulty

1. Irritated, watery, reddish, encrusted eyes or eyelids
2. Recurring sties
3. Complaints of not seeing well
4. Dizziness, headaches, or nausea following close work
5. Blurred or double vision
6. Excessive rubbing of eyes
7. Difficulty while doing close work, child tilts head, shuts one eye, thrusts head forward, is irritable, or blinks frequently while doing close work
8. Difficulty judging distances
9. Avoidance of close work
10. Loss of place while reading
11. Reverses or confuses letters

In sum, academic performance is influenced by ability or general intelligence, motivation, and sensory capacity. Since the usual goal of both parents and school personnel is to help the child to achieve at the optimum level in the classroom, achievement is a frequent target of formal behavior management procedures. However, either a formal or an informal assessment of sensory capacity, motivation, and intellectual ability is always a necessity. The reason for such caution is that the child may be educationally or physically handicapped and the introduction of a formal behavior management program could cause the youngster great stress and frustration, if other needed services are not provided concurrently.

The meaning of the term *educationally handicapped* and it's implications for the child, parents, and the school staff are defined by a public law, which assures that all handicapped children receive a free and appropriate public education. The child's and parents' rights under this law were discussed in Chapter 1. In this chapter, the relevant categories of handicaps will be discussed. If these potential problems are not ruled out, beginning a formal behavior management program while the child remains in the regular classroom could prove troublesome and not in the child's best interests. In addition, the presence of any of these problems indicates a possible need for special educational help, which should be provided by the child's school.

Mental Retardation

Mental retardation is defined by deficits in general intellectual functioning and adaptive behavior, which adversely affect a child's educational performance. General intellectual functioning is measured with an individually administered test of intelligence. These tests are constructed so that a test score (IQ) represents that individual's relative standing within a standardization group representative of the U.S. population. An average score is 100. IQ scores that place an individual in the lower 2% of the population are generally considered to represent mental retardation. This would be an IQ score of 70 or below on most intelligence tests. However, the exact score used to define mental retardation (and thus make the child eligible for special services) varies from district to district being as high as 85 (16th percentile) in some areas. Different terms are also used around the country to indicate mental retardation.

In addition to impaired intellectual ability, a child must also show concurrent deficits in adaptive behavior to be considered retarded. Adaptive behavior refers to the effectiveness of individuals in meeting the standards for personal independence and social responsibility expected for their age and cultural group. Standards of adaptive behavior vary with the age of the child. At age 5 or 6 the focus of assessment would be upon skills such as tying shoes and dressing, while at the adult level the focus would be upon vocational and social behavior. Adaptive behavior is usually assessed using a standardized instrument such as the Vineland Social Maturity Scale, the newer Vineland Adaptive Behavior Scales, or the

American Association on Mental Deficiency's Adaptive Behavior Scale, School Edition. The items on these scales are answered using data from interviews with adults having significant amounts of contact with the child, teachers and parents being typical respondents. For a more detailed discussion of issues in the assessment of adaptive behavior, see Witt and Martens (1984).

A child who shows deficits in both adaptive behavior and general intellectual ability is likely to find much of the regular classroom work too difficult. Consistent failure in the regular classroom is likely depending, of course, upon the degree of the deficit. Special educational help would probably be necessary to supplement regular classroom work. Any formal or informal behavior management program must be designed to take into account the child's current level of performance. Children who are mentally retarded are likely to respond very well to such programs because of their concrete and structured nature. It should also be noted that a retarded child may show other behavior problems discussed in this chapter.

Giftedness

Giftedness is not a mental handicap in the usual sense of the word but it can create problems for the gifted child, parents, and other school staff members. Giftedness is commonly defined by an IQ score above 130 (that is, the upper 2% of the population), or special talents in academic areas, creativity, leadership, or arts. Unidentified gifted youngsters can be very troublesome. Sometimes they do poorly in typical classroom work, because from their perspective the work may be boring and repetitive. They are also likely to give strange, creative, or funny answers to questions. These children are not a behavior problem, but special efforts must be made to foster and not smother their talents. Behavior management programs that reward performance in regular classroom work with opportunities to engage in more challenging activities may be beneficial (e.g., Ehrlich, 1982; Whitmore, 1980).

Learning Disabilities

A specific learning disability exists when there is a deficit in one of the *basic psychological processes* involved in using written or spoken language. It may be manifested by problems in listening, reasoning, speaking, reading, writing, spelling, or arithmetic. Handicaps that result from mental retardation, sensory or motor handicaps, or environmental handicaps are excluded from the category of learning disabilities. This is the definition embodied in Public Law 94-142. (See Appendix C of *The Handbook of School Psychology*, Reynolds & Gutkin, 1982; or Kirk & Chalfant, 1984.) Unfortunately, this definition depends greatly upon undefined terms and does not provide concrete guidance as to how one identifies a learning disabled child.

Current educational practice and state laws tend to focus on the concept of a discrepancy between achievement and ability in classifying children as learning disabled. That is, when achievement is unexpectedly lower than what would be predicted from an assessment of intellectual ability, a learning disability is presumed to exist. The method of conducting such an assessment is to compare the results of an individually administered ability assessment with performance on individually administered tests of achievement. When achievement in a subject area is significantly lower than what one would expect given knowledge of intellectual ability, a learning disability is said to exist.

The most common type of learning disability usually involves low achievement in reading. A typical child with a learning disability is likely to have an average IQ score, which is at or near the 50th percentile. Yet achievement in reading is far below the average for the child's age and grade, around the 10th percentile or lower. The actual magnitude and even the method for determining whether there is an ability-achievement discrepancy varies across school districts and states. However, the general principle remains the same: a learning disability is defined by performance in an area of school achievement that is much lower than expected achievement as predicted by individual tests of intelligence.

Children of average or above average intelligence who show evidence of a learning disability are likely to be somewhat frustrated by their inability to achieve in a specific subject area. Some care must be exercised that any behavior management programs to improve academic performance are compatible with the child's current functioning level in that area of achievement. If the child is presented with goals beyond his or her capabilities, such as answering questions about a passage of reading when it is not known whether the child has the skill to even read the passage, great frustration may result and the child's achievement could worsen. Thus, in planning for the academically disabled child, it is important that behavior management programs be compatible with the educational goals for the child. However, when a child is identified as potentially having a learning disability, an assessment of motivation for performing academic work should not be neglected since poor motivation may account for low achievement.

Serious Emotional/Behavioral Disturbance

The category of serious emotional/behavioral disturbance is defined by special education law and elaborated by state and district guidelines. Generally, it includes behavior problems that adversely affect educational performance. Problems named in the rules for implementing Public Law 94-142 include an inability to build or maintain satisfactory interpersonal relationships, inappropriate behavior or feelings, depression, and a tendency to develop fears or physical symptoms associated with school or personal problems. Also included are children who have an inability to learn not explained by intellectual, sensory, or health factors. Although state educational agencies have been slowest in developing programs for emotionally disturbed children, most who meet the above guidelines will qualify for some type of special educational help.

Formal behavior management programs for such children are usually appropriate and effective. The behaviors targeted in behavior management programs will usually include intellectual performance, as well as other behavior deficits or inappropriate behavior.

Summary

The goal of this discussion has been to introduce school personnel to the considerations involved in identifying children who could benefit from formal behavior management programs directed at improving academic performance. In general, such programs are appropriate under any circumstances where achievement is low. However, there are several circumstances under which additional adjustments must be made. These adjustments typically include curriculum, help from specially trained teachers, and adaptations in the regular education classroom.

Assessments designed to determine the existence of any of these problems can be initiated by parents, classroom teachers, or other school personnel. Parental permission is always required for an assessment. Teachers are usually given some formal training in recognizing these problems, but parents do not receive such training and must rely, instead, on their own observations, expectations, and the guidance they receive from the school. In order to assist in making a decision whether to proceed with a formal evaluation, the following questions may help all those concerned to make a decision. These questions should only be considered guidelines, not hard and fast rules. An affirmative answer to one or more questions indicates a possible need for an individual assessment by a school professional, such as a psychologist, special education teacher, or other specialist.

Question 1   Does the child do very poorly in school, perhaps performing about a year or more behind students in the same age group in all subject areas?

Question 2   In addition to poor school performance, does the child have difficulty coping with children of his or her age and perhaps prefer playing and socializing with younger children?

Question 3   Is the child at or below average in schoolwork but frequently surprises teachers and parents with his or her intellectual accomplishment at home, such as by reading difficult books or showing thorough knowledge of subjects that interest him or her?

Question 4   Does the child perform at or above average in most subject areas but experience great difficulty and/or failure in one or more areas? Is this pattern similar to that of any blood relatives?

Question 5   Do observers ever get the impression that the child is at least average if not above average but "just doesn't get it" in one or more subject areas?

Question 6 Does the child show any of the indicators of visual problems listed in Table 6.2?

Question 7 Does the child manifest any of the indicators of hearing problems listed in Table 6.3?

Question 8 Does hyperactivity, depression, anxiety, lack of social skills, inappropriate behavior, or any other indicator of emotional disturbance interfere with the child's academic performance?

Affirmative answers to any of these questions should not be considered evidence that the child has a problem requiring special educational help; instead, it should be regarded as raising the possibility of such a need. A conference involving the child's parents and teachers, and the school principal, psychologist, and special education staff should be sufficient to indicate whether additional individual assessment is necessary. If the decision is not to conduct further assessment or the assessment results do not indicate the presence of a serious problem, but academic achievement is nevertheless below expectations, then establishing a formal behavior management program remains a possibility. Such a program should be designed so as to avoid creating a "no-win" situation for the child. That is, the levels of performance for which the child is rewarded must initially be within a reasonable range. Additional information and outlines of prototype programs are presented in Chapter 10.

OTHER BEHAVIORAL PROBLEMS

Social Skills Deficits

Social skills training is such a broad area as to require an entire book for thorough coverage. Social skills encompass behavior ranging from sharing a toy at 5 years of age to conversing with a person of the opposite sex in adolescence. However, deficits in social skills easily fall within the range of problems which might benefit from formal behavior management programs. Several general considerations are involved in planning and implementing such programs. Cartledge and Milburn (1986) have edited a book that provides a thorough treatment of the topic. If additional information is desired the reader is referred to this source.

In planning an intervention involving a deficit in social skills, the first consideration would be to define the deficit in concrete, workable terms. The new skill the child is expected to learn must also be appropriate from other perspectives. First, it must be congruent with the developmental status of the child. Second, the new skill should be reinforced by the child's peers. It is also important that thorough baseline data be collected prior to beginning a program. Control observations of a socially successful peer would reveal whether the particular deficit defines a skill that socially successful peers are using.

Training in social skills may be relevant under a variety of circumstances. Social skill deficits are likely to be identified when the child is hyperactive or depressed. In the case of the depressed child, social withdrawal and lack of participation in group activities are likely to be observed. Hyperactive children are prone to be disruptive or aggressive, which also indicates a deficit in social skills. In both cases, the programs described in Chapter 11 may be useful. In the case of hyperactive children, concurrent programs may be necessary to improve academic skills and decrease disruptive behavior. Also, the programs outlined in Chapter 7 can be adapted to include components related to social skills.

Another area of social skills is assertion. Recall from the first chapter that adults who conduct behavior management programs with children are likely to experience the most success when their requests to children are made in an assertive manner. Furthermore, a definition of assertive behavior required explanation of three terms: assertion, nonassertion, and aggression. Training in being assertive and avoiding aggression and nonassertion is frequently provided to adolescents who show social skill deficits. This approach is also briefly discussed in Chapter 11.

Aggression

Aggressive behavior in children, particularly physical aggression, almost always demands the attention of adults who observe it. As noted in Chapter 1, adult attention can frequently be responsible for maintaining the intensity or frequency of aggressive acts. Aggressive behavior can include hitting, shoving, kicking, biting, scratching, forcefully taking objects away from others, yelling and screaming at others, or any other behavior that violates the rights of another. As the child becomes older, this list might be expanded to include lying or malicious gossip and taking credit where it is not due. A problem in dealing with aggressive behavior in our society is that to a great extent aggressive behavior is encouraged, especially in males (e.g., Eron, 1980). Athletic and business competition are two areas where aggression is particularly noticeable and highly rewarded.

The assessment of aggressive behavior is very similar to the assessment of social skills deficits. The problem may be conceptualized as the presence of excessive violation of the rights of others with a concurrent deficit in behaviors that will allow the child to reach goals without violating others' rights. A behavior management program, then, would be most beneficial if targeted at both the excessive aggressive behavior and the social skill deficit that is likely to exist. Another consideration is the information revealed in baseline observations. The question would be from what sources and how often is the child's aggressive behavior rewarded, as for instance, by gaining access to toys or being first in the lunch line. As stated in Part 1, thorough baseline observations can be extremely helpful and revealing in planning a behavior management program.

Goldstein and Pentz (1984) review a variety of psychological skills training approaches that have been tried with aggressive adolescents. They concluded that the research literature clearly shows that aggressive youngsters can learn interpersonal skills, prosocial alternatives to aggression, and aggression-management or aggression-inhibition behaviors. However, as is often the case, the authors noted the absence of demonstrations that the effects of the training generalized outside the training environment or over a long period of time. Thus, if the issue of generalization to other environments is given attention, the methods of social skills training discussed in Chapter 11 may provide appropriate interventions for aggressive youngsters.

Delinquency

A detailed discussion of delinquency is beyond the intended scope of this book. However, it may be useful to consider the problem from the perspective that has been developed so far. A juvenile delinquent is a child, below a given age specified by his or her state of residence, who has committed a crime. The specific laws and procedures vary from state to state but the general principle behind having the label is that the child does not suffer the consequences of being labeled a criminal by the adult court system. However, the actual label is not nearly as important as the *behavior* of the youth or child. Data exist indicating that 75% of "normal" individuals admit to delinquent behavior. In addition, the majority of those caught do not experience legal consequences for their behavior.

There are two major issues in the management of delinquent behavior. First is the issue of monitoring behavior so that delinquent acts can be identified. The most prevalent juvenile crimes (i.e. stealing) are likely to provide the delinquent with substantial rewards, so that unless the behavior can be monitored, it is likely to continue at a high rate. The second issue concerns administering consequences for delinquent behavior. Because institutions are typically overcrowded, most juvenile offenders are released or placed on probation, which would not be a very significant consequence.

Almost the entire range of approaches for managing behavior discussed in this book would be relevant for dealing with delinquent behavior. In the home and school, behavioral contracts (see Chapter 4), which specify that improvements in academic and social behavior are to be exchanged for opportunities to earn money or escape from aversive situations, might be negotiated. The assistance of a probation officer could prove invaluable in such situations. Again, the emphasis should be upon developing new, more useful competencies in the delinquent rather than loading the contract with penalties for undesired behavior.

Institutionally based programs for delinquents tend to be either custodial in nature or emphasize academic and social skills training. Token reward systems, point systems, and/or behavioral contracts are used to implement such training. The token reward system described in Chapter 10 could be adapted to such purposes. For references to successful programs for juvenile delinquents, see the chapter on juvenile delinquency in Schwartz and Johnson (1985).

Teenage and Preteenage Alcoholism

Numerous television specials, newspaper and magazine articles, and school officials have voiced concern over the prevalence of alcoholism among children and youth. Prevalence rates aside, from the school and family perspective, even a single alcoholic child is one too many. Because drinking alcoholic beverages is such a dominant activity in our society, it is sometimes difficult to recognize problem drinkers whether adults or children. Yet, any formal or informal behavior management program targeted at a drinking youngster is unlikely to be successful unless drinking behavior is also targeted for change. For a more complete discussion, see the book, *Young Alcoholics*, by Alibrandi (1978).

Professional intervention is almost always necessary for the teen or preteen alcoholic. The entire family is likely to be involved in a system, of which the teen alcoholic is only one part. A major impediment to obtaining help is recognizing that a problem exists in the first place. Furthermore, many of the problems discussed in this book may either be signs of alcoholism (i.e., academic failure) or the direct result of alcoholism. In either case, behavior management programs are likely to fail unless the drinking is also targeted for change. Thus, the success of some behavior management programs will depend upon the ability of responsible adults to recognize the possibility that the youth may have a drinking problem.

DSM-III provides criteria for two levels of chemical (including alcohol) misuse. *Substance abuse* is characterized by a pattern of pathological use, impairment in social or occupational functioning, and a minimum length of 1 month. For *alcohol dependence,* tolerance (drinking larger and larger quantities) and withdrawal (a hangover or other unpleasant sensations after the cessation of drinking) are necessary in addition to the criteria for alcohol dependence. Signs of pathological alcohol use include daily need for alcohol to function adequately, inability to reduce or quit drinking, repeated unsuccessful efforts to stop drinking, binge drinking, and blackouts. Signs of social or occupational impairment include violence, absence from work (or school), job loss, legal problems related to drinking such as traffic accidents, and arguments or difficulties with friends or family because of alcohol use.

Parents or teachers may be seeing the effects of alcoholism if any of the following behaviors are observed: personality changes and/or mood swings, irresponsibility, association with a "drinking" crowd, consistent reports from others about the child's drinking problems, an arrest for driving while intoxicated, fights with others, general dishonesty, bottles in bedroom or car, dwindling liquor supply at home, smell of alcohol on breath, deteriorating relationship with family, "drunk" behavior, or irresponsible driving. If a drinking problem is suspected, professional consultation is probably the most reasonable route to take.

Victims of Child Abuse and Neglect

One of the themes incorporated into this book has been a strong and consistent bias against the use of painful forms of punishment to modify children's behavior. One reason for this bias is the possibility that physical "punishment" can too easily become "abuse." When this happens a deterioration in both home life and school performance is likely. Because of the profound impact that child abuse has upon the victim, it is imperative that all school personnel be familiar with the signs of child abuse. Efforts to manage the behavior of an abused child that do not deal with the abusive home situation are missing the point.

As was the case with the alcoholic child, school staff members who come in contact with an abused or neglected child are most likely to have a positive impact upon the situation if they can at least recognize the problem. Behavior management is likely to be unsuccessful if the underlying cause of a child's problem behavior is abuse. Most states have child abuse reporting laws that protect anyone who "in good faith" reports suspected child abuse from legal action and, furthermore, requires professionals (teachers, physicians, psychologists, etc.) who have contact with suspected abuse victims to report their suspicions to an appropriate agency. Remember, like any other categorization of children, the label *child abuse victim* is initially an hypothesis subject to revision, confirmation, or rejection. The following discussion is intended to alert those who work with children as to when the hypothesis is warranted. Consultation with a social work agency, school psychologist, school principal, or telephone counseling service is mandatory when child abuse is suspected.

Child abuse can be divided in several categories: physical abuse, sexual abuse, emotional abuse/neglect, and physical neglect. Within these categories, one could place the majority of neglectful or uncaring parents who fail to cooperate with the school in the resolution of their child's problem behavior. So as to balance the perspective somewhat, such parental behavior may result from a lack of motivation, lack of parenting skill, a history of one of the parents being an abuse victim, or a host of other causes. It would be unfair, then, to condemn the parents since the entire family is the logical focus of intervention.

Physical abuse is the easiest type to detect, since many of the indicators are visible marks and bruises. Such signs of possible abuse include bruises in different stages of healing or in unusual places, unusually shaped bruises suggesting contact with an object, "stocking" or "glove" burns suggesting the limb may have been dipped in a hot liquid, or inappropriate treatment of the child's injuries in terms of bandages and medication. The child's behavior may also be an indicator of abuse if any of these signs are present: the child expresses fear of the parents, the child cries frequently, the child seems "different," the child is withdrawn or shy, the child appears depressed, the child inappropriately accepts strangers, the child seems hesitant or afraid to go home, the child is hyperalert to the social cues of the parent, the child behaves very differently when the parents are present than when they are absent, or the child is frequently absent from or late to school.

A common characteristic of abusive parents is that they tend to show ignorance of the developmental sequence in children. Teachers and others who contact the parents directly are likely to find such parents have unrealistic expectations for their children. In addition, they typically lack support systems such as relatives and friends, may be socially isolated from other parents, may offer absurd or inconsistent explanations for their child's injuries, may be uncooperative or passive in encounters with school personnel, may show signs of a drinking problem, may describe the child as "different" or "bad," or they may appear "different" or "strange" themselves.

Physical neglect is also accompanied by a cluster of indicators that generally center around the quality of parental care. Obvious indicators include signs of malnourishment, inappropriate clothing given the weather conditions, torn or dirty clothing, dirty appearance, lack of needed medical attention, and the child frequently is tired and falls asleep in class. Neglected children may also be avoided by their peers for various reasons such as because they smell bad.

Sexual abuse is more difficult to detect but might be indicated if the child manifests complaints of genital or abdominal pain, sexual behavior or language unusual for the child's age, excessive fear of being touched, severe nightmares, acting out, running away from home, signs of depression or anxiety, chemical abuse, a dramatic change in school behavior, evidence of a sudden change in relationships with parents, or evidence that the child assumes the role of "parent" at home. Victims of sexual abuse are about ten times more likely to be girls than boys.

Emotional abuse and neglect are difficult to prove or detect and are unlikely to elicit responses from social or legal agencies. However, any programs that deal directly with the children of such parents are likely to be made more difficult if parental support and cooperation, beyond signing necessary documents, are not obtained. In such cases, it may be helpful to remember that most children are capable of learning to behave appropriately in school regardless of the home situation. Also, one healthy response to a neglectful home situation is for the child to become attached to a trustworthy adult outside of the home.

Abuse and neglect of children are difficult problems with which to cope. The various indicators just listed provide a reasonably complete listing, but the individual needs also to rely on judgement and subjective feelings in entertaining the hypothesis that abuse or neglect underlies the problem behavior of the child. If either the subjective impression or objective evidence is strong, then additional consultation should be obtained.

Children of abusive parents are likely to be depressed, act out, and have less than a normal belief in their ability to control significant events in their lives. Social skills training and other formal programs may be beneficial and could be successful in changing behavior without any change in the parents.

CONCLUSION

The problems reviewed in this chapter represent a broad sampling of those school personnel are likely to encounter. This has not been an exhaustive listing by any means but the great majority of problem behaviors are likely to fall into one of the categories discussed here. The remainder of Part 2 will concern specific intervention strategies for these problems. With a flexible approach to using the general principles outlined in Chapters 1-5, plus using the approaches in the following chapters as guides, school personnel should be able to cope successfully with a majority of the problem behaviors they encounter.

chapter 7

HYPERACTIVITY: MANAGEMENT OF INATTENTIVE, IMPULSIVE, AND DISRUPTIVE BEHAVIOR

This is the first of five chapters designed to illustrate the principles discussed in Part 1. These remaining chapters parallel the discussion of behavioral problems presented in Chapter 6. Within each of the chapters in Part 2, formal behavior management programs are presented in the eight steps described in Chapter 4. The goal is to present a widely varying collection of programs and techniques, which can be applied across a variety of problem situations.

One key to successful behavior management is to remain flexible within the boundaries of valid techniques and to adjust programs according to any new information obtained or evidence that the program is not successful after a reasonable trial. Continuation of the assessment process is necessary because it is always possible that facts were overlooked or hidden from school personnel. New facts could lead to revised hypotheses about the child, which may have a profound effect upon how behavior problems are interpreted and remediated. Changes in the child or the child's environment could also indicate a need for a change in behavior management strategy. An apparently harmless cold could cause a temporary hearing loss, or a formerly pleasant home could be disrupted by the stresses of divorce, a newly born child, or other events. Thus, no matter how reasonable and sound a hypothesis about a child's behavior may appear to be, it must not be considered as written in stone. Instead, it is always subject to revision, as are the behavior management programs designed to improve the child's problem behavior.

A second important consideration in the application of formal behavior management programs is the extent and nature of parental involvement. As noted previously, a behavior management program will be most effective when behavior management in school is consistent with behavior management at home. Although this is a simply stated principle, its application can require great skill and diplomacy. This is particularly true when the assessment reveals that parental responses to the child's problem behavior actually contribute to the problem.

Chapter 5 discusses how to encourage a child's parents to try new techniques of behavior management, while avoiding the appearance of blaming the parents for the problem, since this is likely to elicit denial and defensiveness, which will make further work with them difficult. Where appropriate, suggestions relevant to extending formal behavior management strategies to the home have been provided for many of the behavior management programs discussed in this and the following chapters.

IDENTIFYING AND MANAGING HYPERACTIVITY

The focus of this chapter is upon managing the behaviors associated with hyperactivity. Chapter 6 presented a detailed discussion of the characteristics of hyperactivity. In review, hyperactivity is indicated by problems in three areas: inattention, impulsivity, and hyperactivity. The present chapter will outline detailed procedures for managing each of these three behavior problems. Although hyperactivity, according to *DSM-III*, is present only when all three behavior problems are identified, it is not necessary to categorize a child as hyperactive before following the procedures outlined here. If a child manifests one of these three behavior problems to such an extent that school performance suffers, then a procedure for dealing with that problem may be beneficial, regardless of whether the two other problems are also present. The most important focus of behavior management procedures is upon behavior, not the label.

This does not imply that the label *hyperactive* is not serious. A child whose behavior meets the criteria listed in *DSM-III* for attention deficit disorder with hyperactivity is likely to be very disruptive and performing poorly in many or all academic subjects. In addition, the child's parents are also likely to be experiencing some degree of frustration and lack of confidence in their parenting skills.

When a "hyperactive" child comes to the attention of school staff members, it is most often for one of two reasons. First, the child's teacher may have initiated a referral or asked for advice from a colleague regarding the child's disruptive classroom behavior or poor academic performance. Second, the child's parents may have contacted the school asking to have their child evaluated since they, themselves, may have noted signs of hyperactivity. A fairly high degree of parental sophistication in this area is to be expected, since articles on hyperactivity appear frequently in the popular press.

One approach to the treatment of hyperactivity is the use of prescribed medication. Stimulants such as amphetamine (Dexedrine), methylphenidate (Ritalin), and pemoline (Cylert) are often prescribed for the control of hyperactivity. These medications have been shown to reduce activity level and negative behavior but do not have equally positive effects upon learning or performance of hyperactive children in other areas. In addition, side effects such as reduced appetite and growth have been reported in children taking these medications. Thus, the school staff person may hear frequent anecdotal reports of children who were diagnosed hyperactive and then improved greatly under a regimen of prescribed medication. However, the research literature indicates that learning and academic achievement, the behaviors of greatest importance in the schools, will not necessarily improve when medication is prescribed (Barkley, 1979; Barkley, Karlsson, Strzelecki, & Murphy, 1984; Hinshaw, Henker, & Whalen, 1984; Kerasotes & Walker, 1983).

However, various behavioral strategies have consistently proven effective in the management of hyperactive behavior and academic deficiencies (e.g., Lahey, Delamater, & Kupfer, 1981). In reviewing studies that compared the effectiveness of medication and behavioral strategies, Lahey et al. concluded that, in most cases, it would be reasonable to begin treatment based upon behavioral strategies, adding medication only if satisfactory effects were not produced by the behavioral intervention. In the reality of the school setting, where the use of medication is beyond the control of school personnel, it would seem most reasonable to use behavioral interventions whenever possible and discourage the use of medication until it is determined that behavioral interventions are ineffective. In those cases where medication has already been prescribed, it should not interfere with the use of behavioral strategies. If such strategies prove effective, it may be worthwhile to suggest that the child's medication be reduced or eliminated, if only temporarily, to determine whether it is contributing positively to the effectiveness of the treatment program.

Another important consideration in the management of hyperactive behavior is the desirability of maintaining consistency between the home and school. This involves formulating a general plan for dealing with the child in both the school and at home. Communication and consultation between the home and school are very important and can determine whether a program succeeds. Although a child may learn to behave appropriately when different rules are in effect at home and at school, learning will be more efficient if the two environments are consistent with each other.

Consistency and "structure" are ubiquitous concepts in dealing with hyperactive children and merit additional comment. A highly structured environment is one in which most of the controls on behavior are external to the child. Consistency refers to the degree to which rules and their consequences are administered without variation. Linn and Hodge (1982) showed that hyperactive children tend to regard important life events as out of their control. Thus, the external environment must provide behavioral control through consistent rules and consequences. Any general approach to managing a hyperactive child must take this into account.

Baumrind (1983) provides an interesting discussion of the issues involved in the development of internal control in children. Her conclusion was that for normal children, firm parental control leads to better self-regulation of behavior than when control is subtle or when children are not aware that compliance is expected. Thus, the eventual development of internal control of behavior seems to require, at least in the initial stages of learning, firm and consistent external limits. This can be provided by a well-designed and well-executed behavior management program.

Because severely or even moderately disruptive behavior is likely to interfere with the academic progress of the child and his or her classmates and create an unpleasant home environment, it seems reasonable to begin management of hyperactive behavior by reducing disruptive behavior. At first glance, this may seem to contradict the general theme of this book, which is to emphasize positive reward and increased skills. However, the assumption here is that the level of disruptive behavior is so great as to prevent progress in other areas and perhaps interfere with the learning of other students. As soon as a program begins to reduce disruptive behavior toward acceptable levels, other programs to increase the skills the child is lacking should begin.

Decreasing Disruptive Behavior

Contemplating a formal program to decrease disruptive behavior assumes that informal methods (see Chapter 3) were unsuccessful. In addition, the disruptive behavior is assumed to occur at a frequency high enough to interfere with the normal function of the classroom and would make it difficult to begin programs to increase appropriate behavior. Two techniques for decreasing disruptive behavior in school will be discussed and then adaptations required for their use at home will be considered. The section ends with a brief description of a technique for decreasing disruptive behavior while rewarding desired behavior, called the *Good Behavior Game plus Merit.*

Reducing the frequency of a behavior, as the reader will recall from Chapter 2, can be accomplished by either presenting something aversive or taking away something that is desirable when the behavior occurs. Timeout is an aversive event that may be conveniently presented when a behavior occurs, while a technique called the *response cost lottery* (Witt & Elliott, 1982) or a simple response cost system mediated by free tokens (e.g., Salend & Allen, 1985) may be used to take away something desirable. A step-by-step plan for implementing either procedure, following the steps discussed in Chapter 3, follows.

Step 1: Identify the Problem. As already noted, this formal behavior management program is designed to decrease the frequency of disruptive behavior. When such a program is first considered, the disruptive behavior may be somewhat loosely defined but is likely to consist of speaking out and shouting, aggressive behavior, noncompliance, or other behaviors that interfere with the normal functioning of the classroom. As noted earlier, the child need not be categorized as hyperactive for the program to be useful. The focus of the program is upon specific behavior that interferes with the child's success in school.

Step 2: Refine the Definition of the Problem. In this very important step, a written description(s) of the target behavior(s) should be developed. Consultation with other school staff members can be very helpful to assure that the behavioral descriptions are objective and well defined. For instance, assume that in Step 1, the problem behaviors were identified as aggression and shouting. The goal is to develop clear and workable definitions of these behaviors, which can be used throughout the remainder of the behavior management program. An acceptable definition of aggression might be any physical contact with another child or the teacher that would be considered aversive or unwanted. This may include pushing, shoving, biting, hitting, taking objects, and/or other behaviors observed to be disruptive and to which the victim reacts with avoidance or defensive behavior. Shouting would be a little easier to define and would include verbalizations that are much louder than the child's normal speaking voice occurring at times when such behavior is not authorized. It would probably be necessary to specify the places and times when shouting was to be punished with timeout.

Step 3: Assess the Baseline Rate. If an adequate description of the target behavior was developed in Step 2, then a convenient recording system is all that is necessary to begin assessing the baseline rate. Since each instance of the undesired behavior must be recorded, a portable record sheet, such as a 3 × 5 card with blocks for each hour or half-hour of the school day, might be convenient. Each time one of the target behaviors occurs, a single mark should be made in the correct time block. Additional notes, such as teacher responses to the behavior, should be made on the back of the card. The baseline period may extend for as long as necessary, but several days to 1 week should be adequate. In the case of high magnitude aggressive behavior which may lead to injury of other children, it may be prudent to begin baseline observations and the management program at the same time. See Chapter 3 for more detailed descriptions of methods for recording baseline observations.

Step 4: Identify the Reward and Contingency. This step takes place while the baseline observations are being conducted. The purpose is to formulate the rules for dealing with the target behavior. Two different procedures will be described, timeout and the response cost lottery.

Timeout can be carried out easily when advance preparations have been made. One key is to have a timeout area selected and prepared in advance, and for the teacher to be mentally prepared to quickly and calmly administer timeout whenever it is required. Chapter 4 includes some additional suggestions. To summarize the requirements of effective timeout, remember that the timeout location must be a boring one that does not allow the child to participate in social interactions. Timeouts should be administered quickly and calmly along with a brief statement of the reason for timeout. When the timeout period (5 to 10 minutes) expires, the child should be released from timeout unless he or she in engaging in disruptive behavior. If disruptive behavior is occurring at the scheduled end of the timeout period, then the period should be extended until the disruptive behavior has ceased. In extreme cases, a rather long timeout period may be necessary, but it is very important that the child not gain anything from disruptive behavior. However, note that state laws may set a limit on the length and acceptable locations of a timeout period.

The response cost lottery requires a bit more effort to communicate the idea to the child but, once begun, can be administered more easily than timeout. It is very similar to the assertive discipline technique but has the advantages of making a much more noticeable event contingent on disruption and providing more immediate consequences. It requires that several students be involved and would be appropriate for special education classes of limited number or a group of several disruptive students. A common pattern would be where a "ringleader" causes most of the trouble, while receiving lots of social reinforcement and attention from a small group of peers.

The procedure begins with each child in the target group receiving slips of paper, which are placed under a 3×5 card taped on three sides to the child's desk. The number of slips of paper given to each child is determined from the baseline data. Whenever a rule is violated (the rules could be written on the 3×5 card), the teacher removes one slip of paper from the child's supply. Thus, the number of slips with which the child begins the day should be equal to or somewhat below the average daily frequency of disruptive incidents, so that with some improvement in behavior the child is likely to end the day with at least a few remaining slips. At the end of the school day, each child's leftover slips are labeled with the child's name and placed in a jar.

At the end of the week a slip of paper is drawn from the jar and the child whose name is on the slip receives a predetermined reward. Thus, each time during the week that the child is discovered breaking a rule, his or her chances of winning the lottery decrease. This should be carefully explained to the children involved, although it may require at least a week before they understand what it means to lose one of their slips.

An alternate version of this procedure would be a response cost token reward system, in which the child begins each day with a set number of tokens and loses one for each rule violation during the day. Then, at the end of the day or week, the leftover tokens would be used to "purchase" from a menu of rewards. Baseline data would be used to set reasonable "prices" on the reward menu so that the most desirable reward would require the greatest amount of acceptable behavior during the preceding week. Both the lottery and purchasing rewards with tokens can be quickly conducted at times when only the target children are present, such as at the end of the school day or during time with a special education teacher.

Salend and Allen (1985) employed such a technique to modify out-of-seat behavior and inappropriate verbalizations in two second-grade boys labeled as *learning disabled*. In their procedure, each boy was given a predetermined number of tokens. If the boy had at least one token remaining at the end of a 20-minute resource period, it could be exchanged for an agreed-upon reward. The authors found that the response cost contingency was effective in reducing inappropriate behavior to zero occurrences at the end of the program. In addition, they found that the program was equally effective whether the contingency (removal of a token) was administered by the student or the resource teacher.

Lewis and Blampied (1985) successfully employed a similar procedure to manage time on-task and out-of-seat behavior of nine children. In this procedure, children administered tokens to themselves contingent upon either being on-task or being in their seats. The procedure was successful in increasing these behaviors to acceptable levels and illustrates an alternative method of employing token reinforcement procedures with older children.

Step 5: Begin the Program. After the careful planning in Steps 1-4, this step should be easy. However, it should not be forgotten that observations must still be collected so that Step 6 can be performed. An easy way to collect the data when response cost procedures are used is to record the behavior and time on the forfeited slips of paper as they are collected. When the timeout procedure is used, data should be collected in the same way as during the baseline period. However, the details of the timeout administration, such as its length and the number of times it was necessary to extend the timeout period because of continued disruptive behavior, should also be recorded.

Caution should be exercised in the use of timeout, because careless application could result in injury to a child and/or violation of the child's rights. For instance, a violation of fire safety codes may result if a timeout area is so secure that a child can not easily escape from it. Also, state laws may set limits on the use of timeout and provide specific limits upon such parameters as the length of timeout or the location of the timeout area. It seems advisable for the school staff member using timeout for the first time to obtain consultation from others in the same school district who are familiar with the use of the procedure. As noted earlier, timeout areas need not totally isolate the child. A single chair or desk, well away from other children but close enough that classroom instruction is not missed, can be very effective with kindergarten and early primary children. Older students can be placed at a desk surrounded on three sides by walls that prevent social communication but give the student an area on which to work and write.

Step 6: Observe the Effects of the Program. This step, it will be recalled, is a continuation of Step 5, except that some expectations of change should begin to be confirmed. One to three weeks, about two or three times the length of the baseline period, is a reasonable time within which to anticipate observable change. Of course, the careful baseline observations that establish the range of expected frequencies of the target behavior are very important at this time. Any decrease or downward trend in the frequency of the target behavior should be considered justification for continuing the program without modification. If the downward trend continues, programs to increase desirable but deficient skills can begin. At the same time, the procedures for fading out the program and promoting generalization can be instituted. These procedures are described in Step 8.

Note that it is very important that some reinforcement be available to the child. If academic and/or social skills are lacking, then the rewards that other children experience in the classroom will be unobtainable for the target child. A return to less desirable means of obtaining attention can be expected if the program is faded out while the child lacks other skills that contribute to success in the classroom. Therefore, a concurrent program to improve deficit skills is an important part of the general approach to reducing the occurrence of disruptive behavior.

Step 7: Modify the Program, If Necessary. What if, despite the best effort of those involved, the timeout or response cost procedure did not work? First, it is very important not to become discouraged, because initial efforts at implementing a behavior management program can fail, even when very experienced behavior therapists are involved. Second, it is also important not to attribute the failure to the child. The source of the problem is in the environment that has been structured and failure is an indication that it is time to consider what adjustments may be necessary and beneficial.

Consider, the timeout procedure. Why might it fail to reduce the frequency of behavior? First, in order to be effective, timeout must be at least mildly aversive. If observations show that the child is amusing himself or herself during the timeout period, the timeout location could be changed. Another possibility is that the timeout is too short. Lengthening the timeout period could be an effective adjustment but a number of considerations suggest that 20 minutes should be the maximum length of timeout. If timeout is ineffective, it could also be the case that the timeout is a reinforcer because it allows the child to escape disliked seatwork. One option for dealing with this difficulty is to be sure that the child has something to do in the timeout location. In extreme cases, it may be feasible for the child to earn his or her way out of the timeout by completing certain tasks.

Another way of occupying a child during a timeout period is to have him or her write or copy an essay about the incident or behavior that led to timeout. Workman (1982) and Swift and Spivack (1975) both describe a technique of giving the child a typed essay that describes the targeted misbehavior, its negative consequences, what the child should have been doing, and the positive consequences of the desired behavior. The typed essay is written to address the child's particular behavior problem. and is copied by the child during the timeout period. Since it may be difficult for a classroom teacher to prepare an essay for each anticipated behavioral problem or even to anticipate what problems may occur, it may be effective to assign the child the task of composing an original essay. The essay would answer general questions about the incident that led to timeout. These questions might consist of the following: What did I do wrong? Why is it wrong? What was I *supposed* to be doing? What good things will happen if I do what I'm supposed to do? The resulting essay could then be used as a basis for discussion of how to avoid problems in the future.

The most likely problem with response cost procedures is that the child does not understand the connection between behavior and the reward or the reward is not attractive enough. Some direct negotiation with the child on this issue could be very rewarding to those involved. In any case it is important that the behavior management program be successful before Step 8 is undertaken. Otherwise the gains may be lost, at least temporarily. For other suggestions regarding how to modify an unsuccessful program, see Chapters 3 and 4.

Step 8: Fade Out the Program. The general goal of fading out the program is to substitute the child's internal controls for the external controls on behavior provided by the behavior management program. However, when disruptive behaviors are the target, fading out the program involves somewhat different procedures than those discussed in Chapter 3, where the focus was upon programs that use positive reinforcement to increase behavior. Consistent application of timeout will cause the disruptive behavior to decrease, but long-term reductions will occur only if the child learns new skills to replace disruptive behavior. Thus, two mechanisms are involved in fading a program involving timeout. First, timeout will be used less frequently as the target behavior decreases. Second, as academic and social skills improve via other programs, disruptive behavior should remain an acceptably rare occurrence.

The response cost procedure can be faded out by decreasing the frequency that tokens may be exchanged for reward. Price increases (due to inflation?) may also be announced. The secret of success in fading out the program is to make the early changes in the program as small as possible. If behavior should worsen, then reinstate earlier and demonstrably effective stages of the program.

Extending the Techniques to the Home

An important part of the process of encouraging generalization of the child's behavior to other environments can be to train the parents of the child in the use of the techniques employed in school. The eight-step program just described is designed for use in the classroom but can easily be adapted to the home. In fact, as behavior programmers, parents have distinct advantages over school personnel because of the greater flexibility they have in the selection of timeout areas and reward menus. Cooperation between the school and home increases the chances of success and the efficiency of the program. Important areas for cooperation are in the definitions of problems common to both environments and in the procedure for administering consequences. If the response cost procedure is employed, some items on the reinforcer menu could come from the home. Ideally, there should be very little difference between the home and school application of procedures to decrease disruptive behavior. The general goal is to maintain the consistency of environmental responses to disruptive behavior as the child goes from one environment to another.

Combined Management of Disruptive Behavior and Academic Productivity

As noted previously, control of disruptive behavior does not guarantee that behaviors conducive to learning will increase. Thus, it is typically necessary to employ behavior management strategies specifically designed to improve academic performance in programs designed to control disruptive behavior. The following procedure is based upon a study by Darveaux (1984). In this study, the disruptive behavior of two boys, at risk for placement in a classroom for behaviorally impaired students, was greatly decreased while the percentage of assignments completed almost doubled, using an intervention called the *Good Behavior Game plus Merit*. The intervention combined contingencies for reducing disruptive behavior with a contingency for increasing academic productivity. The study employed an ABAB design (baseline, intervention, return to baseline conditions, return to intervention conditions), which demonstrated that the intervention alone was responsible for the observed behavior changes.

To begin the procedure, the class is divided into two teams. The intervention consists of two contingencies. First, for each violation of a classroom rule the child's team receives a single point. If the entire team keeps its point total under five during a predetermined period of time, that team receives a reward such as candy, access to free time, or story-time. Baseline observations, consultation with others, and previous experience should be used to determine an acceptable number of points. The rules in effect for the Darveaux study were not talking without permission, no excessive noise, staying in one's desk area, remaining still while seated, and not tattling on other children. Of course, one would expect this procedure to be effective with any reasonable set of classroom rules.

The second contingency involves a positive reward for desirable behavior. The children earn "merits," which consist of the words "one merit" printed on an index card. Five merits acquired by the children on a team result in the loss of one of the team's accumulated points. Thus, through good behavior, the children on a team can reduce their point total and thereby receive a reward for keeping that total below five. Merit cards were distributed for completing an arithmetic assignment at or above 75% accuracy and active class participation in Darveaux's study. However, "merit" cards could be awarded for any target behavior deemed important to an individual child or the group as a whole. Thus, in order to conduct this intervention, a minimum of prior preparation would be necessary. This would include a list of classroom rules and ways that children could earn merits, a supply of merit cards, plans for providing access to rewarding activities, and a method of conducting baseline observations.

With respect to baseline observations, the simplest approach would be a count of rule violations prior to beginning the program. Presumably, classroom rules are objective, concrete, and measurable, but it may prove necessary to give this component of the program careful attention. The count of rule violations could focus on both an individual child and the entire classroom, depending upon the goal of the program. Additional data could also be included, such as the particular rule violated, the name of the rule violator, the time of day, and/or the type of activity in which the class was engaged. Alternately, a time sampling procedure may be used to obtain objective observational data regarding the behavior of a particular child (see Chapter 3). The baseline data would be useful in setting the criterion for acceptable behavior that results in access to a reward. In addition, it could prove important should a special education team be assembled to consider special services for the target child or children.

Once the Good Behavior Game plus Merit has been initiated and positive effects have been observed, the question of generalization must be considered. One strategy for the practitioner would be to make the intervention a permanent component of the classroom structure. A disadvantage of this strategy is that the children remain subject to external structure, when the ultimate goal of the classroom teacher may be to promote self motivated behavior and independence. If this is the case, a couple of alternative approaches could be used.

First, the program could be slowly faded until most of its components had been removed entirely. Two variables can be manipulated in this respect. The number of merit cards necessary to erase one of the points could be slowly increased so that greater productivity would be required of the classroom as a whole in order to offset the penalty for disruptive behavior. Another variable that could be changed is the period of time between rewarding activities. That is, in the initial stages of the program, the children might receive access to a rewarding activity if fewer than five points were accumulated during a single day or independent work period. This could be changed in a number of ways. For instance, access to a rewarding activity could be made contingent upon 2 or 3 days of having fewer than five points at the end of the day. Similarly, the students could be allowed access to a rewarding activity for having accumulated fewer than, say, ten points during an entire week. Using changes such as these, the program could eventually be entirely eliminated or a level of structure with which the classroom teacher was satisfied could be maintained with the Good Behavior Game plus Merit.

An alternative approach might be to fade out the group contingencies and focus the rules of the game only upon children who are exceptionally disruptive. Then, the same techniques discussed above could be used to fade out the game for the individual students.

The Good Behavior Game plus Merit represents one of many viable strategies for intervening when children are disruptive in school. The advantage of the procedure is that it combines negative contingencies (loss of access to rewarding activity) for disruption with positive rewards for desirable behavior. However, this could be accomplished in other ways as well. For instance, timeout for disruptive behavior could be employed concurrently with one of the behavior management programs described in Chapter 10. The choice of an appropriate strategy will depend upon the particular needs of the target student and the needs of the classroom teacher.

INATTENTIVE AND IMPULSIVE BEHAVIOR

As noted in Chapter 6, the type of behavior that was once called hyperactivity is now labeled Attention Deficit Disorder with Hyperactivity according to *DSM-III*, placing the primary emphasis upon attentional processes rather than hyperactive behavior. Factor analysis of teacher ratings of inattentive, impulsive, hyperactive, aggressive, and anxious behavior of 9-year-old children has also suggested that inattention is the "core dysfunction" in hyperactivity (McGee, Williams, & Silva, 1985). McGee et al. found that ratings of inattention were most strongly related to academic and motor abilities while antisocial, hyperactive, and worry ratings were associated with family backround measures. Consequently, the most significant target for behavioral intervention within the school may be the attentional skills of children who show signs of hyperactivity.

Regardless of whether a child has been categorized as hyperactive, learning to attend to specific aspects of the environment is crucial to academic development and survival. Consider a simple task, such as crossing the street. The child must be taught to stop and look for oncoming cars and, if necessary, wait until it is safe to cross. The child who impulsively dashes out into the street without attending to the possibility of oncoming cars may end up in real physical danger.

In the classroom, the problem is no less difficult or important than outside the classroom. The child must attend to the subtle differences among the letters of the alphabet as soon as he or she enters kindergarten. This is not as easy as it sounds. The lines and angles that make up letters are very similar. To discriminate the differences among them, it is necessary to attend to very subtle aspects of the letters. For instance, in discriminating between *b* and *d* the child must note that the crucial difference is in the direction that the letter points. As school progresses, the child must "pay attention" to selected aspects of more and more complex stimuli. Students who do not pay attention often become the subjects of referrals for academic and behavioral problems.

The most useful type of attentional skill is selective attention, the ability to attend selectively to a particular aspect of the environment. This skill is brought into play as soon as the child enters school. In fact, as Staats (1971) points out, the child's ability to attend and discriminate specific stimuli is presumed to be well developed when the child begins kindergarten. The child whose attention cannot be directed at certain aspects of the environment, such as the shape of letters, certainly will have a difficult time at school and at home.

When teachers say, "Pay attention!," they usually expect their students to sit up straight and make good eye contact. However, even though a child may appear to be looking at the appropriate area of the room and listening carefully to instructions, it is not certain that information is being processed, because the child might be daydreaming or thinking about something unrelated to the classroom activity. Thus, focusing a behavior management program upon posture and eye contact may lead to improvements in behavior and the appearance that the child is attentive, but academic performance will not necessarily improve (Ferritor, Buckholdt, Hamblin, & Smith, 1972; Jones & Kazdin, 1981). An alternative approach is to focus directly on the skills that contribute to learning.

The basic problem of inattentive or impulsive children is that they appear to act "without thinking," that is, too quickly or illogically to have properly analyzed the particular requirements of a problem-solving situation. Thus, one method of remediating impulsive/inattentive behavior might be to train the child in verbal and cognitive skills necessary for analyzing a task and responding correctly. A substantial empirical and theoretical literature has developed around interventions designed to accomplish this with children. These types of interventions are typically called *cognitive-behavioral techniques.*

One of the most frequently cited articles in the area of cognitive-behavioral interventions is by Meichenbaum and Goodman (1971) entitled, "Training Impulsive Children to Talk to Themselves: A Means of Developing Self-Control." The title accurately describes what these authors set out to do. The underlying theory is very simple: Much of what people do is mediated by self-generated verbal instructions. Therefore, one way to learn new skills or to improve old ones is to learn an appropriate set of verbal mediators to go along with that skill.

Meichenbaum and Goodman taught their subjects to formulate questions about the nature and demands of a task, answer these questions in the form of cognitive rehearsal and planning, verbalize appropriately while performing the task, and reinforce themselves for good performance. The results of two studies in which the effects of such training were assessed indicated that the program was successful in modifying impulsive behavior. In addition, their results indicated that modeling of the procedure by a trainer may be an important component of the training.

A similar procedure has been used by Palkes, Stewart, and Freedman (1972). In their procedure, four cue words with illustrative line drawings were used: stop, listen, look, and think. They showed that the self-directing commands could be used to modify the maze performance of hyperactive boys. Unfortunately, only the children's maze performance was assessed so it is not known whether classroom behavior or academic performance was improved by this treatment.

More recent studies (Argulewicz, Elliott, & Spencer, 1982; Brown & Conrad, 1982; Kendall & Braswell, 1982b) indicate that these types of training procedures can be useful in remediating problem behaviors of hyperactive boys, and academic deficiencies of teacher-referred (Thackwray, Meyers, Schleser, & Cohen, 1985), and emotionally disturbed (Swanson, 1985) children. Harris, Wong, and Keogh (1985) edited a special issue of the *Journal of Abnormal Child Psychology* devoted to cognitive-behavior modification with children.

Kendall and Braswell (1982b) conducted a group-oriented training program for children (85% boys) in grades three through six, who were referred by their teachers for "non-self-controlled" behavior. The experimental, cognitive-behavioral treatment group received twelve 45- to 55-minute sessions, two sessions per week. The treatment package consisted of a variety of tasks in which the emphasis was upon training in verbal self-instructions via modeling, social reward for correct responses, response-cost contingencies for errors, and token reward for successes.

The self-instructional training was designed to teach a five-step problem solving approach to the children. The steps were problem definition, planning an approach, focusing attention, selecting an answer, and self-reinforcing for correct performance. One interesting feature of the program is that the therapist met with the teacher of each child to determine what situations were likely to elicit non-self-control. These situations were then employed in role plays of problem solving in social situations.

A large number of dependent measures were employed in this study, but the results can be briefly summarized. First, both specific skills were learned and general classroom behavior improved. A second important result was that the cognitive component of the program was shown to add to the effectiveness of the treatment package. Finally, these authors confirmed, again, one of the most robust generalizations from the behavior management literature, that generalization of new skills and behavior to situations other than the treatment environment needs to be an explicit component of a successful treatment package.

Kendall and Braswell (1985) have elaborated their techniques in a recently published book, which focuses on applying the technique with individual children. The program they describe consists of several components embedded within a token system. In each session the child begins with 20 tokens. Whenever mistakes are made — such as going too fast, omitting a step, or getting the wrong answer to a problem — the child loses a token. The rationale for employing the response cost contingency is that the loss of a token is a potent cue to remind the child to stop and think before answering. In addition, the technique avoids the problem of rewarding the child for impulsive guessing, which occasionally results in a correct answer. An important component of the response cost procedure is that the child is given a brief explanation of why the token was taken away, so that future improvement is possible.

In addition to the response cost contingency, the child is given opportunities to earn bonus tokens. One way of earning bonus tokens is by accurate self-evaluation of performance within a training session. This is accomplished in the following way: First, the trainer evaluates the child on a How I Did Today chart, which consists of five alternatives: not so good, OK, good, very good, and super extra special, with one point assigned to not so good and five points assigned to super extra special. After the trainer rates the child, the child rates him- or herself. The child receives a bonus token if his or her rating comes within one point of the trainer's rating. This procedure was implemented to enhance generalization of the training.

Another way for the child to earn bonus points is by completing homework assignments. These assignments consist of describing situations where the problem-solving procedures were or could have been used in real-life situations. The assignments are "graded" for accuracy and difficulty. The main function, again, is to enhance generalization from the training environment to other situations.

The following paragraphs describe two programs for remediating inattentive or impulsive behavior. The first technique is easily adaptable to special education or regular classrooms. It involves systematically encouraging children to verbalize the steps in solving a problem and is directly related to the studies just cited. The other technique consists of one-on-one instruction in how to approach tasks in a nonimpulsive manner, which could be provided by a regular or special education teacher or a school psychologist.

Step 1: Identification of the Problem. The general problem is defined as inattention or impulsive behavior, either as an isolated problem or in the context of other behaviors that accompany hyperactivity. For a complete review of relevant assessment techniques and issues, see Kendall and Braswell (1982a). One of the measures discussed by Kendall and Braswell is a rating scale for self-control in children. The scale (Kendall & Wilcox, 1979) consists of 33 items, which are rated on a seven-point continuum by a child's teacher. The scale covers a broad range of behaviors and was designed to measure generalization of behavior management programs beyond the specific training environment. The measure could prove to be a valuable assessment tool because it could easily be used to assess both a target child and a control child. Also, it would be a good way of determining the broad effects of a treatment program.

Impulsive behavior is indicated when the child acts too quickly to have processed the relevant components of the problem and, in addition, typically makes mistakes when work is completed too quickly. This may happen in a variety of situations, ranging from completion of seatwork to social situations that result in anger and fights. The child who requires a lot of individual instruction in order to understand the nature of an assigned task is also likely to be approaching schoolwork in an impulsive or inattentive manner. Inattention can be indicated when the child is unable to repeat or perform the essential elements of a task that has been presented via group instruction. Of course, behavioral indicators—such as not looking at the teacher, bothering other students, playing with objects in and around his or her desk, and being out of seat during group instruction are all behavioral indicators of inattention and impulsive behavior.

A key element in any definition of impulsivity and inattention to school work is the concept of ability level. It is important to know whether the child is capable of doing the assigned work. If a child is not capable of doing the work, he or she is likely to appear inattentive and/or impulsive, when the actual problem may be an academic handicap. What is necessary in identifying inattention and impulsivity is independent evidence that the child is capable of doing the assigned work. The accepted way to answer this question is to conduct an individual assessment of the child. Such an assessment could consist of an individual intelligence test or a period of individual instruction in which attention to the task can be closely monitored. It is important that a child be taught at a level that does not produce frustration, so that any program to modify academic habits will work.

Step 2: Refine the Definition of the Problem. Successful performance of school work is the ultimate indicator of proper attention and reflection. However, lack of success in performing school work may be the result of a variety of problems. Thus, the considerations discussed in Chapter 6 and the behavior management programs discussed in Chapter 10 could prove relevant in this context. Whether the decision is to use one of the programs discussed in this chapter or some other plan, it is always possible to change strategies if one program or another is unsuccessful.

As discussed by Meichenbaum and Goodman (1971), who were among the earliest to apply these techniques, previous research has suggested that children learn to use internal speech to guide their behavior in a gradual progression. Early in development, adult speech serves to guide and direct a child's behavior. Later, the child's own overt speech serves this function. Finally, the child's inner speech (thoughts) serve to guide and regulate behavior. Given that this is a universal progression, it might be hypothesized that impulsive and/or inattentive children have failed to learn to control their behavior via covert verbalizations. This is the essence of how the problem of inattention/impulsivity is viewed from this perspective. The question for the school staff member to ask is whether this model might have validity for remediating a particular child's behavior.

What, then, are some specific indicators that training in verbal mediation of problem solving might be beneficial? Meichenbaum and Goodman (1971) employed a pretest in which children were given instructions to slow down while performing a task. Those children who did not slow down were included in the treatment group. This informal test might serve as a general indication that a child could benefit from training that teaches him or her to verbally control behavior. Other indicators might include inaccurate responses or an inability to respond to questions regarding the nature of an assigned task, an inability to respond accurately to a request to "tell me what you're doing," or any of the signs of impulsivity or inattention discussed in Chapter 6. A teacher might also be requested to answer the questions on the Kendall and Wilcox rating scale.

Step 3: Assess the Baseline Rate. The goal of this formal behavior management program is to improve academic performance and on-task behavior, which are the most important indicators of impulsivity and inattention. All teachers keep detailed records of academic performance, so this measure should be no problem. On-task behavior is difficult to measure because so much activity is taking place in the classroom and often little time is available for observation. However, if no consultative help is available, a time sampling procedure can provide a valid measure of on-task behavior. The time period can be from 10 minutes to 1 hour in length, with 20-30 minutes probably being sufficient for most purposes. Two characteristics of the time period are important. First, it should occur at about the same time each day. Second, the children should be engaged in the same activity during each observation period.

For example, a good observation period might be while the class is working on arithmetic worksheets which occurs on Monday, Wednesday, and Friday at about 1:10 to 1:45 P.M. The observation period might be minutes 10-30 of the work period (a 20-minute interval). Observations could be recorded by dividing the 20-minute period into 120 10-second blocks, or 80, 15-second blocks. At the end of each interval, the target child is observed and judged to be on-task (carefully defined according to the activity taking place) or off-task. A checkmark is recorded on the record sheet, which has already been divided appropriately. The percent of time on-task equals the number of checkmarks divided by 120 or 80. Observation of one or two control children or observing each child in the classroom for 3- or 4-second periods will enable a comparison of the target child with the class average. Separation of the observation into teacher-directed (e.g., lecture and instruction) and independent work periods may also be revealing. These and other observation techniques are also discussed in Chapter 3.

Step 4: Identify the Reward and Contingency. The first issue to resolve is how to work with the child, individually, or as part of the regular classroom during group instruction. The main considerations would be the availability of time and consultative help. Success with these types of procedures has been obtained with sessions ranging from 10 minutes each over several days to a single 2-hour training session. Within this range, it should be possible to reach some sort of accommodation. At the beginning of training, the most effective procedure would probably be to work with the individual child for a short daily period, planning on a total of perhaps 9-12 sessions of 20 minutes each. Group instruction may then be added to provide additional practice in the techniques and to boost the probability that the training will generalize to the classroom.

The goal within each training session is to help the child toward deriving correct answers to assignments. The method is to encourage use of a procedure that involves five cues to which the child responds: LISTEN, ASK, HOW, DID, and REWARD. This is a modified version of the original series of cues (Meichenbaum & Goodman, 1971; Palkes et al., 1972). In the earlier version cards with the cues and symbolic line drawings were used as reminders. The entire series of questions and cues follows. These cues could be copied onto cards and presented one at a time to the children, or a large poster could be used during group instruction. To begin, the instructor brings the child into the teaching setting and says that he or she will be doing some worksheets in a special way today.

- L   LISTEN to instructions.
- A   ASK myself what I'm supposed to do.
- H   HOW do I do it?
- D   DID I do it right?
- R   REWARD myself for doing it right.

The goal is to train the child to use the steps shown above to solve each problem on the worksheets. This is accomplished by first explaining the steps to the children while they look at each of the cards. The instructions should explain that each card tells the student what to do. For the first problems, the child is requested to say everything out loud so that the instructor knows what the child is doing. The instructor should model responses for the student on the first two problems. Begin with the first card, LISTEN to instructions, and then read the instructions for the worksheet: "Put an X on the square that has the same number of things as the first square." Relevant worksheets, which are consistent with the child's level of performance, should be selected. Then, show the second card, ASK myself what I'm supposed to do, and read it to the child. Afterwards the instructor should model an appropriate understanding of the directions such as by saying: "What am I supposed to do? I should find the box over here (point) that has the same number of things as this one (point)."

Next, show the third card and say: "How do I do it? Let's see. I can count these in the first box, and then count to see which one of these is the same. Then I put an X on it." Perform all the steps correctly and then show the fourth card and say: "Did I do it right? Let's see. I'll count how many are here (count out loud) and how many are here (again, count out loud). Yes! There are five in each one. I did it right!" Finally, show the fifth card and say: "Reward myself for doing it right. Good for me! I did it right and used all the steps to help me."

For the second problem on the worksheet, the instructor should follow the same sequence except that an error should be made the first time through. When the error is "discovered," go back to the first step and rework the problem correctly.

Self-praise for getting the problem correct and catching the error should be part of the REWARD step.

The third problem on the worksheet should be done by the child with as much help and prompting from the instructor as necessary to get the child to proceed correctly through the sequence. On subsequent problems help should be decreased as the child's skill increases. Praise and attention from the instructor should follow the successful completion of each step. Eventually, praise should be limited to the correct answers preceded by correct completion of all five steps. It is likely that several sessions will be necessary before the child begins to show mastery of the problem-solving sequence.

It may be the case that the child is uncooperative or noncompliant. If this occurs, the instructor can reward appropriate behavior with candy, dried banana chips, stickers, or tokens. Alternately, a token program with response cost contingencies for misbehavior, responding too quickly, failing to use the steps, or wrong answers, as employed by Kendall and Braswell (1985), could be used. This procedure, coupled with copious verbal praise from the instructor, should be sufficient to get the child on task. If not, additional consultation or a change in the initial goals of behavior management is probably necessary.

Step 5: Begin the Program. Once a schedule has been arranged, materials have been prepared, and a place to conduct the training has been found, the program may begin. Although baseline data would include academic records and behavioral observations from the classroom, the instructor should also keep records of the training sessions. First, some notes should be taken on the general behavior of the child during the training sessions. These notes may reveal much that is of value to know regarding the child's approach to school work and suggest other behavior management programs that may be more beneficial. A second source of data is the child's responses to each problem. The instructor should record whether or not the child responds appropriately to the five LAHDR steps. A prepared mimeographed sheet could be used for this purpose. Checkmarks or "smiley faces" could be used to indicate correct responses and the recording sheet could also serve as a basis for a token system, if desirable.

Steps 6 and 7: Observe the Effects of the Program and Modify It as Necessary. Since behavioral observations are based upon classroom performance, it is likely that few effects will be observed until specific training to promote generalization to the classroom has been conducted. This may require specific training on tasks the child performs during the observation period. Yet, even with such training, the child may not use the problem-solving steps when working independently. This can be directly addressed during the individual training sessions by teaching the child to whisper and silently say the answers to the questions posed by the LAHDR technique. In addition, the cards may be given to the child to use as reminders during class. The cues could also be written on a single card which is taped to the child's desk. Alternately, group instruction in the technique could be given to the entire class.

In any case, it may require specific effort to teach the child to use the technique in the classroom, assuming that training was successful in the individual sessions. However, by the time specific training has been conducted in the classroom, positive effects upon both on-task behavior and academic performance should be visible. If not, the behavior management programs for improving academic behavior discussed in Chapter 10 may be useful.

In their cognitive-behavioral program, Kendall and Braswell (1985) included several components designed to promote generalization beyond the training environment. These components included homework assignments and self-evaluation of daily performance. In addition, their program includes a progression of tasks beginning with concrete, worksheet-type activities to emotionally laden material in role plays of social situations. Another way of labeling this progression is to say that it goes from concrete cognitive-behavioral training, focusing on a specific task, to a more general, conceptual approach, which would generalize to other problem situations. Thackwray et al. (1985) showed that teaching a general problem-solving strategy improved performance in academic areas not included in the original training.

The LAHDR technique described in this context must be regarded as representing the most concrete end of the progression, since it is designed to provide steps relevant to solving concrete academic problems. Alternately, a more general series of steps might be similar to those employed by Kendall and Braswell (1985): (a) recognize the existence of a problem and identify its relevant features, (b) identify a strategy that would result in a probable resolution of the problem, (c) consider the various solutions suggested by the strategy and evaluate their potential effectiveness, and (d) go ahead and execute the plan and objectively evaluate the results. Evaluation would include self-reinforcement for an appropriate solution and coping positively with failure by resolving to do better or trying a different strategy or solution. The LAHDR steps could be modified thus:

- L   LOOK at the problem.
- A   ASK myself what my goal is.
- H   HOW can I reach the goal?
- D   DECIDE upon a course of action.
- R   REVIEW the results and REWARD myself or try again.

Another potential problem with the procedure suggested here is that it may be too abstract for younger children. Brown, Meyers, and Cohen (1984) employed a much more concrete sequence of cues using a schematic stoplight. The stoplight consisted of three colored circles against a black background. The top circle contained a picture of an owl which served as a cue to "stop and think." The second circle contained a picture of a turtle with a checkmark below it, serving as cues to go slow and look carefully, and then go back and check the answer. The third circle contained a smiley face, which cued successful use of the procedure and self-praise. This self-instruction training technique was successful compared to the results of two carefully matched control groups. It was also found that the training generalized to both similar and dissimilar tasks. The authors attributed their results to several factors, which may be relevant in the planning of such interventions.

First of all, they noted that the length of the intervention (nine sessions, about 30 minutes each) coupled with the use of a concrete, visual cue may have enhanced retention of the self-instruction sequence. Second, the self-instructions were a combination of task-specific instructions and general instructions "not anchored to a specific task." The use of a general self-instruction strategy rather than a task-specific strategy would tend to enhance generalization to novel tasks and situations. This principle is supported by other research (cited in Brown et al., 1984). Finally, the authors suggested that the young age (4- and 5-year-old preschoolers) of their subjects may be related to the success of self-instruction training.

Step 8: Take Steps to Fade Out the Program. Efforts to strengthen generalization and fade out the program have been included in earlier steps. By the time Step 8 is reached, the child should be using LAHDR or a more general approach to guide progress through most independent work and the steps should be performed silently. Occasional prompts or help from the teacher may be necessary but the ideal goal is to provide the child with about the same amount of individual help as is typical for other students of similar ability.

Group instruction conducted within a classroom may enhance the effects of the program. Such training would follow the basic outline established above but could also move on to broader issues, say, solving classroom problems such as rule violations or social conflicts. Success would depend at least partially upon generating feedback from students, indicating that they were attending to the task and using appropriate steps to solve the problem. In addition, it may be necessary to give at least occasional individual attention to the target student to assure he or she responds appropriately to tasks.

As in all behavior management efforts, communication between home and school can greatly increase the chances for success and the efficiency of learning. If parents are aware of the training procedures, they can be encouraged to model some of their own problem-solving behavior out loud in the presence of their child. In addition, they could provide some degree of monitoring of the child's performance of homework. It may be helpful for the parents to observe use of the LAHDR system in school, so they can provide some relevant help at home. If the child is too young to do homework, the LAHDR system may still be useful knowledge for the parents, since they can then provide models of problem-solving behavior and guide the child in problem analysis in nonacademic contexts.

Regardless of the situation and degree of parental involvement, the parents should at least be aware of the school's efforts to improve the child's behavior and academic performance.

An Alternate Strategy for Remediating Impulsivity and Inattention

Another program for dealing with impulsive behavior was described by Berger (1981) and published in the *School Psychology Review*. Although the generalizability of the case study is in doubt because only a single child was involved, the program described by Berger has much in common with the LAHDR technique. Both procedures employ cognitive mediators to train a skill that is incompatible with impulsive, inattentive behavior. In addition, Berger's procedure has a design that allows ready transfer from the situation in which training takes place to the classroom. Also, the technique's procedures can be more easily used and reinforced in the home. The basic procedure consists of training the child to shoot a basketball and build towers of blocks in a nonimpulsive manner. A description of the program follows.

Step 1: Identify the Problem. The problem in Berger's case study was the behavior of an 8-year-old boy, medically diagnosed as being hyperactive. Observations indicated that he was very disruptive and spent only 30% of his time engaged in assigned tasks. Medication significantly reduced off-task and disruptive behavior but accuracy of completed seatwork dropped to near zero. A preliminary observation indicated that the boy could control his high rate of activity when rewarded with candy for doing so. According to Berger (1981), the ability to exhibit self-control is an important prerequisite for using this procedure.

Step 2: Refine the Definition of the Problem. As in the previously described behavior management program, Berger conceptualized the problem as being the absence of self-control skills. However, the emphasis was not upon verbal mediation of problem solving but upon establishing external controls for inhibiting hyperactive and disruptive behavior. At the same time the program emphasized learning to anticipate the consequences of actions and make appropriate behavioral adjustments to compensate for predicted results.

Step 3: Assessment of the Baseline. Berger did not specify his procedures for recording classroom observations. However, the goal of the program was to improve classroom behavior and academic performance so that the baseline observation procedures described earlier would be appropriate. Recall that the two areas tracked were academic performance and on-task behavior in the classroom. Teacher-maintained records were used to track academic performance and a time-sampling procedure was described for tracking on-task behavior. In the time-sampling procedure, a period of about 10-30 minutes, during which the class is regularly engaged in the same assigned activity, is selected. Observations are recorded by dividing the observation period into equal intervals and noting on a prepared data sheet whether the child was on-task at each observation point. These data are then used to compute the percent of time the student was on task.

Step 4: Identify the Reward and Contingency. The training in this case involves teaching the child how to shoot a basketball and how to build a tower out of blocks. For a highly impulsive or inattentive child, these are difficult tasks and the goal of training is to teach the child a nonimpulsive, attentive approach that could generalize to the classroom. The child is taken to the school gym or playground and given the opportunity to earn candy, points, or tokens for making three shots in a row or six out of ten. The child is then given specific instruction including how to push off using his or her legs, how to hold the ball, how to aim, and instructions to "think the ball through the hoop." The child is also told to wait 10 seconds between shots.

In the following sessions, the child is conditioned to respond to the words, "Stop! Think!" accompanied by a hand signal, whenever he or she is about to shoot "impulsively." Here, impulsiveness is defined as not waiting 10 seconds between shots and not following other instructions. As the child's skill improves, the requirement for being rewarded is increased and other games (including challenging the instructor) are added for variety. Two contingencies are involved in the training: one is the natural contingency of making baskets; the other is the reward for successful shooting. Both rewards are more likely to occur if the hand signal and verbal prompt (Stop! Think!) are obeyed or if a nonimpulsive approach to shooting is taken.

In the second phase of the program, the child is required to earn basketball time by building towers from wooden blocks. Berger's criteria was that the tower had to be taller than 2 feet or use all of the blocks. Only one block was allowed to touch the floor as a base. During this phase the child is coached just as during basketball shooting. This would include reminders to "Stop and think!" about what was being done, the current status of the tower, and how another block would affect its balance.

Step 5: Begin the Program. Once baseline data concerning academic performance and behavior had been collected, the actual training began. Berger experienced success using three 20-minute sessions of basketball shooting per week for 17 sessions followed by 35 additional sessions, which also included tower building. The number and timing of sessions for other children would vary with both performance during training sessions and performance in the classroom.

Step 6: Observe the Effects of the Program and Strengthen Generalization Beyond the Training Environment. These steps rely on the sound judgement of the instructor for their success. It is not possible to provide objective criteria against which to judge the success of the program. However, both classroom observations and behavior within the training situation should be observed. In order to promote generalization from the training environment to the classroom, Berger taught the hand signal and verbal prompt to the classroom teacher, who was to use them when the child left his seat, was not attending to work, or was playing with other students. Once the hand signal and verbal prompt are learned by the classroom teacher, they should be used at the teacher's discretion.

Other steps could be taken to promote generalization of learning beyond the school gym. One method would be to employ the training procedure with worksheets and other academic projects. This may require additional individual training. As with all programs in this chapter, it may be useful to refer to the programs in Chapter 10 if academic performance does not improve.

Step 7: Modify the Program If Necessary. As Berger notes in his article, the success of his program depends in large part upon the interaction between child and instructor. This interaction, which was neither described in detail nor monitored by Berger, consisted of encouragement, physical skill training, "challenges," and "conditioning" of the hand signal and verbal prompts. Unfortunately, the exact meaning of "conditioning" in this case is not clear. Presumably, what is meant is that the signals began to be associated with reward whenever the child followed the instructions. That is, reward is much more likely to follow a carefully planned and executed shot than an impulsive or careless one. Success at tower building was also likely to be governed by similar rules.

It seems that the most appropriate modifications of the procedure would involve the nature of the signal and the interaction between child and instructor. More specific instructions or prompts, such as "Stop and aim!" or "Stop! What will happen?" may work better at first. In addition, the success of the verbal prompt and hand signal in the classroom depends at least partially upon the child's level of academic functioning and maturity. If the child's skills are weak, more specific training may be beneficial, such as those described elsewhere in this book.

Step 8: Fade Out the Program. Fading out the individualized portion of the program can be accomplished by initially skipping an occasional session and then slowly scheduling less frequent meetings. As the end of the program is reached, monthly sessions on an irregular schedule can provide "booster" training. Hopefully, success experienced in academic performance and peer relationships will provide intrinsic reward for the child.

One of the advantages of Berger's program is that the activities upon which it is based can easily be used by the parents at home. It requires some caution to provide parents with the information necessary to execute the procedures in this chapter. I recommend that parents be introduced to simpler procedures, such as the home-based program for mastering basic facts described in Chapter 10. If parents can master and understand this rather simple, straightforward procedure, then they and their child might benefit from instruction in more sophisticated procedures. If the parents appear cooperative and concerned, extending some of the techniques discussed in this chapter to the home may be very helpful. Ideally, parents should observe training sessions early and late in the school's management program, then be instructed in techniques similar to the ones they observed.

If a decision to proceed with parental training is made, several important issues must be considered. Initially, the parents must be given a simple but accurate introduction to the basic principles of child management as explained in Part 1. Two general points are of particular importance: First, the parents must be made aware of the need for consistent application of behavior management techniques. Second, an awareness of the nature of their child's behavior problem *in strictly behavioral terms* should improve their understanding of general principles and lead to more consistent use of management techniques at home. Ideally, with experience the parents will see the value of behavior management and share responsibility with the school for dealing with their child's problem behavior.

CONCLUSION AND COMMENT

This chapter was concerned with the behavioral indicators of hyperactivity. All the techniques described here have empirically demonstrated validity; however, the techniques for decreasing impulsive and inattentive behavior are fairly recent additions to behavior management technology. While the research data base for these techniques supports their continued use, some cautions are in order. First, techniques which involve verbal cues and problem-solving strategies have been most successful with younger children, although Berger's (1981) case study involved an 8-year-old boy. Second, generalization from the training tasks to other school work has also been problematic. For this reason, the procedures recommended and described in this chapter include training on a wide variety of tasks and recommendations for a wide range of procedures, designed to promote generalization beyond the training situation. Finally, continuous observations of classroom performance and behavior are necessary to ensure that the procedures are valuable in the context in which they are applied.

chapter 8

MANAGEMENT OF CHILDHOOD DEPRESSION AND RELATED BEHAVIOR

Childhood depression is defined by a cluster of behaviors, which can include sadness, unhappiness, crying, loss of interest in pleasurable activities, low self-esteem, social isolation, sleep difficulties, elevated or depressed activity level, poor academic performance, fatigue, difficulty in concentrating, poor appetite, weight loss, and expression of suicidal intent. Within the school, poor academic performance, expression of suicidal thought or intent, social skill deficits, or indications of low self-esteem may bring such children to the attention of practitioners who elect to conduct further assessment and perhaps intervene. Chapter 6 covers the problem of identifying depressed children in greater detail, while this chapter focuses on intervention strategies.

The problems associated with childhood depression may be categorized in three separate areas: behavior, cognitions, and environment. The behavioral signs include sadness, social isolation, poor academic performance, difficulty in concentrating, failure to engage in reinforcing activities, and other behaviors discussed in Chapter 6. Cognitions include the thoughts and attitudes that interfere with optimum functioning and may even continue the depression. These beliefs may include feelings of helplessness, incompetency, or lack of control over significant life events (grades, for instance). The child whose statements indicate a belief that he or she is "dumb" or incompetent would be likely to make half-hearted, failing attempts at classroom work. The cognitive component of depression may be extremely important, because the interpretation of life events greatly influences how one behaves.

Environmental events, such as abuse (Kazdin, Moser, Colbus, & Bell, 1985), parental alcoholism, or divorce (Drake, 1981), are often associated with depression in children. A focus on remediating the behavioral or cognitive signs of depression may be unsuccessful if the child lives in an abusive or neglectful home. Thus, while this discussion will focus on managing the behavior and cognitions associated with depression, the school's professional staff must remain alert for indications of other problems requiring intervention. In some cases, a resolution of the child's problems in school may require far-reaching environmental changes at home. Family counseling or a referral to social service agencies may prove superior to behavior management programs conducted exclusively within the school.

OVERVIEW OF THE TREATMENT OF DEPRESSION AND ASSOCIATED BEHAVIOR

The behaviors associated with depression in children range from academic problems and hyperactivity to poor relationships with peers. Many of these problems are discussed elsewhere in this book. Peer relationships and social skills are discussed in Chapter 11, academic problems in Chapter 10, and hyperactivity in Chapter 7. Given the variety of problem behaviors associated with childhood depression, what characterizes it as a *unique* problem requiring an entire chapter of coverage?

The primary characteristic of depression in either children or adults is a persistently depressed mood. While occasional sadness is expected to occur in most children, a mood disturbance severe enough to interfere with normal activity for an extended period of time is unusual and is almost certain to arouse the attention and sympathy of adults. Once the attention of adults is focused on the child, a thorough assessment may reveal a significant number of the other behaviors that accompany severe depression, such as changes in sleep patterns, depressed appetite, diminished concentration, and social isolation. It is the presence of a *cluster* of behaviors associated with childhood depression that brings it a unique character. The cluster of behaviors implies more about the child than the presence of just a single behavior and has broader implications for intervention.

The implications for intervention are threefold. First, depression can be a life-threatening condition and the possibility of self-harm must be guarded against. Second, childhood depression is a problem that often requires a broad intervention plan involving the school, the child's parents, and sometimes other referral agencies. Third, it is possible to view depression as a medical problem, which is amenable to treatment with prescribed medication (see Weller & Weller, 1984). Consequently, children showing signs of depression are sometimes referred to a psychiatrist or pediatrician. Reynolds (1984) suggests that medication may be the optimum treatment for children who may be suicidal since higher risk would be involved in conducting a lengthy behavioral treatment program.

Even if medication is prescribed, a behavior management program may be needed to help the child return to a normal level of functioning in the school. A child whose behavior includes all or most of the indicators associated with depression may indeed be a serious case for even the most skilled behavior programmer. A team approach involving multiple resources—including psychiatric consultation, parental participation, behavior management programs, and environmental restructuring—may be the most effective and cost efficient strategy for managing childhood depression.

Explanations of depression from a social learning perspective emphasize the role of reinforcement in the life of the depressed individual (see Carson & Adams, 1981). From this perspective the depressed individual is seen as either not correctly interpreting rewards, not having skills to earn them, having the skills but not behaving so as to receive rewards, or lacking opportunity to earn reinforcement. *Consequently, the primary goal in the remediation of childhood depression and associated behavior is to increase the amount and frequency of reinforcement that the child receives from the school.*

A wide range of specific interventions may be employed to reach this goal. Behavior management programs to improve specific skills in either the academic or social area may increase the amount of reinforcement the child receives. It may also be fruitful to provide training with a cognitive base to improve the child's skills at interpreting rewards, predicting when they are most likely to be delivered, and delivering rewards to others.

If a child shows a significant number of the behavioral and physical signs associated with depression, it is likely that academic performance will be poor due to difficulty in concentrating, poor organization, and excessive off-task behavior. The child's self-esteem is also likely to be low, a feeling that may be exacerbated by continued academic failure.

If observations indicate the child's academic productivity is low, initial efforts may be directed at improving on-task behavior, using one of the programs described in Chapter 10, such as a home note. Alternately, the programs described in Chapter 7 to improve problem solving and self-control could be useful. If the child is producing inaccurate work, the problem is more complicated because other factors could be causing the poor performance such as a learning disability, mental retardation, or even boredom if the child is gifted. Thus, careful assessment is necessary before beginning a behavior management program directed at academic productivity.

In attempting to improve the academic performance of a depressed child, it is important that considerable success be experienced in the early stages of the management program. This could be accomplished by starting with easy tasks or by rewarding behavior that the child is clearly capable of emitting. The goal is to ensure that the child experiences success and the rewards that accompany it. By making a concurrent effort to see that the child appropriately labels successes, the child's self-esteem should improve.

Another problem likely to be experienced by a child showing the cluster of behaviors associated with depression is in social interactions with peers. Jacobsen, Lahey, and Strauss (1983) noted, in a study of 109 normal children, that measures of childhood depression were correlated with unpopularity and conduct problems. Thus, children who show signs of depression are likely to show social skill problems. Chapter 11 presents a detailed discussion of methods for improving the social skills of children.

The remainder of this chapter will focus upon the problems of social isolation and low self-esteem. Techniques for remediating these problems are discussed in the sections that follow. A pair of illustrative case studies will also be presented to clarify application of relevant strategies for remediating depression and related behavior in children. Finally, the chapter will conclude with an outline for a general approach to remediation of depression in children.

INTERVENTION STRATEGIES FOR SOCIALLY ISOLATED CHILDREN

One of the few generalizations to come out of the literature on socially isolated children is that there is little agreement among clinicians and researchers as to its nature and taxonomy (see recent reviews by Conger & Keane, 1981; Wanlass & Prinz, 1982). The ambiguity lies in the measurement and dynamics of social isolation in any particular child. Social isolation can be assessed by either observing the extent of the child's interactions with peers or using sociometric measures in which the child's peers are asked to supply information, such as with whom they like to work or who they consider their best friend. Unfortunately, the effects of interventions on these measures are frequently contradictory with few studies showing improvement in both measures.

Another important issue is whether isolation results from a performance deficit or a skill deficit. A performance deficit means the child is capable of social interactions but does not emit such behavior for some reason; that is, the child possesses the necessary skills but is not performing. A performance deficit should respond to a formal or informal behavior management program in which the child is rewarded for social interactions with peers.

On the other hand, a program to simply reward the occurrence of social interactions may be unsuccessful because the child lacks the needed skills. If this is the case, a detailed observation and analysis of the child's behavior is necessary because the dynamics that underlie the child's isolation will influence the intervention strategies. Consider the following possible explanations of the child's isolation: (a) The child fears social interaction and therefore withdraws from it. (b) The child is teased by peers for wearing dirty clothes, being uncoordinated, having a bad smell, or other reasons. (c) The child is aggressive, annoying, or obnoxious, and is avoided by others. (d) The child has specific social skill deficits such as not knowing how to play cooperatively, ask questions, or take a turn in a game.

(e) The child is a recent arrival in a class with established cliques. (f) The child interacts frequently with adults but not with peers. (g) The child could be categorized as depressed, retarded, language delayed, hyperactive, psychotic, autistic, physically ill, or as having other problems that result in social isolation.

The various hypotheses on this list, which is meant to be suggestive rather than exhaustive, can require different actions on the part of the professional. Basically, three courses of action are possible. First, social isolation may suggest other problems such as child abuse/neglect or retardation, which should be ruled out by further assessment. Second, social isolation may result from a skill deficit, which suggests that new social skills need to be learned by the child. Third, it is possible that social isolation/withdrawal reflects a performance deficit, which can be effectively managed by arranging that social interaction with peers is rewarded.

The behavior management program that follows is designed to remediate social isolation that results from a performance deficit. As noted above, a number of factors may underlie a performance deficit. One of these might be that the child is depressed. However, child abuse, a recent move to a new school, aggressive behavior, a loss in the family, or fear are alternative causes of social isolation. Although other assessment and intervention might be required, it is reasonable to focus a formal behavior management program directly on the problem of social isolation, as long as there are no major skill deficits. A discussion of issues in remediating social skill performance deficits concludes the present section. Chapter 11 also contains information of value in this context.

Step 1: Identify the Problem. Social isolation/withdrawal is relatively easy to identify. The basic issue is the quantity and quality of social contact with peers. Initial concerns are likely to center around issues such as the child spending too much time alone or being excluded from social interactions and play. However, as noted earlier, later observations and assessment may reveal that other, more serious or pervasive problems underlie the child's isolation and indicate that these problems should also become a focus of intervention.

Step 2: Refine the Definition of the Problem. Although the initial concern is social isolation, the goal is not to decrease social isolation but to increase normal social interactions. This goal, of course, requires more than simple observation of the target child.

As should be evident by now, assessment of the baseline rate of a problem behavior is not always a simple matter of counting occurrences of a discrete behavior. Social isolation/withdrawal is certainly no exception since a complete assessment requires at least two formal measures and consideration of at least two additional issues. Thus, I suggest that assessment of social isolation be conducted in two stages. In the first stage, several issues must be addressed simultaneously, so a running behavior record is the most reasonable assessment method. A running behavior record consists of a running narrative of behavioral events. The goal, vague though it may be, is to gain an understanding of the nature of the child's isolative behavior.

The initial observation should at least provide answers to these questions: Does the child's behavior cause other children to stay away? Is the child teased or harassed by others? If so, why? Does the child interact normally with anybody at any time, such as with adults in the classroom? How does the child behave outside the classroom? Does the child make unsuccessful attempts to approach other children? What seems to be the most important characteristic of the child that leads to isolation?

Once these questions and any others that arise have been answered, it should be possible to decide upon a course of action. One alternative is to revise the hypothesis that social isolation captures the nature of the problem. Perhaps, the child behaves hyperactively or lacks important social skills. An alternative hypothesis is that the child shows other signs of depression that deserve immediate attention or certain environmental factors should be the subject of intervention. In these instances, it may be more reasonable to reconceptualize the issue, provide training in social skills, or pursue other courses of action. On the other hand, if the child is at least moderately skilled socially and the isolative behavior can be reasonably assumed to be a performance deficit, the second stage of the assessment process can begin.

Step 3: Assessment of the Baseline Rate. Given the time limitations that plague most school personnel, a time-sampling procedure is the most reasonable approach to establishing a baseline for isolative behavior. The important variable in time sampling is to select an appropriate period in which to conduct observations. Since the concern is social isolation, a period of time with many opportunities for socializing would be required. For young children, a free- or play-time would be good; for older children, a discussion period, recess, or lunch might present good situations in which to observe. It may also be wise to consider using a multiple baseline approach. A multiple baseline design consists of recording observations from two or more different environments, while focusing treatment on only one environment. This allows assessment of the degree of generalization of the management program.

Once a setting and time for recording observations have been determined, a recording scheme must be devised. Such a scheme should be based upon mutually exclusive categories (i.e., a behavior fits only one category) and include any behaviors that were observed significantly often during the initial observations. The behaviors should be operationally defined, using the information in the narrative record. Such a scheme might include all or some of the following categories:

- PP: positive interaction with peers
- AP: aggressive interaction with peers
- PA: positive interaction with an adult
- AA: aggressive interaction with an adult
- IP: isolated play

The final step is to combine all of these elements and proceed with the actual baseline observations. This is accomplished by dividing the observation period into 4- or 5-second intervals and recording the behavior occurring during each interval. The most convenient method is to use a prepared mimeographed sheet divided into the appropriate number of squares, recording the code for the behavior category in which the child is engaged during each interval. During the baseline period, any inadequacies in the coding system should be corrected by eliminating uninformative categories and adding new ones as necessary. The percent of intervals during which the child was engaged in each of the categorized behaviors can be computed daily and recorded or plotted to summarize the observations. Chapter 3 contains a more detailed discussion of observation methods.

Although this intervention is intended to focus upon isolative behavior, it may also be informative to use a sociometric measure of the child's popularity and peer relationships. A variety of methods exist for conducting sociometric assessments. One method is to reproduce several dozen copies of a list of pupils in the class asking all students to circle the names of their peers in response to questions such as, "Who do you like to play with?" or "Who are your friends?" The sociometric status of the target child is measured by counting the number of times his or her name is circled in response to each question. The sociometric measure is administered before and after the behavior management program.

In order to develop age-, sex-, and grade-appropriate intervention goals, it is helpful to observe socially competent control children of the same age and sex as the isolative child. These observations can then be used as standards against which to judge the effectiveness of the intervention program for the socially isolated child.

Step 4: Identify the Reinforcer and State the Contingency. It is, or should be, intrinsically rewarding for children to interact socially with their peers. The aim of programs designed to improve social skill performance is to allow the naturally reinforcing consequences of peer interactions to come into play. A successful program is not restricted to merely programming reinforcers for interaction with peers. Other environmental manipulations can improve the chances of success. Hops (1983) recommends employing a combination of procedures in interventions with socially isolated children. The techniques most frequently mentioned in the research literature are contingency management, symbolic (filmed) modeling, coaching, structuring of activity and play material, and peer socialization. My recommendation is that the formal behavior management program focus upon rewarding increased duration and quality of social interactions, while the environment be structured in such a way as to enhance the probability that interactions will be rewarded and new skills learned.

The general goal would be to reward the isolated child for increasing initiations of social interactions and for developmentally appropriate duration and quality of the interactions. Some caution is necessary since it is possible to produce behavior that appears somewhat "artificial," if the frequency of initiating interactions is emphasized rather than the duration and quality of interaction (Conger & Keane, 1981). A variety of approaches to providing contingent reward for appropriate nonisolative behaviors are possible. It may, in fact, be necessary to try several approaches before one is found that produces positive effects. The most likely cause for isolative behavior resulting from a performance deficit is that adult attention is inadvertently being paid to the child when he or she is alone. If this is the case, it is necessary to reverse the contingency, paying attention to the child only when he or she interacts appropriately with peers. Naturally, operational definitions of preferred behaviors are those established during baseline observations of the isolated child and same sex peer. If adult attention does not have the desired effect, either a token system or a consumable reward could be tried.

The reward structure in this program can be varied according to the needs and maturity of the child. Its basic structure is that isolative behavior is ignored and socializing at appropriate times is rewarded with adult attention, points, or, if necessary, a consumable reward. The definition of appropriate socializing will also vary with the context, but concrete, operational definitions should be established prior to the start of the program using observations of socially competent control children. Recall, also, that the child's isolative behavior is presumed to be the result of a performance deficit, meaning that the child is demonstrably capable (i.e., at home) of emitting appropriate social behavior.

Step 5: Begin the Program. Once sufficient baseline data have been collected, the program can begin. If the program consists of rewarding appropriate socializing with adult attention, it is not necessary to inform the child that a change in contingencies is about to occur. However, it may be helpful to suggest to the child a couple of times that it might be more pleasant to join in group activities rather than staying by themselves. It may be even more helpful to suggest a specific activity and how they might be able to participate. Caution must be exercised that these interactions do not continue to reward the child's isolative behavior.

For older children who receive reinforcement via some type of token system, some explanation of the program may be necessary.

Step 6: Observe the Effects of the Program and Take Steps to Strengthen Generalization Beyond the Training Environment. Periodically, behavioral observation should be obtained using the same technique employed to collect the baseline data. Obviously, the expectation is that isolative behavior will decrease. Informal observations should indicate that the child is being reinforced by his or her peers and that social interactions are being maintained by these natural contingencies.

If the multiple baseline technique was used to gather baseline data, determining the generalized effects of the intervention program will be a simple matter of comparing more recent observations to the baseline data. Again, the expectation is that positive change will be found. The key to generalization of socializing to other environments lies in the natural contingencies that one hopes will affect the child. That is, other children should be rewarding the child's attempts at social interaction, so that adult attention or other rewards become unnecessary for maintaining the behavior.

Step 7: Modify the Program, If Necessary. If the program does not result in positive effects within a reasonable time period, perhaps 2-3 weeks, various modifications can be considered. The most basic modification would be to change the reinforcer. If a token system is being used, renegotiation of the reward menu could improve performance. Similarly, adult attention may not be particularly rewarding for some socially isolated children, who would consequently show no improvement in social interactions. For such children, a change in the reward may lead to improved behavior.

One aspect of this behavior management program that should be carefully monitored is the reactions of the child's peers to attempts at initiating social interactions. The assumption that the child's behavior is the result of a performance deficit may be in error. This would imply that some form of social skills training may be more appropriate. The following section describes one approach, while other issues in social skills training are discussed in Chapter 11.

Step 8: Fade Out the Program. The goal of any program to decrease a child's social isolation should be to intervene as necessary to modify the child's behavior to the extent that natural contingencies take over and the child "fits" into the social scheme of the classroom. As this occurs, the formal behavior management program can be faded out by decreasing the frequency of reward and raising the criteria for reinforcement.

Careful monitoring of the effects of fading out the program should be performed, especially in the early stages. As noted above, the expectation is that social interactions with peers will continue at a reasonable rate and that the child will gain some positive reinforcement from these interactions. If this does not occur and the target behavior returns to an unacceptably low level, other approaches to the problem may be worth consideration. These approaches might include reexamining the role of environmental factors in the child's behavior, revising the goals of the program, seeking the assistance of a clinical psychologist or psychiatrist, or making a referral to other professionals within the school system. The behavior management programs described in Chapter 11 may also be helpful.

Social Isolation as a Skill Deficit

A socially isolated child might not respond to the behavior management program just described, if he or she lacks the skills needed to participate in social interactions. In such cases, simply rewarding social interaction will not be successful because the quality of the child's interactions will not lead to rewarding responses from other children. Thus, the child will remain isolated. The solution is to teach the child some skills as well as reward social interaction.

Rather than attempt to teach every component of socializing with peers, it may be more efficient to teach general strategies for interacting effectively. Oden and Asher (1977) studied the effect of coaching children's social skills upon peer acceptance. The basic approach consisted of giving socially isolated children specific coaching in how it might be fun or enjoyable to play a game with another person, followed immediately by an opportunity to practice the same skills with a peer. Afterwards, the effectiveness of the strategies was reviewed with the child. Peer ratings of the desirability of the target child as a play partner showed improvements across time and at a follow-up assessment a year after the intervention.

Finch and Hops (1982) suggested an intervention program for socially isolated children involving four components. The first component consists of tutoring the child in social skills necessary for successful interaction with classmates. The second component consists of giving the child an opportunity to earn rewards during recess by practicing the skills taught in the tutoring sessions. In the third component, the child is given a peer partner and assigned to an academically related task, which provides additional practice in social interaction. Finally, the child is given practice in predicting his or her own behavior on the assumption that those children who are taught to do what they say will actually increase their rate of social interaction. Each of these four components will be examined in some detail. (See also Ladd and Mize, 1982, for a general discussion of social skills remediation from a social learning perspective.)

Tutoring a child in social skills basically means to use informal behavior management techniques to help a child develop social skills that will result in positive feedback from peers. These techniques would include shaping, prompting, rewarding with praise, modeling, and ignoring inappropriate behavior. The program described by Finch and Hops includes training in how to initiate an interaction with others, how to respond to an initiation, how to keep an interaction going, how to praise others, and how to be cooperative. Reams could be written detailing the definitions and behavioral components of each skill. On the other hand, pretreatment observations of both the target child and a socially skilled counterpart should be sufficient to clarify the problem area and indicate which skills the child needs to learn.

In the second component, the child is given an opportunity to practice skills learned in the tutoring session. Points are awarded for playing and interacting with others during recess. Special helpers are selected to help the child earn the rewards, which can be exchanged for activities or treats shared by the child's classmates. A more formal structure could be added to this portion of the intervention by gathering pre- and postintervention data regarding the child's level of social interaction on the playground.

Finch and Hops call the third component of the program joint task. In this component, partners are assigned to the target child, who then work together on an academic task requiring social interaction, taking turns, and cooperation. This provides the child with additional structured opportunities to practice the newly acquired skills.

The last component of the program consists of having the child tell the instructor what he or she is going to do in the upcoming period of recess or free play and then report back to the instructor after the period to discuss what occurred. A partner is assigned to the child to corroborate the reports and provide a definite opportunity to engage in social activities. A more structured intervention of this type is described in Chapter 11, in which the goal is to teach the child to think about behavior before acting. Giving the child practice in predicting his or her own behavior should increase the child's ability to formulate strategies of or dealing with various social situations.

In sum, the program described by Finch and Hops (1982) may be helpful in remediating social isolation when lack of social skill underlies the isolative behavior. The success of such a program would depend upon an assessment that accurately describes both the nature of the skills deficit and the skills shown by the child's socially successful peers. Then, skillful application of informal and formal behavior management techniques should help the unskilled child acquire at least some of the social behaviors of his or her socially successful peers.

A case study of an intervention technique similar to the general model described by Finch and Hops was described by Petersen and Moe (1984). The Petersen and Moe study was conducted with a 9-year-old girl, whose "bossy," aggressive behavior resulted in rejection by her peers. The preintervention assessment consisted of interviews with the child's parents and teachers, a sociometric assessment, and behavioral observations of the child's inappropriate social behavior.

The intervention consisted of several strategies designed to both decrease inappropriate behaviors and improve social skill. The major portion of the intervention was conducted in a one-on-one structured teaching situation. The emphasis in the early sessions was upon identifying the negative consequences of being bossy or aggressive and teaching positive social behaviors, such as how to approach other children, smiling, taking turns, playing with others, making requests, and letting others do what they want. The emphasis was upon teaching the child the consequences of her negative and positive behaviors so she "could learn the effects of her behaviors on other children's feelings and behavior."

After instruction was completed, various situations that had occurred recently were role played. Praise and smiles were used to reward correct responses. In addition, positive consequences of correct actions and negative consequences of incorrect actions were pointed out. Specific feedback was also given for correct and incorrect responses. When an incorrect, inappropriate response to one of the role play situations was emitted, the situation was repeated until all behaviors emitted in that situation were correct.

Another aspect of the role playing exercise was that role plays of negative social behavior were practiced with the child playing the part of another child and the instructor playing the role of a child showing the negative behaviors. Then the negative consequences of the instructor's behavior were discussed, emphasizing how the child felt about the actions of the adult. I believe it is important to emphasize the cognitive component of this intervention. The child was given specific training in anticipating the consequences of her own behavior and emitting appropriate social behavior.

The next phase of the training consisted of observing a "good" model of social behavior and discussing her behavior and what she did to which other children responded positively. The next two phases consisted of a supervised game with peers during recess. Initially, the child was given feedback in the same manner as in the role playing exercises. Then, direct supervision of the game was eliminated.

One very interesting aspect of the procedure was that the child was reminded to look at the faces of other children to see whether they liked what she was doing or saying. The authors noted that the discovery that information about another's feelings could be gained through nonverbal cues was a revelation for their subject. This is an intriguing clinical observation that deserves additional follow-up by these and other researchers.

Petersen and Moe reported strong effects of their procedure which persisted through follow-up observations conducted at the beginning of the next school year. However, interpretation of this demonstration should be done cautiously since only one subject was involved. Nevertheless, the techniques employed were sound and the results were highly favorable. It seems that both informal techniques just described may have some utility in remediating social skill deficits.

INTERVENTIONS FOR REMEDIATING BEHAVIOR ASSOCIATED WITH LOW SELF-ESTEEM

Depression, in both children and adults, is very much a cognitive phenomenon. That is, what the depressed individual thinks has an important role in maintaining the behavior associated with depression. For example, if a child believes he or she is "dumb," school work is not very likely to be viewed positively. Therefore, why bother with it? Furthermore, difficulty in concentration and distractibility due to concern about other events are likely to contribute to the child's difficulties by making school work even more difficult.

If a child believes that nobody likes him or her, it follows that the child is not very likely to initiate social interactions. Again, other behaviors associated with depression may help confirm the child's self-perception. A sad child is just not likely to be a very "fun" playmate, and rejection by peers may be the consequence of sadness, crying, negative statements, or other behaviors associated with depression. The combination of negative self-perception and inept social behavior is likely to confirm the child's negative self-perception and exacerbate the problems associated with depression.

Consequently, it seems reasonable that an alternate approach to remediation of depression is to modify the cognitions of the child. If a child could be taught to say "I can do my work" rather than "I am dumb," successful completion of classroom work seems more likely. Hollon (1984) has suggested that one approach to remediating depression in adults is to encourage them to test their cognitions against reality and learn to discriminate "beliefs" about themselves from the "facts." For instance, if a depressed adult claims he or she is incompetent and unemployable, a test of that hypothesis could be arranged by having the individual apply for several jobs or begin this task by assembling the materials needed for a resume. Depressed individuals often do not initiate behaviors because of a belief that they will fail, but when they actually try to do something, they experience at least some success. By having the person engage in "tests" of his or her beliefs, behaviors associated with depression can be improved. For children, it may also be useful to subject their negative self-statements to a behavior management program (cf., Frame, Matson, Sonis, Fialkov, & Kazdin, 1982).

Low Self-Esteem

Low self-esteem is a significant part of childhood depression and can often be one of the signs that initially brings attention to the child. Low self-esteem can be defined as a belief that one is inferior, worthless, or possesses inferior abilities. Such beliefs can interfere with the performance of normal activities. The existence of low self-esteem is shown by statements children make about themselves. If a child frequently makes negative statements, such as "I'm dumb," or "I can't do this," then self-esteem is assumed to be low.

Phillips (1984) studied the effect of teacher praise for positive self-referent statements upon a measure of self-esteem in third, fourth, and fifth graders. Phillips found that both the frequency of positive self-referent statements and scores on a self-esteem inventory increased as a result of the intervention. The subjects of the study were essentially normal and it would not be certain that the method would also be effective with children who display the cluster of behaviors indicative of childhood depression. It is possible that a depressed child may not emit enough positive self-referent statements to be affected by positive feedback. One method of avoiding these potential pitfalls would be to reinforce children for making positive statements about themselves while concurrently applying cognitive-behavioral techniques to the problem of changing the negative patterns of self-talk that depressed children are likely to show.

More specifically, the step-by-step program described here involves two basic components. The first component is a simple plan to reinforce the depressed child for positive self-statements. The second component involves an adaptation of the LAHDR technique first introduced in Chapter 7. The value of the LAHDR technique in this context is that it provides a structured problem-solving situation to confront the depressed child with evidence of his or her personal effectiveness. By structuring a situation in which success will be experienced, rewarding the child for that success, and teaching the child to appropriately label his or her successes, it should be possible to reduce the incidence of several important signs of depression and improve the child's overall level of functioning.

Step 1: Identify the Problem. Depression, whether in childhood or adulthood, is at least partially a *cognitive* phenomenon; that is, a child's thoughts can influence behavior in a way that reinforces depression. A depressed child may think negatively about himself or herself, predict failure, misattribute success to irrelevant variables, attribute failure to internal and stable personal characteristics (e.g., "I'm dumb"), mislabel successes as failures, cope with failure by withdrawal or helplessness, and/or show other distorted interpretations of reality. These cognitive distortions are likely to result in such a low level of academic productivity that behavior management programs to simply increase output and accuracy may not succeed. Instead, direct intervention to improve the child's problem-solving techniques may be necessary.

Identifying cognitive distortion requires astute observation of the child's behavior in the classroom. The child's verbal and emotional expression while confronted with academic tasks would provide an indicator of cognitive processes. Signs of frustration or sadness such as crying, being off task, throwing things, avoiding work, frowning, failing to enjoy "fun" activities, or excessively demanding help, may all be signs that the child's cognitions about academic accomplishment are interfering with optimum performance. What is said by children also indicates their cognitive perspective. Negative statements about themselves, their accomplishments, and the future would provide the most concrete indicators of cognitive distortions.

Step 2: Refine the Definition of the Problem. One way to obtain a more refined view of the child's cognitive style is to employ an objective measure of self-concept or depression. Numerous such measures are available, such as the Piers-Harris Children's Self-Concept Scale (Piers, 1984), the Behavior Evaluation Scale (McCarney, Leigh, & Cornbleet, 1983), the Personality Inventory for Children (Wirt et al., 1977), or the Children's Depression Inventory (Kovacs, 1980/1981; Finch, Saylor, & Edwards, 1985). Asarnow and Carlson (1985) describe an instrument called the Depression Self-Rating Scale (DSRS) which could be quickly administered and allows the administrator to classify children as depressed or not depressed, according to *DSM-III* criteria with an accuracy of about 75%. However, an interesting finding was the identification of subgroups of children who tended to deny depressive symptoms. Thus, multiple sources of data are needed when it is believed that a child may be depressed.

When it is suspected that a child may be so depressed that social adjustment or academic achievement is being inhibited, a school psychologist or similar professional should almost certainly become involved in the treatment program. Parental permission would also be needed prior to administering any objective measures such as the DSRS. The existence of unhappiness and depression also implicates a potential need for special services for handicapped children.

If it is determined that a child shows a significant number of the general signs associated with depression, including cognitive distortions, it is important to reconsider some explanations of the problem that may interfere with behavioral programming. Most important, the assessment should include information about the child's home. Abuse, family alcoholism, divorce, a major loss, or similar events could underlie the problems shown in school. An intellectual problem, such as a learning disability or retardation could also lead to frustration, a negative self-concept, and poor academic performance. Finally, diminished sensory capacity could also explain these problems. Thus, before undertaking intervention with a child who appears depressed, several alternative explanations of the child's behavior should be ruled out.

Frequently, family dynamics will play an important role in a child's depressed behavior. Ideally, any behavior management program in the school would be conducted concurrently with family therapy and parental training in behavior management techniques. Unfortunately, the reality is that parental cooperation is sometimes difficult to obtain and home problems may continue to interfere with school performance. Consequently, school practitioners will need to determine what degree of parental cooperation can realistically be obtained and work to manage the child's behavior as effectively as possible within these parameters.

Once family and environmental factors in the child's behavior are understood, and it is determined whether evidence of low self-concept is a component of a general syndrome of childhood depression, the definition of the identified behavior deficits can be sharpened. The primary indicator of low self-concept in this context is poor academic performance. Records in the child's cumulative file, and the teacher's record of classroom performance for the current school year would be the best and most relevant sources of data. If academic performance is, indeed, below expectations, more concrete questions could be posed. First, does the child fail to complete assignments or complete assignments but do so incorrectly? Second, what degree of academic success and positive feedback does the child experience? If any behavioral or academic incentive programs are used in the classroom (e.g., assertive discipline, points, stickers), how does the depressed child compare to other children in the classroom? Finally, how does the depressed child compare to other children in terms of general academic progress?

If the child's academic progress is below expectations, the next step is to determine whether low self-concept and cognitive distortions underlie the child's academic difficulties. The most concrete indicator would be statements such as "I can't do it," "I'm stupid," or "I won't be able to get any right." Excessive demands for individual help, signs of frustration, or off-task behavior might also be observed. Observations during any individually administered academic or intellectual assessment (e.g., a WISC-R) can be extremely informative. Verbalizations and test-related behavior can both reveal the child's attitude toward academic performance.

With a depressed child, any attempt to eliminate inappropriate verbalizations, off-task behavior, or other behavior that interferes with academic productivity via punishment, such as timeout, or a response cost contingency, may backfire. The negative feedback from such contingencies may confirm the child's self-defeating cognitions and actually lead to a further decline in performance. Instead, the focus must be upon the child's behavior deficits, academic performance, and positive self-talk. If academic performance, alone, is the problem—that is, negative self-concept appears not to be involved in the child's poor academic performance—refer to the programs described in Chapter 10.

However, if the child's behavior reveals that cognitions are likely to be interfering with performance, the problem is to increase the child's positive statements about himself or herself. More specifically, one would like to see the child emit a greater frequency of general positive statements about herself or himself, cope with failure in a positive way, cope with success by self-reinforcement, and make positive predictions about future performance.

Thus, to refine the definition of the problem for children who appear depressed and show signs of low self-concept, two areas require consideration. First, academic performance needs to be improved. Second, the statements that mediate the child's academic performance must be improved to include positive statements about himself or herself, and positive predictions about future success.

Step 3: Assess the Baseline Rate. The nature of childhood depression is that it affects several aspects of the child's life simultaneously. Therefore, attempts to remediate behaviors associated with the general syndrome are likely to be fairly complex. In the present context, the goal is remediation of low self-esteem and its accompanying indicators. Directly establishing baseline rates of "self-esteem" is not possible because the term is a mediating construct, which represents the internal state of the child and consequently cannot be directly measured. The pool of behaviors that can indicate low self-esteem is quite large and the behaviors discussed here are only a representative sample of relevant behaviors. Consequently, the baseline measures that follow may not be sufficient for capturing the needs of a particular child. If other behaviors seem more representative of the child's problem, then these behaviors should be assessed.

A large portion of individual cases will involve deficits in academic performance, which can be accurately monitored by taking two types of data. First, the child's overall level of academic performance can be monitored via the classroom records kept by all teachers. The only caution is that areas selected for detailed monitoring involve approximately similar conditions of performance across time. Different types of worksheets and testing conditions may confuse the issue of looking at performance. That is, different procedures of monitoring performance should not be compared directly. This would include methods such as timed versus untimed tests or multiple choice worksheets versus short answer worksheets. In each area of academic progress being monitored, a constant method of assessment, such as a weekly test administered in the same format, should be adapted as the criterion measure of progress.

A second measure of progress is on-task behavior. Under most circumstances, on-task behavior would be difficult to measure unless a time-sampling procedure is employed. Chapter 3 contains detailed descriptions of time-sampling procedures for monitoring on-task behavior. Recall that this procedure consists of careful observation of a child for a limited time period, which occurs at about the same time and involves the same activity at each observation. The observation period is divided into equal intervals and the child's behavior is classified as on- or off-task at the end of or during each interval according to the requirements of the classroom activity taking place. A second child, a group of children, or the entire class should also be observed to determine a realistic level of on-task behavior.

The cognitive component of low self-esteem can be observed using the same basic time-sampling technique. The difference would lie in the type of behavior observed and exactly how it was tallied. One method would be to record the number of positive self-referent statements and the number of negative self-referent statements made by the target child within a specified observation period. In order to encourage a moderately high rate of verbalizations, the observation period should be a semi-structured period, in which the class as a whole is free to move about within limits and socialize.

Since time may be of some importance, it may be necessary to limit observation periods to one or two of each type (on-task and self-referent statements) per week. Recall that it would be important to conduct each type of observation under relatively constant conditions.

The third format for obtaining baseline observations is in one-on-one problem-solving situations conducted by the child's teacher or another school practitioner. The precise structure of the problem-solving situations will depend upon the age, intelligence, and achievement level of the target child. Classroom worksheets or other materials would be appropriate. The structure of this type of observation period could vary widely, but the general goal is to obtain data about the child's cognitive approach to problem solving. The least structured format would be to simply ask the child to talk about how each problem is solved. The child's statements could then be categorized in the following manner:

- TO: task-oriented statement
- OT: off-task statement
- NS: negative self-referent statement

- PS: positive self-referent statement
- SR: self-reinforcing statement
- SP: self-punitive statement

A prepared sheet listing these categories could greatly facilitate data collection. Naturally, any method of recording data that captures the child's behavior could be used. This categorization is meant to be only suggestive, not all-inclusive.

With these baseline observations taken over 1 or 2 weeks, with two or three sessions per week of each type of data, it should be possible to determine in even more detail whether this program will remediate the child's depressed behavior. The major intent of the contingencies described in the following step is to employ the one-on-one situation to tutor the child in more appropriate verbalizations.

Step 4: Identify the Reinforcer and Contingencies. Once it has been determined that negative self-referent statements are occurring at a frequency above the norm for the classroom and that these statements appear related to poor academic performance, an approach is required to replace this behavior with a more positive outlook. The suggestion here is that two approaches be employed, either simultaneously or individually, depending upon the constraints of the situation and needs of the child. The first approach is to reinforce *positive* self-referent statements with praise and attention. The second approach is to directly teach the child appropriate verbalizations using the LAHDR approach to cognitive-behavioral modification discussed in the previous chapter.

Reinforcement of positive self-referent statements can be accomplished in a number of ways. The simplest rule is for the classroom teacher to praise the target child each time a positive self-referent statement is noted. A positive self-referent statement is defined as any statement that makes a positive reference to the self reflecting happiness, self-praise, a positive feeling, or self-confidence. For example, if the child says, "I did well on my worksheet today," the teacher could answer "I'm glad to hear you say that." Alternately, the teacher could paraphrase the child's statements or reinforce their contents by agreeing with them (i.e., "Yes, you did well today"). The child could also be reinforced for any behavior incompatible with signs of depression, such as making a joke, smiling, contributing to the classroom discussion, or positive social interactions. To avoid making the target child the center of attention, it is probably best to treat the positive self-referent statements of other children in the classroom in the same manner. Perhaps attention could be given to the target child about half the time. An additional advantage is that the target child would be able to observe others being rewarded for the desired behavior, which could enhance learning via modeling and vicarious reinforcement.

A more subtle way of reinforcing the child for self-referent statements would be to use a token reward system. One advantage of tokens is that they can be presented to a child with minimum disruption in the flow of instructional activity. They can also be employed in a broad program to improve both academic performance and other classroom behavior. A token program may be most useful in cases where the depressed child is not rewarded by adult attention. A token reward system would be flexible enough to give the child a wide choice of backup rewards, some of which could be provided by the child's parents.

During baseline observations, it may become evident that the child spends most of her or his time behaving in a way that reflects depression. Consequently, a program to reward nondepressed behavior, such as positive self-referent statements, may be unsuccessful because the child rarely emits nondepressed behavior. While it is possible that observation of other children receiving rewards for nondepressed behavior could cause the target child to increase it, the school practitioner may need to become actively involved in teaching the requisite skills.

One of many approaches that might meet with success is the LAHDR approach, discussed in Chapter 7. In this approach the acronym, LAHDR, represents each of five cues to which a child is taught to respond: LISTEN, ASK, HOW, DID, and REWARD. In Chapter 7, the goal was to teach the child to use these cues in order to derive correct answers to problems. The point of the procedure was to train the child to approach tasks in a reflective rather than impulsive manner. The value of this training procedure for a child showing signs of low self-esteem is as a method of teaching several important behaviors the child lacks. These behaviors include accurate assessment of past performance, self-rewarding of correct performance (coping with success), predicting future performance, and coping appropriately with failure. Additional advantages of this procedure are that the child can be taught to improve work habits in general, and a more general form of the same procedure can be employed in teaching social skills. The latter is important because social skills deficits are often associated with childhood depression.

Recall that the goal within each training session was to help the child derive correct answers to assignments, using the five cues presented in Table 7.1 of Chapter 7. The training begins by bringing the child into the area set aside for individual work and stating that the child and practitioner will be doing some worksheets in a special way today. Then, the instructor introduces the child to each step in the LAHDR sequence, explaining what it tells the child to do and perhaps giving an example or two of each step. Cues in the form of a chart or individual cards illustrating each step should be provided for the child to use during the initial training sessions. Eventually, the child can be given a small card with the steps written on it for reference during regular classroom activities. If a token reward program is used, the rules should also be explained to the child at the beginning of the first session and reviewed at the beginning of each subsequent session.

The actual training begins with the instructor modeling the sequence of steps for the child while solving the first problem. While doing so, the instructor should model statements reflecting self-confidence and pleasure such as "This is fun!" or

"I'm doing a good job!" The first time through the sequence should be without error, but on the second or third trial the instructor should make an error, discovering it during the fourth step (DID I do it right?). The error should be corrected by repeating the entire sequence. The final step, REWARD, should be given special emphasis in this case, with the instructor modeling good coping skills by saying something such as "I made a mistake, but that's okay because I found it and still got it right."

After a few problems have been modeled by the instructor, the child can be guided through the steps. In contrast to Chapter 7, where the emphasis was upon teaching a reflective approach to problem solving, the emphasis should be upon positive self-referent statements and coping appropriately with both success and failure. Because the typical depressed child is likely to show bland effect, it may be necessary to use techniques such as shaping and prompting to help the child produce appropriate responses. For example, a smile may initially be regarded as an acceptable self-reward in lieu of a verbal statement or the child could be told what to say when rewarding himself or herself.

It is also likely to be the case that much of the success of the program will depend upon the relationship between the instructor and the child. It may be necessary to spend the first few sessions just establishing rapport. This could be accomplished via talking, having the child draw pictures, or perhaps playing an informal game with the child. In order to maintain the child's interest and keep the basic activity as nonthreatening as possible, the context of teaching the child the LAHDR steps could be a game such as checkers or tic-tac-toe. At a later stage of training, academic activity could be substituted for the game.

Once rapport has been established and training has begun, the instructor may wish to record formal observations to document the child's progress across sessions. A simple tally of the number of positive self-referent statements made by the child during a given period of time, such as the last 10 or 15 minutes of each session, would be a relevant indicator of progress. Informal notes about each session should also be taken. These notes could be valuable for indicating any behaviors that should be observed in formal manner.

Step 5: Begin the Program. The program can be started once adequate baseline observations have been obtained, a place for conducting the individual sessions has been located, and the worksheet or game activities have been selected. Remember, an individually administered behavior management program that requires taking the child out of the regular classroom should not be conducted without parental permission. The baseline data should be examined to determine whether there is a need for an individually administered behavior management program. If the child is not benefitting from regular instruction because low self-concept and its observable components are interfering with performance, a need for remediation probably exists.

Step 6: Observe the Effects of the Program and Strengthen Generalization Beyond the Training Environment. Positive effects of the program should first be observed within the training environment, which is the reason for some objective measure of progress within the training environment. Once the child begins to master the problem-solving steps accompanied by a reasonable frequency of positive self-referent statements, it is reasonable to expect to see some generalization to the classroom. Generalization may be enhanced by introducing elements from the classroom into the training situation; for instance, teaching the child to use positive self-referent statements and the LAHDR steps while completing worksheets that have been assigned in the regular classroom.

A technique used by Kendall and Braswell (1985) was to give the child homework assignments. A relevant assignment in this context would be to have the child tell about one or two events or projects in which she or he did well, coped successfully with an error, or rewarded himself or herself. In the early stages of these assignments, it may be very helpful to obtain some information from the classroom teacher prior to meeting with the child. If the child has difficulty with the assignment or is reticent to discuss classroom events, the instructor can assist the child by prompting and shaping. For cognitively sophisticated children detailed self-monitoring of behavior, moods, and responses to various situations may be helpful.

It may also be helpful to integrate elements of the individual training program into the regular classroom. A card taped to the student's desk, a large poster, or a bulletin board display illustrating the steps in problem solving, placing special emphasis upon self-reinforcement, can serve as a cue to the target child and all those in the classroom. A few sessions of group instruction by the classroom teacher may also enhance the effectiveness of the training. Of course, regardless of whether a formal behavior management program is being conducted, the classroom teacher should be rewarding the child with praise, attention, or even tokens for positive self-referent statements. Backup reinforcers for the tokens could be provided in the individual sessions.

Step 7: Modify the Program, If Necessary. Suggestions for modifications of this program have been presented; the key is to be flexible. If a token reward system is being used, an infinite variety of backup reinforcers can be tried. If the child appears extremely resistant to change, referral to a medical doctor, family therapist, or social agency should be considered. A revision of the original hypotheses about the child may be necessary.

Additional assessment data may also reveal that other behavior management programs discussed in this book are more appropriate such as those discussed in Chapters 10 and 11. Chapter 7 and 11 contain other suggestions regarding the use of cognitive-behavioral techniques.

Step 8: Fade Out the Program. To fade out this type of program requires two conditions. First, data from the baseline observations should indicate that the effects of the training are generalizing to the regular classroom. Second, the frequency of individual sessions should be decreased slowly. A "diploma" or other reward can be used to mark the end of the formal training and occasional booster sessions can be scheduled on an irregular and increasingly less frequent basis. Rewards from both the classroom and from the child should be occupying the child's attention, so that the importance of the individual session decreases.

CASE STUDIES

In order to illustrate the principles and interventions just described, a pair of case studies are presented. The cases are intended to illustrate both the behaviors associated with childhood depression and the wide variety of interventions that may be necessary to help such children.

Jack

Jack, a 7-year-old first grader, was referred for an evaluation by his teacher, who noted that he did not do his school work unless closely supervised, did not attend to classroom instruction, and showed signs of frustration and emotional upset, including crying and excessive self-criticism. An interview with Jack's teacher indicated that her major concern was Jack's apparent inability to organize the components of a task and focus his attention upon completing it. Jack's mother also reported problems managing his behavior at home.

A behavior rating scale completed by the child's teacher revealed a multitude of problems in the classroom. The most serious problem was off-task behavior. Other areas of concern were self-blame, poor impulse control, poor academic achievement, excessive suffering, and resistance to adults. A classroom observation confirmed that Jack spent most of his unsupervised time engaged in irrelevant, off-task behaviors. In addition, Jack seemed to lack the ability to cope with frustration and failure. This was illustrated succinctly by his behavior during an intellectual assessment. When he was unable to complete one of the tasks in the examination, Jack pushed away the materials thereby losing points he could have gained for partially completing the task. Other behaviors that interfered with his test performance included attempting to engage the examiner in conversation, perseverating on his errors, and giving up on tasks before time limits expired.

Jack also indicated a lack of confidence in his ability to perform, criticized his performance, and appeared anxious. He inquired about his times on many timed tasks and wanted to read all the notations recorded by the examiner on the test protocol. It was concluded that the results of the assessment probably represented a minimal estimate of Jack's ability and that in the absence of interfering behaviors he could be expected to perform somewhat better. However, Jack scored just above average (61st percentile) on the intellectual assessment and no signs of learning problems were revealed. It seemed, then, that Jack was capable of satisfactory performance but that a variety of behaviors were interfering with classroom achievement.

Many of the behaviors shown by this child were suggestive of the cluster of behaviors associated with childhood depression. These behaviors included self-criticism, poor academic performance, crying, and an apparent inability to concentrate on academic tasks. Jack was living with his divorced mother and had recently moved to a new town. School records indicated that he had been referred for behavior problems by his previous school. Thus, it is possible that his behavior could have been related to the turmoil that surrounded the divorce of his mother and the consequent loss of his father, who was living and working in a distant city.

A variety of interventions were chosen to remediate Jack's behavior. Several of them were very practical. First, to help Jack organize his work and complete tasks, a schedule of daily activities was taped to his desk. This schedule listed both the task and the materials required for it. A second intervention was to obtain a new pair of sneakers for Jack. Observations indicated that his old pair was too big for him, which caused him to appear awkward and uncoordinated in physical education class and while walking around. Finally, Jack's desk was crowded with unnecessary supplies such as an excessive number of crayons and tablets. Some of these items were eliminated or replaced.

Two formal behavior management programs were initiated. First, Jack occasionally would emit tantrums. Jack's classroom teacher was instructed to present him with a brief timeout, or "cooling off" period, whenever such behavior occurred. Jack's mother was also given instruction in the use of timeout. (See Chapter 7 for a detailed guide to using timeout.) In addition, Jack's classroom behavior was monitored with a checklist of desirable behavior and good behavior was rewarded by his mother. Chapter 10 discusses the implementation of such programs.

Jack's teacher was also given detailed instruction in how to apply informal behavior management procedures to some of Jack's behavior problems. We worked mainly at defining Jack's undesirable behavior in concrete terms and developing some strategies for dealing with them. This included ignoring inappropriate behavior, looking for and prompting positive self evaluations so they could be praised, and discussion of alternative ways of handling situations that resulted in tantrums. Finally, it was also recommended that Jack's second-grade teacher be informed of his behavior problems and the methods of dealing with them that had been effective so that some degree of continuity and consistency would be maintained from year to year.

The general impact of these interventions was positive as indicated by the teacher's report. However, it would not be possible to identify which components of the intervention were most effective. It was my personal impression that the informal behavior management procedures and practical interventions had the greatest immediate impact.

Michael

Michael, an elementary school student, received individual resource room help from the school's learning disabilities teacher. He was referred for a periodic reevaluation, which is required by special services law. Conversation with the child's teacher revealed that Michael's behavior in the classroom was very unusual and caused the teacher a great deal of concern. These behaviors included frequent crying over minor events, crying and pouting over most attempts to correct errors in classroom work, and a belief that other students were "picking" on him, even when ongoing activities had nothing to do with him. Michael's behavior was tolerated in the relatively protected environment of the elementary classroom and the child's teacher was consistent in ignoring inappropriate behavior. However, there was concern over how Michael would behave in the relatively less structured environment of the junior high school to which he would be transferring the following school year.

An intellectual assessment revealed that Michael's ability fell in the average category. However, he showed strengths in the area of nonverbal intellectual skills and a relative weakness in the area of verbal skills. These findings are typical of children labeled *learning disabled.* Michael's mother was asked to complete the Personality Inventory for Children (Wirt et al., 1977) which provides a broad description of child personality. Items endorsed by the child's mother resulted in significant elevations of the Depression and Anxiety Scales. Elevations of these scales are typically associated with sadness, unhappiness, problems in self-concept, emotional lability, excessive worry, isolation, trouble falling asleep, nightmares, and an excessive need to avoid personal error. In short, the parental perspective on Michael's behavior was consistent with observations in the school.

Michael was also asked to complete several self-report instruments. The results indicated that Michael did not show any significant concern over his behavior pattern. However, observations during the intellectual assessment indicated an excessive concern with performance.

Interviews and phone contacts with the parents, and reports of school contacts with the parents indicated that Michael's behavior had a long history and that parental conflict and inconsistency may have been an important factor in his behavior. Interviews with the teacher and classroom observation indicated that the classroom teacher's responses to Michael's behavior were appropriate. He was ignoring inappropriate behavior and attempting to point out alternative interpretations of incidents to Michael once he calmed down after being upset. Given that it appeared Michael's parents would have experienced great difficulty cooperating with a school-based behavior management program, a home note system to reduce emotional outbursts was not attempted.

The major intervention procedure was to refer the child for a psychiatric evaluation, at the school district's expense. The outcome of this evaluation, which involved a more thorough assessment of family system characteristics than was possible in a school-based assessment, was that medication for the child and family therapy were recommended. The family chose not to communicate with the school regarding the efficacy of the family therapy or even regarding whether the recommendation was being followed over the long term. It is frequently the case that behavior problems observed in the school are related to events and family characteristics outside of the influence of those in the school. In such cases, the best that may be accomplished is to specify the nature of the problem and give those involved an opportunity to see that a problem exists and point out possible routes toward improvement.

A GENERAL MODEL
FOR REMEDIATING CHILDHOOD DEPRESSION

The basic model employed in this book is an eight-step formal behavior management program. Using this procedure, a behavior for which remediation is desired is identified, defined, and measured. Once measured, it is subjected to environmental contingencies which bring about the desired change. Continued measurement of the behavior provides feedback to indicate the success or failure of the intervention program and whether modifications are needed.

Childhood depression is defined by a cluster of behaviors any one of which may or may not be present in a particular instance. Thus, it is not possible to present a step-by-step procedure that will be effective in remediating the problem. This is not to say that such procedures are not useful in dealing with depression; they are. However, in dealing with such a complex entity as childhood depression, a more complex approach is needed. What follows is a description of one such approach.

Look at the Original Referral Question

The first step in dealing with virtually *any* problem that appears in the school is to evaluate the implications of the original referral question. That is, are there any hints that depression may be a part of the problem? Such hints could come in a variety of forms. First of all, the original referral problem may, itself, be obviously linked with depression in children. Such problems might include excessive crying, obvious signs of sadness, or hyperactivity. On the other hand, less obvious indications of depression may be present such as a suggestion that "low self-concept" is interfering with classroom performance. Finally, it may be that the person who initially notices the problem has a strong belief that there is more to the problem situation than first meets the eye.

In the early stages of problem identification and definition either a formal or informal behavior management program may be devised to remediate the problem initially identified. The options at this stage include all of the step-by-step procedures described elsewhere in this book, along with any modifications that might seem useful. If the problem resolves, no further action may be needed. On the other hand, the presence of behaviors that suggest depression or difficulty with the behavior management program may indicate that additional steps need to be taken.

Expand the Assessment Process

At this juncture, the assessment process can be expanded to specifically address the issue of whether or not the child's behavior is characteristic of depression. The general assessment procedure described in Chapter 3 can be followed, adding specific questions relevant to depression to the process. At this point, a school psychologist or other special education staff members are likely to be involved in the assessment. The questions that should be pursued include: does the child evidence any sleep or appetite disturbance? Has the child spoken about death or suicide? Does the child appear to be in any danger of hurting himself or herself? Does the child cry frequently, look sad, or show any other signs of persistent mood disturbance? What does the long-term history of the child's academic performance look like? Are there any signs of declining performance? Is the child's activity level consistent with that of peers? Does the child show interest in activities that would be regarded as rewarding to most of his or her peers?

If the answers to the above questions indicate that the child could be categorized as depressed (see also Chapter 6), it will be necessary to assemble the team that will deal with the child and consider various treatment options. One of the most important options to consider is whether to refer the child to additional agencies both within and outside the school district. If the assessment reveals that the child is severely depressed and is seriously in danger of harming himself or herself, emergency hospitalization should be considered. If this question cannot be answered by the school's assessment team, referral to a clinical psychologist or psychiatrist should be considered. The assessment may also reveal that the child's behavior is directly related to the family's structure in one way or another. This finding could prompt a referral to an agency specializing in family therapy or a legal agency, if abuse or neglect is the causal factor.

Set Priorities for Intervention Within the School

Regardless of whether agencies outside the school system have become involved with the child, the school continues to have some responsibility for providing help. It remains important that the actions of those involved with the child continue to be coordinated. Interventions attempted within the school can range from agreeing upon an informal behavior management program, to be conducted by the classroom teacher, to individual counseling, conducted on a daily or weekly basis. Recall that three major areas can be the subject of intervention: behavior, cognitive skills, and the environment.

Virtually any of the formal behavior management programs described in this book could be of use in the case of a child identified as depressed. However, the selection of a single behavior or even a small group of behaviors for intervention does not assure that resolution of the child's problem will follow a successful behavior management program. Consequently, it is crucial that the child's *overall* progress be monitored by the team. If this is not done, individuals within the school might become complacent while major portions of the child's life are still in turmoil. Keep in mind that adults in the child's school can be important sources of support and positive feedback when other adults in the child's life are not capable of performing such functions. Thus, key supports should not be removed without considering the overall impact.

FINAL WORD

Childhood depression is the only childhood behavior problem that can lead to self-inflicted fatal consequences. In addition, childhood depression is closely associated with environmental problems from which society has taken a great interest in protecting children. For these reasons, a large portion of the present chapter was devoted to general issues in remediating depression rather than step-by-step behavior management programs. Those of us who are experts in childhood problems—whether they be academic, psychiatric, psychological, physical, or behavioral—need to be aware of the impact that childhood depression can have upon any facet of a child's life and, when depression is suspected, take appropriate action to alleviate the child's distress.

chapter 9

BEHAVIOR MANAGEMENT STRATEGIES FOR ANXIETY AND FEAR

Children with strong and irrational fears can present a frightening spectacle to an observer: uncontrollable crying, fierce resistance to approaching the fear-evoking stimulus, vomiting, stomachaches, violent tantrums, arguments, running away, nightmares, and other associated behaviors. The attempts of a family or classroom teacher to cope with such behavior can place a strain on all those involved. Normal educational progress can be impossible when a child shows signs of a phobia because the child is not in school or is behaving in a way that makes learning impossible. The parents of such a child are also under a great strain since even the simplest activities, such as going to bed or leaving for school and work, may become catastrophic events for the entire family.

Some fears are not obviously debilitating. It would be an unusual circumstance where fear of the dark, fear of social interaction, or even test anxiety had an obvious negative effect upon school performance. In the case of test anxiety, it would require a perceptive teacher to attribute poor performance to anxiety rather than lack of motivation and study habits. Yet, fears that are not accompanied by obvious negative effects upon school performance may eventually come to the attention of professionals in the schools via referrals from the student, parents, or a classroom teacher. When such referrals appear, a detailed assessment may reveal that academic performance is, indeed, impeded by fear or anxiety. It may then be desirable to implement a behavior management program to improve performance and help the child cope better with the fear-evoking stimulus.

As noted in Chapter 6, theoretical approaches to remediation of anxiety and phobias are somewhat broader than the techniques of behavior management based upon the use of positive reinforcement. Thus, prior to describing step-by-step procedures for remediating anxiety and fear, a general overview of techniques for managing anxiety will be presented.

TECHNIQUES OF MANAGING ANXIETY

In general, techniques of managing anxiety and fear can be placed in one of two categories. In the first category are those techniques based upon positive reinforcement. The second category includes techniques that have their theoretical base in classical conditioning. Recall from Chapter 6 that positive reinforcement and classical conditioning differ in the rules for delivery of an appetitive stimulus. When positive reinforcement is used, the appetitive stimulus is delivered contingent upon a particular behavior. When classical conditioning is used, the stimulus is delivered contingent upon the appearance of another stimulus. The rationale for using classical conditioning in remediating fear or anxiety is that these responses are elicited by a particular *stimulus*. Thus, it is reasonable to eliminate fear by substituting a *different* response to the same stimulus. For instance, if a child with a debilitating fear of dogs could learn to relax in the presence of dogs, the fear would be eliminated.

Techniques based upon positive reinforcement have a similar logic. By rewarding appropriate coping behavior it is possible to substitute reasonable coping strategies for the fearful behavior. For example, if a child showing signs of school phobia is rewarded for completing school work, increasing the amount of time spent on academic work has the effect of leaving less time for behaviors associated with fear. Thus, by increasing the frequency of more desirable behavior, a phobia may be eliminated.

In essence, both positive reward and classical conditioning are likely to contribute to resolving a debilitating fear. When rewards are delivered for appropriate behavior in the presence of a fear-evoking stimulus, that stimulus has been paired with the reward. The effect, then, is to both reward appropriate behavior and reduce the fear-evoking properties of the stimulus.

Techniques of remediating fears based upon the classical conditioning model include relaxation techniques and flooding. Techniques more firmly rooted in positive reinforcement include reinforcement and shaping, teaching various coping strategies, modeling, and vicarious extinction. See Morris and Kratochwill (1985) for a recently published review of behavioral techniques for treating children's fears and phobias.

Relaxation Techniques

The basic goal of relaxation techniques for remediating anxiety or fear is very simple: the child is taught to relax in the presence of the fear-evoking stimulus. This can be accomplished in a number of different ways. One way is via counterconditioning. An example of this technique, discussed in Chapter 6, involved the child whose fear of rabbits was eliminated by having the child eat meals in the presence of a rabbit. Recall that the rabbit was moved closer and closer to the child while he ate over a period of 2 months. Eventually, the child was able to approach the rabbit without any signs of fear.

Presumably, what happens in counterconditioning is that the fear response to the object is replaced or counterconditioned by the response to food. The pediatrician who gives a lollypop to each child she or he examines is employing the same technique on a smaller scale.

Systematic desensitization is the name given to another method of remediating fears. In this method, the child is taught by a therapist to relax by tensing and relaxing various muscle groups until the child is able to attain a more or less completely relaxed state within a reasonable time period. Concurrent with relaxation training, the child and therapist construct a hierarchy of scenes, which will be imagined by the child while in a relaxed state. This hierarchy of scenes begins with one that is nonthreatening and proceeds to scenes that more and more closely resemble the feared stimulus. For instance, if the problem was fear of school, the least threatening scene might be driving by the empty school building on a Sunday afternoon. The most frightening scene on the hierarchy might consist of being in a crowded classroom with a number of activities taking place at the same time.

After relaxation training has been completed, the next step in systematic desensitization is to have the child relax with the instruction that any time anxiety or fear is experienced, he or she is to raise a finger. Then the child is instructed to imagine the least threatening scene in the hierarchy. If no fear is signaled, the trainer instructs the child to imagine the next scene in the hierarchy. The trainer then continues to proceed up the hierarchy until even the most threatening scene can be imagined without any reported fear. If fear is reported to one of the scenes, then the trainer backs up a couple of scenes and proceeds to more threatening scenes once again. The transition from one scene to a slightly more threatening one can also be eased by inserting additional scenes in the hierarchy.

What is hoped to be accomplished in systematic desensitization is that the child, once training is completed, will be able to confront the fear-evoking situation without experiencing debilitating anxiety. In practice, it may take additional training before the child is fully competent in dealing with the stimulus. The theory behind the technique is much the same as for counterconditioning. Presumably, the child learns to relax in the presence of an imaginary presentation of the feared stimulus, and the relaxation response comes to replace or at least inhibit the fear. Then, the same relaxation response is dominant when the child is confronted with the actual stimulus. Only fairly recently have relaxation training techniques been employed to remediate the fears and anxieties of children. The research literature indicates relaxation training techniques are generally effective in treating problems of schoolchildren. However, most writers lament the absence of controlled studies, long-term follow-up, and analyses that point to the effective component in these techniques. Hatzenbuehler and Schroeder (1978) defined desensitization as consisting of two different but related processes. One process consists of pairing either real or imaginary representations of feared stimuli, presented in a gradual manner, with a response incompatible with anxiety such as relaxation or a pleasant image. Because the subject is not required to emit any specific responses to the feared stimuli they call these techniques "passive association." The other process, "active participation," places the greatest emphasis upon rewarding active responses toward the feared stimuli. However, pairing is not eliminated but is more an implied component of the procedure.

These techniques can be regarded as being on a continuum of gradual exposure to the anxiety-eliciting stimuli with passive association representing the least amount of exposure and active participation representing the greatest amount of exposure. Hatzenbuehler and Schroeder suggest that the optimum strategy for treating phobias may relate to the degree of interfering anxiety present at the start of treatment. They hypothesize that desensitization procedures are necessary only when fear responses are so extreme that they interfere with voluntary, active responses toward the feared stimulus. If a child responds with severe panic to the feared stimulus, it would be impossible to reward approach responses or other appropriate behavior with any effectiveness. Passive association techniques could then be useful in reducing panic and allowing the child to begin approaching the stimulus so active participation can be rewarded.

Richter (1984) concluded that both behavioral and academic problems can be effectively treated with relaxation training, conducted over an extended period of time and accompanied by some form of supportive and/or educational training to help children learn how and when to use relaxation techniques in real life. He also suggested that treatment generalization is enhanced when role playing and practice of problem situations are included in the treatment. Forman and O'Malley (1984) also found that relevant skill training may be an important component in enhancing treatment success.

Another method of accomplishing desensitization is to gradually and directly expose the child to the fear-evoking stimulus. *In vivo* is the term often used to describe such techniques. By making the exposure gradual, coping or relaxation responses are made to dominate over debilitating anxiety. Methods of gradual exposure to a fear-evoking stimulus would most often involve reinforcement and praise from the trainer along with exposure to the stimulus.

While gradual exposure is one way of desensitizing a child to a fear-evoking stimulus, another way is to expose the child directly to the fear-evoking stimulus with no preparation whatsoever. *Implosion* and *flooding* are the names given to this technique. Implosion involves imaginary exposure to the feared stimulus in a greatly exaggerated form, while flooding involves actual exposure to the feared stimulus (Ross, 1981). One rationale behind these techniques is that the child's responses to the feared stimulus simply extinguish along with the avoidance behavior that keeps the child away from the feared object. What this means is that the exposure to the stimulus must continue until the fear has, indeed, extinguished noticeably. Otherwise, the exposure may become another learning trial that strengthens the fear rather than weakening it.

Techniques Involving Positive Reinforcement

An alternate way to view phobias is to assume that they result from the *absence* of skills needed to cope with the stimulus that evokes fear. From this perspective, it follows that intervention programs be directed at the deficit skills identified during the assessment of the problem behavior. Consider how this perspective can be applied to the problem of school phobia. One view of school phobia would hold that the core problem is the fear or anxiety elicited by school-related stimuli. The fear of school, then, causes the child to avoid school. Remember that behavior that causes something unpleasant, in this case, school, to be avoided is reinforced by the absence of the unpleasant stimulus. The solution to the problem of school phobia from this perspective is to eliminate the fear so that avoidance is no longer the dominant response.

Another view of school phobia would hold that the core problem is the infrequency of desired behaviors such as leaving the house, walking up to the school, entering the classroom, completing assigned work, and engaging in other activities associated with success in school. The solution is to identify the relevant behaviors and increase their frequency with a formal or informal behavior management program. It would be likely that shaping and successive approximations would be important elements in such a program, because the target behaviors may not be occurring at all. Furthermore, if behaviors were rewarded, each presentation of a reward in the presence of the feared stimulus could also be viewed as a counterconditioning trial. Thus, as noted earlier, the two general approaches to alleviating fear can be difficult to separate.

There are other methods of remediating fears based mostly upon the principles of reinforcement, such as that based upon vicarious learning processes. *Vicarious learning* refers to learning that takes place in the absence of observable behavior on the part of the learner, usually by simply watching someone else. Thus, by having a fearful child watch another child or adult interact positively with the fear-evoking stimulus, the fear can be reduced sufficiently that the child will then approach the stimulus. The model of fearless behavior can be presented live or on film, and the child may be a passive observer or an active participant in the process (Ross, 1981). However, the theoretical issue of just how to explain the results of such procedures remains unresolved. Learning by observation could be considered a way of either teaching new coping skills or as a means of reducing fear. Fortunately, regardless of the underlying process, the outcome is the same.

Several methods of remediating fears can be considered variations on the theme of social skills training. That is, many fears can be viewed as resulting from deficits in social skills. These skills might include being appropriately assertive, interacting with the opposite sex, feeling confident in one's ability, saying positive things about the feared situation, and learning other appropriate verbal mediators. For example, Kanfer, Karoly, and Newman (1975) looked at how three groups of children tolerated the dark. One group repeated statements that related to their competence in remaining in the dark. Another group repeated statements about the positive stimulus characteristics of the dark. A third group repeated neutral statements.

The study, with an essentially normal group of children, showed that repeating competence and stimulus oriented statements increased the children's tolerance of the dark. Although children who reacted extremely fearfully toward the dark were eliminated from this study, it demonstrated the potential usefulness of such training for the remediation of fears and phobias. Bandura (1977) formulated a related theory stating that the behavior of people in stressful situations is mediated by their self-perception of efficacy. Studies have indicated a strong relationship between reports of self-efficacy and behavior in fear-arousing situations.

The usefulness of techniques that employ cognitive mediators may lie in what they can add to other procedures. Biran and Wilson (1981) compared the effectiveness of guided exposure versus cognitive restructuring in the treatment of simple phobias. Guided exposure consisted of the therapist providing aid and support with an emphasis upon task performance issues while the subject attempted a graded series of fear-related tasks of increasing difficulty. The cognitive restructuring technique consisted of presenting the subjects with a theory that related their fear responses to the cognitive responses evoked by the stimuli. Then, the subjects were given instructions in replacing negative cognitions and irrational beliefs with more positive and productive self-statements. The guided exposure technique was clearly superior to the cognitive restructuring technique using a variety of criteria including physiological, self-report, and performance measures.

However, when cognitive techniques are added to a graded exposure technique, it has been found (Butler, Cullington, Munby, Amies, & Gelder, 1984) that the combination is more effective than exposure alone. Thus, cognitive techniques alone may not be the most effective way of remediating anxiety and fear; however, in adults at least, cognitions do appear to play some role in avoidance of fear-eliciting stimuli.

Confronting the Stimulus

Miller (1983) suggests that several essential elements are involved in the treatment of children's fears and anxieties. These elements are establishment of a relationship, stimulus clarification, desensitization to the stimulus, and confrontation of the stimulus. The first element, establishing a relationship, refers to the process of learning about the child, the child's family, and the characteristics of the problem as they see it. Empathetic listening and the development of trust and confidence in the interviewer probably make strong contributions to the establishment of the helping relationship.

The second element, stimulus clarification, consists of determining the stimulus conditions related to the debilitating fear. The importance of thorough assessment prior to beginning a behavior management program has already been discussed, but it is important to reemphasize the necessity of determining the stimulus conditions that control the problem behavior. It is these stimuli to which the child must eventually be desensitized, so it is important that they be well understood by those planning a behavior management program. The third element, desensitization to the anxiety-producing stimulus, consists of implementing an appropriate behavior management program. The techniques that might be involved in such a program have been discussed and step-by-step descriptions of prototype behavior management programs will be presented in the pages that follow.

The last element in the management of anxiety and fear is confrontation of the stimulus. Miller (1983) states that confronting the stimulus is an "absolutely necessary" part of treatment as well as an indicator of treatment success. The attitude of the parents toward forcing a confrontation of the stimulus is one of the key elements in the success of the management plan. Parents may, to some extent, reinforce the child's fear for a number of reasons, such as a history of similar fears or empathy for the discomfort of their child. Miller believes that at least one parent must resolve their ambivalent attitude toward a confrontation of the fear-evoking stimulus and decide that, regardless of the consequences, the child will go to school, sleep in his or her own bed, or otherwise face the stimulus.

This is particularly true for school phobia, which is the fear most often encountered by school personnel. Regardless of the severity of the child's fear, it will be necessary that the child be returned to school as soon as possible after treatment is initiated. Under some circumstances this may prove to be an extremely difficult task. Resistance can be so strong that one parent alone finds it impossible to bring the child to school without the risk of serious injury. However, regardless of the strength of resistance, the child must be forced to return to school at some point in the course of treatment. While it may be possible to ease the transition for some children, for others it may be necessary to go to the child's home and physically bring the child to school.

Because of the prevalence and serious consequences of school phobia, the first step-by-step procedure described in this chapter will focus on remediation techniques for this problem.

A REMEDIATION PLAN FOR SCHOOL PHOBIA

Sometimes a case of school phobia comes to the attention of school personnel in a dramatic way, such as a nearly frantic call from a classroom asking *someone* to please do something about a student who is crying uncontrollably and disrupting the entire class. On the other hand, school phobia can be identified when a secretary comments that a particular student has been missing a lot of school lately and a call to the parents reveals that they are experiencing great difficulty in getting the child to school. Often, the parents are relieved that someone from the school has taken an interest in their problem and are ready to receive some help. At other times, one or both parents may be deeply involved in the problem and keeping the child at home for reasons of their own.

As noted in Chapter 6, school phobia is characterized by avoidance of school. It may be accompanied by physical symptoms, such as complaints of headaches, vomiting, stomachaches, or nausea. The child is also likely to express unrealistic fears about attending school. School phobia usually occurs with the consent and knowledge of the parent(s), who are aware that the child is remaining out of school. On the other hand, older children may be absent from school without the consent of their parents, who may be unaware of where the child is during the day. Differentiating school refusal or truancy from school phobia is not difficult but will certainly influence the nature of the remediation program.

Blagg and Yule (1984) studied a series of consecutive referrals for school phobia. They compared the effectiveness of a behavioral treatment that emphasized returning the child to school as quickly as possible versus hospitalization versus home tutoring. Their findings were that the group treated behaviorally showed a superior outcome to the other two groups. The superiority of the behavioral treatment extended to attendance, separation anxiety, self-esteem, personality indices, and the amount of therapist time involved in the treatment. The formal behavior management program that will be outlined has much in common with the technique used by Blagg and Yule (1984), especially in its emphasis upon returning the child to school as quickly and efficiently as possible. It differs from Blagg and Yule's approach in that immediate confrontation with school attendance can be delayed, while the child is gradually accustomed to stimuli associated with school attendance and rewarded for mastering these situations.

A Step-by-Step-Procedure

Step 1: Identification of the Problem. School phobia is fairly easy to identify. However, once it is identified, the assessment should not come to a complete halt. Other problems could be present. For instance, academic difficulties and failure could be major contributors to the development of the school phobia. In such a case, getting the child to attend school would only be the first step in the process of improving school performance. Other problems, such as a poor self-concept, a learning disability, or poor social skills, may also be potential targets for remediation.

Three sources of information are likely to be involved in the initial identification of school phobia. First, and probably most important, are the school's attendance records. Frequent absences are one of the major characteristics associated with school phobia. A second source of valuable information is the child's classroom teacher, who may observe signs of anxiety in the classroom or provide other information relevant to identifying the nature of the problem. The third source of information is a phone conversation with at least one of the child's parents. This phone call is very important, because the parents eventually must see that the child attends school. Thus, any problems they experience are going to be crucial in identifying school phobia and formulating a remediation plan.

Step 2: Refine the Definition of the Problem. Refinement of the definition of school phobia is very simple. There are two basic issues to consider: First, the child must return to school as soon as possible and maintain an acceptable attendance record. Second, problems secondary to the school phobia, but that continue to interfere with school performance, should be considered as potential targets for remediation. This could include poor academic performance, test anxiety, disruptive behavior, or any other significant problem with school.

If excessive fear is the problem, then the primary goal of assessment is to specify as completely as possible the stimulus conditions associated with fear. However, because the child's parents are responsible for initiating the process of getting the child to school, it is equally important to determine the family systems factors related to the problem of school phobia.

To be more specific, several areas need to be assessed, if the behavior management program is going to address the key issues and have a reasonable chance of success. The first of these issues is the child's behavior. The main question is how does it come about that the child does not attend school? Does the child complain of physical symptoms that cause the parent to keep him or her home for health reasons? Does the child physically resist efforts to transport him or her to school? What kinds of resistant behavior are noted? Does the child resist with crying, tantrums, running away, or hiding?

If possible, some information about the child's behavior in the classroom should also be obtained. An observation of on-task behavior may be very helpful and could become part of the baseline observations. In addition, observations of any behaviors that interfere with accomplishing assigned work should be made informally and precise frequency data should be obtained. If the child has not been attending school, it may be necessary to depend upon second-hand reports until the child has actually returned to school.

Information about the stimulus conditions associated with fear of school is also a necessary component of the assessment. The following information should be obtained: When and where does the child first begin to show signs of fear? Does the child show signs of separation anxiety; that is, does separation from the parents for any reason result in signs of fear from the child? What specific behaviors do the parents and teachers observe that are associated with fear? Does anyone else in the family behave similarly to the target child? What steps in the process of getting to school do not elicit signs of fear? Does the child express worry about school in the evening or on weekends? The information is needed to construct a hierarchy of stimulus events beginning with events that elicit no fear and moving in gradual steps to the most threatening stimulus conditions.

Once the stimulus conditions surrounding the fear have been completely specified, it is then necessary to determine how others, particularly parents and teachers react to the child's behavior. A second question is whether any other members of the family are experiencing problems similar to those of the child. If so, it may be necessary to encourage the family to seek treatment for that individual because the target child may be learning to show fear as a result of modeling by a significant other. The goal is to determine what sources of reinforcement, if any, may be contributing to the maintenance of the problem behavior. Naturally, whether or not a formal behavior management program is undertaken, it will be necessary to arrange that undesired behavior is ignored and desired behavior is rewarded.

It is often possible to deal with some milder cases of school phobia via a phone conversation with the child's parents. In such cases one might expect the child to be attending school but showing signs of discomfort and fear prior to leaving home. The parents may need professional support to do some of the things that they realize may be necessary to force school attendance. In discussing this issue with parents, one should obtain a description of the child's behavior and parental reactions to it. Then one would gently encourage the parents to ignore inappropriate behavior and reward behavior that is appropriate and realistic. A classroom observation or second hand report from the child's teacher can be very reassuring to a parent, if it turns out that the child is showing no evidence of a problem in school.

When the child is avoiding school by reporting physical symptoms — such as stomach pain, headaches, or fever — one should first encourage the parents to have the child examined by a medical doctor. If the doctor discovers no physical basis for the child's complaints, a few simple rules can be instituted to assure appropriate attendance. First, the parent should be instructed to ignore the child's complaints of physical problems. If the child persists with a complaint, then a temperature should be taken and the child allowed to stay at home only if a fever is present. Alternately, the child could be sent to school every day, regardless of complaints, and the school nurse asked to decide whether the child is sick enough to justify remaining at home. Of course, this should be done only with the consent of the nurse. Finally, the days that the child actually remains at home should not be loaded with fun. Since the child is sick, remaining in bed to rest is the most appropriate activity.

Occasionally, it will be discovered that the child's school phobia is deeply entangled within the structure of the family. In such cases, it may be very difficult to implement a successful behavior management program, because the child's parents play such a key role in getting the child to school. In these cases, those in the school may find it necessary to conduct a behavior management program without the cooperation of the parents. In the meantime, referrals to appropriate social agencies may be appropriate. In extreme cases, it may be necessary to take legal action.

Step 3: Assessment of the Baseline Rate. The most important baseline measurement is the child's record of attendance and tardiness. However, this would not be the only behavior of interest. If the child is attending school, then some formal classroom observations will certainly be helpful. The percent of time on task is a very basic measure discussed in Chapter 7, which could be of some value. If the child disrupts the classroom with tantrums or crying, the frequency and/or duration of these behaviors should also be recorded. As noted previously, school attendance is crucial to the child, so it may not be possible to take baseline measurements before the behavior management program is begun. In such cases, baseline data can be obtained from school records and during the early stages of the program.

Another component of the baseline assessment is construction of a stimulus hierarchy, which consists of a list of stimulus situations surrounding school attendance ranging from least to most threatening. I recommend that a stimulus hierarchy be constructed around the following categories and adjusted as necessary to meet the needs of individual children: nonthreatening practice at school attendance (e.g., driving by the school on a weekend), school-related weekend and evening activities, getting up and getting ready for school, leaving the home to go to school, the trip to school, arriving at school and entering the building, entering and remaining in the classroom, and other events that may occur in school (e.g., a fire drill). A specific example of such a stimulus hierarchy follows.

1. The child is riding in a car that passes by the school on a Sunday afternoon.
2. The child is at home watching TV on Sunday evening.
3. It is time to go to bed on a school night and the child is instructed to get his or her school supplies ready for the next day.
4. The child is ready for bed on a school night.
5. The child is in bed trying to fall asleep on a school night.
6. It is time to awaken on a school morning.
7. It is time to get out of bed on a school morning.
8. The child is eating breakfast on a school morning.
9. The child is getting dressed on a school morning.
10. The child goes through the front door on the way to begin the walk to school.
11. The child passes by various points en route to school.
12. The child crosses the last street on the way to school.
13. The child enters the schoolyard.
14. The child enters the school building.
15. The child is walking down the hallway.
16. The child pauses at the entrance to his or her classroom.
17. The child enters an empty classroom.
18. The child is remaining alone in an empty classroom.

19. The child is the only child in the classroom with the teacher.
20. The child is in a crowded but quiet classroom.
21. The child is in a crowded, noisy classroom with a number of different activities taking place at once.

Step 4: Identification of the Reinforcer and Contingency. School phobia is a problem that must be handled flexibly enough to deal with the variety of its manifestations. As noted, milder cases that are in the early stages may be remediated via phone consultation with the parents. At the other extreme are cases that require legal intervention and referral to outside agencies. In this example, it is assumed that the child's phobia is moderate to severe and the parents are concerned and cooperative.

The general approach outlined in this formal behavior management program involves the use of positive reinforcement to reward the child for gradual mastery of the steps involved in attending school. Variations on this procedure and other techniques that may be used to supplement the program will be discussed as parts of Steps 6 and 7.

One thing that must be kept in mind about school phobia is that the goal of any remediation program is to get the child back in school. This sounds very simple and very concrete, but in practice it can also be very difficult. The process of getting the child to school may be accompanied by behaviors that are very difficult to tolerate. Furthermore, the method of dealing with these behaviors is simply to wait until they disappear via extinction. Again, this may be very difficult in practice. The case study and experimental literature on the treatment of school phobia contain a variety of procedures that have successfully returned children to school. These procedures range from programs involving shaping, gradual exposure, relaxation training, and a variety of behavioral contingencies to those that simply have one of the parents bring the child to school until voluntary attendance is no longer a problem. The strategy described begins with token reward for gradual approximations of school attendance followed by reward for attendance and completion of school work. In actual practice, the form of the program will depend greatly upon the judgement of the person implementing the program and the severity of the problem behavior.

The central feature of the program is a hierarchy of stimulus conditions associated with fear and refusal to attend school. While the specifics of the hierarchy will vary from situation to situation, its general form will remain the same from case to case. The key to implementing a particular program is to select a point of entry into the stimulus hierarchy that is satisfactory to those involved. The major risk to be considered in this decision is the negative consequences of entering the hierarchy at a point that elicits behavior beyond the tolerance of the person responsible for the program. For example, if the step in the hierarchy calls for one or both parents to escort the child to school, one must be sure that they are capable of coping with the child's responses. If the child's crying and tantrums cause the parents to take the child home instead of to school, the avoidance behavior of the child is rewarded and those responses actually gain in strength.

The specific reinforcer and contingency are tokens and social praise from significant adults provided for mastery of the steps in the stimulus hierarchy. In addition, the adult conducting the program can also be a model of appropriate behavior. As described in Chapter 4, a token reward program rewards a child for appropriate behavior with tokens, such as points, poker chips, or marbles that can be exchanged for some desirable reward. The value of the tokens as a reward comes from the fact that they can be used to "purchase" back-up rewards. Usually, a menu of several different back-up rewards is offered to the child so that the tokens maintain their usefulness as rewards over a long period of time. The number of tokens required to purchase a reward will vary with the value that the child places on a particular reward.

Alternately, it may be possible to reward the child effectively with praise or perhaps with a consumable reward, such as potato or banana chips. As noted previously, younger children will respond best to rewards that are concrete and immediate.

The exact nature of the formal behavior management program is this: First, a thorough assessment of the problem is conducted and the information is used to construct a stimulus hierarchy like the one shown earlier. Then, using praise, token rewards, consumable rewards, or a combination of the three, the child is rewarded for mastering the elements of the stimulus hierarchy. This phase should probably last about 5 to 10 days. The final goal of having the child enter school is accomplished by escorting the child on a Monday following the original identification of the problem. Numerous variations are possible. However, an important characteristic of the program's implementation is how well the various components of the system work together. The problem of school phobia is extremely difficult to remediate without the cooperation and trust of the child's parents.

Step 5: Begin the Program. Beginning an intervention procedure for school phobia is somewhat different than for other techniques. Parents, teachers, other school staff members, and the child must be appropriately prepared for the child's reentry into school. First and foremost, all interactions with the child should refer to the child's eventual return to school, communicating to him or her that the return is inevitable; that is, the question is not "if" but "when." Second, the child's teachers and other school staff who might be in contact with the child should welcome him or her and not overload the child with work or aversive activities. Likewise, a method for handling complaints of physical symptoms, such as ignoring them or taking the child's temperature, should be arranged ahead of time.

Preparation of the child's parents will require the greatest care. This would be particularly true if it was decided to bring the child directly to school. The child may show a great deal of resistance and it may require some planning to assure that an escort is available for quite a period of time. If it is necessary for personnel from the school to go to the child's home and bring him or her to school, two people should always be involved. This is necessary mainly to prevent injury to the child since resistance can be so strong that one individual would find it impossible to control the child. Most authors recommend that the child's return to school be scheduled for the Monday that follows the identification of the original problem.

The child's parents are almost certainly, and probably inadvertently, rewarding some or all of the problem behaviors associated with resistance to attending school. Great care must be taken to establish a cooperative relationship with the child's parents since they are the most important element in the long-term success of the program. Reframing the child's behavior in terms of a desire to remain in the secure environment of the home and reframing the parents' behavior in terms of their desire to provide a secure environment for the child may enable them to more easily adjust their behavior to the task of getting the child to attend school without absences (see Chapter 5). An advantage of employing the gradual exposure of the child to the stimulus elements of the hierarchy is that the parents can be retrained in methods of rewarding school attendance and associated behaviors, while ignoring those behaviors that interfere with attending school. With this approach, it is possible to ensure that the parents have some of the necessary skills when it is time to confront the stimulus and actually attend school regardless of the consequences.

A program to remediate school phobia begins as soon as the responsible person from the school system makes contact with the family of the child. The school staff should communicate confidence in the ability of the child to return to school and in the parents' ability to participate in the program and bring it to a successful conclusion. The emphasis in all conversations must be upon when, not if, the child returns to school. Once all pertinent data about the problem has been gathered and a stimulus hierarchy has been constructed, the actual program can begin. Consider a concrete example.

Assume that a child has been absent from school for a week and a phone call to the child's parents on a Monday reveals that the parents just can not manage to get the child to school. The first thing to do is contact the parents personally and obtain all the necessary assessment data. An interview with the child's teacher, inspection of attendance records, and search of the child's cumulative file should also be conducted. The data from these sources should be used to construct the hierarchy of stimulus conditions. On Tuesday, a plan should be formulated for returning the child to school on the following Monday, and this plan should be discussed with the parents. For example, the agreed upon program might involve gradual exposure to the stimulus elements in the hierarchy on Tuesday through Friday, having the parents escort the child to school on Monday through Wednesday, and having the child come to school with someone from the school on Thursday and Friday.

The following week can be devoted to continuing the child's successful pattern of attendance, consultation with the parents, and determining whether additional interventions might be necessary, such as implementing a home note program (see Chapter 10). A period of close supervision of the child's attendance should continue for approximately 6 weeks. Also, be prepared for a return to former patterns of behavior on Mondays and on the first day of school following a holiday or a genuine illness.

Step 6: Observe the Effects of the Program and Take Steps to Strengthen Generalization Beyond the Training Environment. The major effect of the program should be to get the child to attend school. However, this may be accompanied by behaviors such as tantrums and crying that require some special handling. If tantrums and crying are disruptive enough to interfere with the classroom routine, then isolation in a quiet area until the child calms down might be necessary. It may be valuable to keep a record of how long it takes the child to settle down. Remember that avoidance is the problem, so the child should not be allowed to escape the classroom without some penalty or contingency, such as having to complete the same work as other students in the class.

Since the goal of the management program is to return the child to the regular classroom as soon as possible, generalization to other environments is not an issue. However, the problem of promoting generalization can appear in two different forms. First, it is possible that returning the child to the classroom is not followed by optimum performance. That is, the child may engage in other behaviors, such as seeking attention and reassurance from the classroom teacher or being off-task for an unacceptable percent of the time. In these cases a supplementary behavior management program to deal with other behaviors may be helpful.

A second issue involving generalization of coping behaviors concerns the possibility that the child may be alright in the presence of certain conditions but show signs of fear and anxiety in the absence of these conditions. The most likely manifestation of such a problem comes from using one or both of the child's parents to escort the child to school. Occasionally, under these circumstances the child behaves appropriately as long as the parent is present in school but shows signs of distress as soon as the parent begins to leave. One solution to this problem is to slowly fade out the presence of the parent over one or several days. An example should clarify how this can be accomplished.

On the first day that the child is escorted to school the child's parent might begin the day remaining very close to the child. As the day goes on, the parent can be instructed to move away, perhaps sitting in the back of the classroom by midday. Then, as the afternoon progresses, the parent can move outside the classroom for short periods of time, which are gradually lengthened. On the following day, the parent could begin by sitting in the back of the classroom, leaving the room again for increasing lengths of time. The goal would be for the parent to drop the child off at school with no need to remain in the school. As time passes, the escort to school may also be faded in gradual steps, perhaps beginning with having the parent bring their child and a friend or neighbor of the child. With successive trips to school, the length of the escorted portion of the trip could be slowly decreased. This procedure, known as stimulus fading, can be useful in any circumstance where behavior is appropriate in the presence of a particular stimulus but inappropriate in its absence.

Step 7: Modify the Program, If Necessary. The description of this behavior management program has been complicated by the fact that so many variations in the nature of the referred problem are possible. Once it has been decided to bring the child to school on a certain date, the options for modifying the program become somewhat limited because the avoidance behaviors will be strengthened if the child is not kept in school. However, it is possible to add one or two components to the program that may enhance its effectiveness. One of these components is relaxation training involving muscle relaxation and imagery and a second is teaching the child to use competence oriented self-statements. These two techniques are described later in this chapter.

Step 8: Fade Out the Program. Fading out the program refers to the process of removing the artificial supports for school attendance, leaving the child able to go to school without problems. While the procedures just described are demonstrably effective in accomplishing this, it is possible for them to miss the main point, that school should be a positive experience for any child. Thus, once the child has been successfully returned to school, monitoring the child's classroom behavior should be continued with this in mind. Just because the child is once again in school does not mean that the problem has been completely solved. It is possible that additional intervention of either a behavioral or academic nature might be helpful. For instance, the child may show signs of an academic handicap or social skills deficits. Assessment and, if needed, intervention may be the best ways to prevent future avoidance of school.

SUPPLEMENTARY TECHNIQUES OF REMEDIATING ANXIETY

While the formal behavior management program just outlined can be useful under a variety of circumstances, other techniques may be employed by themselves or in conjunction with this program. Relaxation training, systematic desensitization, and positive self-statements are three such techniques. In the remaining pages of this chapter, the potential applications and procedures for using these three techniques are discussed.

Relaxation Training

Almost all professional people, especially those working in school systems, are subjected to job pressures that lead to feelings of stress and anxiety. At the same time, most of us have developed methods of coping with work pressures. Hobbies, listening to music, transcendental meditation, counting to 10, jogging and other sports activities, shopping, and taking a drive in the country are examples of mechanisms for coping with stress. One thing that these various activities have in common is that they induce a state of relaxation characterized by the absence of stress-inducing thoughts and muscular tension. Some adults and children have not learned to induce such a state and, for these people, training in techniques of relaxation can be helpful for reducing stress and tension.

Relaxation training can be a useful addition to the formal behavior management program that was outlined for school phobia. In addition, it could be used alone to remediate specific fears, such as test anxiety. As discussed earlier the research evidence for the value of these techniques is slim at this time, although numerous successful case studies exist. Thus, those who opt to use such techniques should carefully monitor their effectiveness and be prepared to change treatment strategies, if needed. Also, reviewers (e.g., Forman & O'Malley, 1984; Richter, 1984; Ross, 1981) seem to agree that relaxation training appears most effective when used in conjunction with other methods, such as skill training and practice in coping with the problem situation. For instance, in treating test anxiety, it would make the most sense to work on both learning to relax and improvement of study skills.

A variety of methods can be employed to induce relaxation in children, but few of these methods can be easily administered in school, where space is limited and quiet rooms with soft chairs are often nonexistent. Within the restrictions imposed by typical school settings, it is possible to teach a child some relaxation skills. Two elements are particularly important in such teaching. First, it is often necessary to give the child some instruction in the meaning of relaxation. Not all children understand what the word means nor do they necessarily have any experience with the behaviors involved in relaxation. Furthermore, they may not know when it would be appropriate to use such skills. Thus, it may be possible to provide a lot of help to children by giving them the vocabulary to label their own feelings (both of relaxation and anxiety), training in relaxation skills, and training in how to apply relaxation skills in problematic situations.

Procedures. Relaxation training consists of instruction in how to relax. This can be accomplished in a number of ways including having the child imagine a pleasant scene, listening to tape-recorded instructions, specific training in muscular relaxation, or engaging in any activity incompatible with anxiety. Systematic desensitization consists of having the child imagine various components of the fear-evoking situation while in a relaxed state. The assumption is that the fear evoked by the stimulus will at least partially be replaced by relaxation allowing the child to begin approaching the stimulus when actually confronted with it.

Another application of relaxation training is to provide the child with a means of coping with the feared stimulus. That is, if the child becomes anxious while in the classroom or taking tests, it may be helpful if they have learned a method of reducing anxiety that allows them to perform at their best. Thus, relaxation training can be applied as part of a program to desensitize the child to the feared stimulus or it can be taught with the goal of providing the child with a skill to help him or her cope with the fear-evoking stimulus.

Saigh and Antoun (1984) compared the effects of systematic desensitization, imagining a series of pleasant images counterposed with a hierarchy of anxiety-evoking scenes, and a control condition upon levels of anxiety and grade point averages of a group of test-anxious subjects. The findings were that systematic desensitization was as effective as the imaging technique, both of which were superior to the control condition. The technique they employed was to select a group of pleasant images based upon group ratings. Five images were selected to be counterposed with a ten-item hierarchy of anxiety-evoking images related to test anxiety. Then, a group of test-anxious high-school age students were instructed to alternately imagine one of the pleasant scenes and one of the scenes from the hierarchy of anxiety-evoking scenes until they reported being able to imagine the anxiety-evoking scene without reporting that they experienced any anxiety. This training was conducted in seven 50-minute treatment sessions. In addition, all of the subjects received three 50-minute sessions of training in study skills.

Since study skills training was given to all subjects, including those in the control group, the effects of the treatment conditions can be attributed to the use of imagery and desensitization. In fact, the control group showed a slight decline in grade point average and a slight increase in reported anxiety indicating that study skills training alone was not helpful.

In applying this technique with individual children, several considerations must be kept in mind. First, it is important to consider the chronological age and cognitive skills of the child. Elliott and Ozolins (1983) concluded from an examination of the relevant research that 7- or 8-year-old children are able to produce and manipulate images. Younger children, on the other hand, are also able to use imagery but these authors question whether they can manipulate images in the ways required by systematic desensitization. Given the ease with which the behavior of children from 4 to about 7 years old can be changed with reinforcement techniques, it would seem prudent to reserve imagery techniques for those 7 years and older.

A second consideration concerns the specific imagery that a particular child is encouraged to employ. Research shows that imagery seems most effective in controlling behavior when its content and elaboration are at least partially determined by the child. Elliott and Ozolins suggest that children may interpret therapeutic instructions in ways not intended by the therapist, so it would be important to monitor the meaning that any particular child assigns to an image he or she is encouraged to conjure up.

A method I found useful in helping children to form images is to have them draw a picture of themselves doing something that is relaxing, makes them feel good, or makes them feel happy. As the drawing is produced, the child can be questioned about its details and encouraged to elaborate upon various aspects of the drawing. Then, it is a relatively simple matter to ask the child to imagine the scene. The child's drawing can then be used to guide the trainer in helping the child form a concrete and relaxing image. As training progresses, every effort to monitor the child's behavior must be made to assure that relaxation is the net result.

Following the procedure employed by Saigh and Antoun (1984), a well-elaborated, relaxing image could then be imagined by the child in alternation with items from a hierarchy of anxiety-evoking scenes related to the child's specific problem. In Saigh and Antoun's procedure, the relaxing image was alternated with the test-anxiety related image until the subjects reported that the image related to test anxiety no longer evoked any anxiety. While this might be fairly easy to establish in high-school age subjects, younger children may need some additional training in order to learn to monitor their subjective feelings of anxiety. Alternately, behavioral indicators of discomfort could be monitored by the person conducting the training.

Another method of desensitization involves a technique called *emotive imagery* and was first used by Lazarus and Abramovitz (1962). In this procedure, the child imagines a credible story involving one of his or her heroes, such as Batman or Supergirl. The story is made up in such a way as to arouse emotions incompatible with anxiety and may involve pride, affection, humor, self-assertion, or other feelings. Then, as the story evolves, items from a hierarchy of anxiety-evoking situations are woven into the story. For instance, the child may be instructed to imagine himself or herself as an agent of their hero or heroine while performing the behaviors involved in attending school.

Elliott and Ozolins (1983) speculate that the success of this treatment would depend upon the detail and creativity woven into the scenes and their ability to shift the focus of the child's concerns away from the debilitating anxiety. They also observe that while the technique has been in existence some 20 years and that dozens of children have reportedly been successfully treated with it, no controlled outcome studies have demonstrated its usefulness in comparison to appropriate control conditions.

Positive Self-Statements. One way of coping with anxiety is to tell oneself not to be afraid. Kanfer et al. (1975) showed that children who were trained to say positive things about their ability to tolerate the dark or to say positive things about being in the dark were able to tolerate darkness longer and tolerated a lower intensity of light than children in a control condition, who recited passages unrelated to being in the dark. Unfortunately, children who showed intense fear of the dark, such as might be encountered in a clinical situation, were excluded from the study. In addition, the children remained in control of the intensity of light in the test room via a rheostat. This condition may have contributed to the results but may be impractical to implement in the field when dealing with a fearful child about to confront a feared stimulus.

Zatz and Chassin (1985) found that children high in test anxiety reported more negative self-evaluations and off-task thoughts than children low in test anxiety. However, test performance was most strongly related to the presence of negative cognitions. Zatz and Chassin suggested that improved test performance might be associated with the absence of negative thoughts rather than the presence of positive thoughts. Furthermore, perceptions of being threatened by evaluation in the classroom tend to debilitate the performance of high test-anxious children. In sum, disruption of negative self-evaluations, increasing positive self-evaluations, and lessening perceived evaluative threat in the test-taking environment appear to be the strategies that are most likely to result in improved test performance. On the other hand, statements directing themselves to remain on-task, and instructing themselves to calm down or other task-related strategies did not facilitate performance.

A similar technique was discussed in Chapter 8 as a method of remediating one of the signs of depression in children. Using the technique with anxious children would involve a similar approach. Prompting children to say positive things about their ability to cope with an anxiety-evoking stimulus could be particularly effective when applied in the context of the behavior management protocol described earlier in this chapter. As is typical, research exploring the parameters within which such a technique is likely to be successful is lacking. Consequently, if a trainer chooses to apply this technique, it would make the most sense to use a broad array of coping statements. Kanfer et al. found that statements related to competence were somewhat more effective than statements related to the stimulus properties of the dark. However, whether these results are practically significant remains to be demonstrated.

Zatz and Chassin (1983) studied the cognitions of test-anxious fifth- and sixth-grade children. They were presented with a list of 40 statements about themselves and asked to endorse those that were correct. The following statements (listed in order of most frequently to least frequently endorsed) were most often endorsed by the high anxious group: "Everyone usually does better than me." "I am nervous and worried." "My mind keeps wandering." "I can't seem to sit still." "The others probably think I'm dumb." "I must be making many mistakes." "I don't do well on tests like this." "I must have a bad memory." When a child is rewarded for making positive self-statements, the trainer may be successful if statements were employed that contradict the above negative cognitions.

In actual practice, training children to use self-statements to cope with anxiety-arousing situations might best be employed in the context of other treatment methods. Competence-oriented statements of a general nature, such as "I'm a brave boy/girl," "I'm smart enough to do well in school," "I like school; it is fun," and "I can take care of myself at school (on the playground, at home, etc.)," can be taught to the child until they can be said without error. Then, when the child says these statements in anxiety-producing situations, reward can be presented in the form of praise, attention, tokens, or something consumable. The reward would then have the dual effect of rewarding the child for behaving competently and counterconditioning anxiety.

ADDITIONAL SOURCES AND A PLEA FOR RESEARCH

Morris and Kratchowill (1983b) have written an excellent book on the behavioral treatment of children's fears and phobias. They provide a thorough review of the research support for techniques plus the necessary detail to apply them. This book is highly recommended to those who wish to know more about the treatment of children's fears. Cautela (1982) provides a description of general procedures useful in the application of techniques involving imagery along with a couple of case study examples. Ross (1981) and the book edited by Walker and Roberts (1983) also contain interesting and relevant chapters.

When severe anxiety impedes the performance or attendance of schoolchildren, the immediate response of those in the school system is to provide some help to the children and their parents. Often, treatments are successful and the technique may even be written up and published as a case study. The reality of the school environment is that research above the level of case studies is rarely conducted. The rarity of some problems, time constraints, and the ethical problems involved in delaying help in favor of placing the child on a waiting list or in a control group all work against the production of good research. However, good research is absolutely necessary if we are to develop techniques that work reliably and have a sound theoretical base.

Thus, to conclude this chapter, I would like to remind the reader to be alert for research opportunities that may be available within their working environment. The study by Blagg and Yule (1984) is a good example of what might be called opportunistic research. Rather than forming a group of subjects and assigning them to treatment and control conditions at the same time, they assigned successive referrals to their two conditions over a 3-year period. Such a design might lend itself particularly well to analyzing the effective components of various treatments. While some degree of planning and a lengthy time commitment are required, the result may be a better understanding of behavioral techniques and how they work.

chapter 10

MANAGEMENT OF ACADEMIC PRODUCTIVITY

Academic performance is a primary concern of professionals in the schools, and numerous techniques are available for managing it. These techniques can be categorized according to their complexity and the age of children for whom they are best suited. As a general rule it is best to begin with the simplest appropriate program that the child will be able to understand. Younger children should respond best to concrete programs that involve immediate, tangible rewards, while older children are likely to respond well to more complex programs that involve intangible rewards and long delays between the target behavior and reward.

Procedures for implementing six different behavior management programs will be discussed in this chapter. These programs are presented according to the age of the children for whom they are best suited, beginning with programs for the youngest children and ending with a sample behavioral contract appropriate for high school students.

A TOKEN REWARD PROGRAM FOR TEACHING BASIC SKILLS

As noted in Chapter 7, when a child enters school, he or she is expected to have several skills, which are important to the learning that will take place in kindergarten. Staats (1971) labeled these skills *basic behavioral repertoires*. A child who is lacking in basic skills, such as being able to attend to a stimulus on command, will almost certainly have difficulty in the early years of school. The child is also likely to present a behavior problem, because he or she is engaged in other activities while the remainder of the class is working on an assigned task or attending to lessons.

When a child lacks basic attending skills, it is possible to deal with the problem either directly or indirectly. Dealing with the problem directly would mean using the techniques described in Chapter 7 to improve attentional skills. An indirect way of dealing with the situation is to use a behavior management program to teach the same skills that are being taught in the classroom, but using more powerful rewards than are received by the typical child. Using more powerful rewards and, perhaps, one-on-one instruction can serve the dual purpose of helping the child to acquire specific skills, such as learning the alphabet, and acquire the more general attentional skills that will be needed for success throughout his or her academic career. Learning to attend appropriately comes about because earning rewards requires both responding correctly and being able to attend to the relevant stimuli. For instance, the child will not be rewarded for learning letters unless he or she learns to attend to the characteristics that differentiate them from each other.

In addition to the development of attentional skills, one might also expect other disruptive or nonproductive behavior to disappear as a result of a token program to teach academic skills. If the child is working hard to earn rewards for desired behavior, the opportunity for undesired behavior is significantly lowered. As noted in earlier chapters, an important consideration is the magnitude of the child's disruptive or nonproductive behavior. If the child is extremely disruptive or inattentive, then a program to teach academic skills may be unsuccessful until other behaviors are brought under control. On the other hand, even a very disruptive child may respond immediately to the offer of a concrete reward for academic performance.

A Step-by-Step Procedure for Mastering Basic Facts

The following step-by-step procedure for implementing a token reward system has broad generality and usefulness. The procedure is presented more as an illustration and example than as a specific method. Token programs can be effective in numerous situations and with children of any age. They are likely to be most effective with younger children when the token is concrete, preferably an object such as a marble, poker chip, or similar item. Older children are typically capable of understanding more abstract tokens, such as points recorded in a recordbook.

Step 1: Identify the Problem. For this example the problem will be defined as a deficit in kindergarten reading readiness skills. Basically, this translates into not knowing the alphabet. Learning one's ABCs is no easy task to accomplish in kindergarten. Not only is the child required to recognize 42 different symbols (the upper and lower case letters), but the sound of each letter must also be learned along with how to write it. Considering how similar some letters appear (e.g., "b" vs. "d" or "F" vs. "P"), it is easy to see how difficult the task can be from the viewpoint of the child. Furthermore, without thorough knowledge of the alphabet, the child is likely to have great difficulty learning to read.

There are numerous reasons that a child in kindergarten may not be learning basic skills at the same rate as his or her classmates. The child's intelligence may fall in a range that means she or he will learn at a slower rate than those of average intelligence. Another possibility is that the child entered kindergarten without basic attending skills due to environmental factors. It is also possible that the child shows the entire cluster of behaviors associated with hyperactivity. The child also may have a physical problem that interferes with learning such as an illness resulting in a large number of absences, ear infections which interfere with normal hearing, or an untreated visual problem. In any of these cases, it could be very beneficial to work individually with the child using the token program to be described, but concurrent remediation of other problems may also be necessary.

Step 2: Refine the Definition of the Problem. The primary goal of a token reward program is to increase appropriate responses. In this example, the desired responses are naming letters, giving their sounds, copying them, writing them from memory, and so forth. The most important point to remember in conducting these programs is that *responses* not stimuli are reinforced. That is, rewards should be forthcoming only when the child has responded appropriately, such as by correctly naming or writing a letter. Note how this contrasts with teaching in a group setting, where the teacher often points to a stimulus and describes its characteristics, then uses worksheets to confirm individual mastery. In an individual tutoring program, the tutor can directly monitor the child's behavior. This assures efficient learning because the tutor can monitor what has and has not been learned so that stimulus presentations can be repeated and other adjustments can be made as needed.

Step 3: Assess the Baseline Rate. Assessment of the baseline rate merely involves determining the child's level of knowledge in the skill area to be trained. If the target skills are recognizing, writing from dictation, and being able to give the sound of the letters of the alphabet, the child's percent of mastery of each skill can be determined with the same method employed in the regular classroom. As always, it is important that the conditions of the baseline assessment be carefully noted so that they can be easily repeated when the child's progress is assessed. Important variables might include whether the testing is done individually, the method of presenting the various stimuli, and how the questions are posed to the child.

If the child shows evidence of other behavior problems in the classroom, such as inattention or disruptive behavior, it may be useful to determine the baseline rate of these behaviors even though they are not directly targeted by the management program. Any of the time-sampling procedures described in Chapter 3 would be appropriate for this purpose. Information about the child's behavior in the regular classroom could be particularly helpful in the final stages of the behavior management program when the goal is to program events so that the child is capable of learning in a regular classroom without the benefit of individual tutoring.

Step 4: Identifying the Rewards and Contingency. The mechanics of a token reward program can be set up in a number of different ways. The tokens can be stickers, pennies, play money, marbles, or any other small objects. I have found that marbles work well as tokens. They can be easily given to a child and various sizes of containers can be filled with them in order to receive the backup reinforcer. Plastic baby bottles work well as the container since they come in different sizes and their tops (minus nipples) are designed so that the marbles are not likely to spill out. Alternative methods of implementing token programs include filling various sized sheets of paper or cardboard with stickers and letting the child "buy" rewards with play money or points. The younger the child, the more concrete the progression toward the reward must be. For this reason, filling a container with marbles may work best with children of age 5 or 6, while points are more suitable for older children.

Once a token system has been found, the next step is to identify the backup reward. This is an important element in the program, since this is what the child actually earns. Therefore, it must be powerful enough to gain the child's attention and motivate him or her sufficiently to remain on task. The variety of possible rewards is endless: candy, snacks, trips, special activities, small toys, and so forth. It is also possible to offer a group of rewards from which the child can choose. The child and the child's parents are the best sources of information about effective rewards.

In theory, the contingency is very simple. The child is rewarded with tokens for correct responses to stimuli presented by the tutor. Then, when the required number of tokens has been earned, they can be traded in for the backup reward. In practice, it is not so simple because of the wide variety of skill levels a child may have at the beginning of such a program. At the highest levels of skill, the tutor may find that the child is attentive, at least attempts a response to each question, and has already mastered at least some of the target skills. At the other extreme, the child may be disruptive, inattentive, and have none of the target skills. In the latter case, it may be necessary to employ the tokens to reward the behaviors that are prerequisite to effective instruction, such as remaining seated, looking at each stimulus, and giving appropriate responses to questions.

As noted earlier, it is crucial that the child's responses be rewarded. This is easy enough when the child responds correctly, but it is important to remember that a learning trial takes place for certain only when the child responds. When the child does not know the correct response or gives an incorrect response, it is important to have the child repeat the correct response while looking at the stimulus. One way to use the token system to accomplish this with ease is to give the child two tokens for a correct response without help and one token for a correct response with help.

Step 5: Begin the Program. In essence, the program begins with baseline measurements of the child's current knowledge. To place the token system in operation, the child is told a very simple rule such as, "If you fill this with marbles, then you can have ____ ." It is possible, of course, to elaborate by telling the child how marbles can be earned, but this can just as easily be communicated by action. If the child does not appear to understand immediately, continue with the program as planned anyway. Once the child has filled up the container a couple of times, he or she may get the idea.

Step 6: Observe the Effects of the Program and Strengthen Generalization Beyond the Training Environment. If the program is effective, two things should be observed. First, the child should be learning the material as expected according to the goals of the program. This can be tested by readministering the baseline measurements. The second observation should be that the child is, in general, learning more efficiently. That is, the child works well, stays on-task, and begins to show signs of being motivated to please the tutor. Behaviors that interfered with learning prior to the beginning of the program may be observed less often. Depending upon the child's level of accomplishment prior to the start of the program, varying amounts of time may be required before positive effects are observed.

Because a token reward program is usually implemented via one-on-one tutoring, generalization to the regular classroom will require some special effort. The first step is to wean the child from dependence upon the token reward program. This is accomplished by slowly increasing the amount of work required in order to earn a token. In addition, the tutor can offer challenges to the child such as five tokens if he or she answers a series of review questions without error. The eventual goal is to have the child working at a high rate for minimal material rewards. However, praise and positive attention from the adult tutor should continue at a high rate.

The problem of moving the child's learning activities from the tutoring environment to the classroom is not an easy one and may involve some trial and error to discover a program that works. A first step in this direction might be to offer a reward to the child for successful performance of a classroom activity, such as completing a worksheet or art project. As the child begins to experience success with simple classroom projects and the tutoring program brings the child's level of accomplishment into line with the regular class, the child can be given the responsibility of learning things in the regular classroom. With careful planning, the tutor can test the child's acquisition of classroom material eventually providing reinforcement only when classroom material is mastered without the help of the tutor. As the child reaches this level of competence, the classroom teacher can take over the functions of the tutor in a manner that begins to approximate the regular classroom. Other programs described in this chapter may then be useful to ease the transition.

Step 7: Modify the Program, If Necessary. If the program is not effective, there are several alternatives. First, if the child appears not to grasp the value of the tokens, their relationship to the reward can be made more direct by decreasing the number necessary for earning a reward. In the most extreme case, it may even be necessary to employ a consumable reward, such as a piece of candy or a banana chip, in the initial stages of the program. Then, the child can be taught to exchange a single token for a consumable reward. Once this concept has been mastered, it should be possible to increase the number of tokens required for a reward so that learning can proceed at a reasonable rate without having to wait for the child to eat after each stimulus presentation.

If the child's nonproductive behavior interferes with the learning process, it may be necessary to target the undesirable behavior directly, using any of the programs described elsewhere in this book. For instance, high magnitude disruptive behavior could be reduced by using timeout or, if absolutely necessary, a response cost contingency. It is very likely that a child unable to learn in the regular classroom will show more than one behavior problem. Thus, more than one contingency may be required to teach the child the skills necessary for academic survival in the regular classroom.

Step 8: Fade Out the Program. Fading out the program involves continuation of the techniques discussed under Step 6 such as fading dependence upon the rewards and promoting generalization to the regular classroom. An issue that could be important to fully integrating the child into the regular classroom is the child's relationships with peers. If the child was not functioning well in this environment or has been absent from it for long periods each school day, the child's social status among his or her peers may be low. Part of the program for integrating the child back into a regular classroom could be targeted at this issue. One possibility is that the child could earn treats or snacks for the entire classroom for reaching milestones in his or her learning. Any part of the program that makes the regular classroom a more rewarding place will pay great dividends as the program is faded out.

A PROGRAM FOR REWARDING MASTERY OF BASIC FACTS

Much of what is learned in school consists of memorized lists of individual facts, such as letters of the alphabet, state capitals, countries, arithmetic facts, continents, or vocabulary words. Failure to master certain basic facts can cause a child to fall further and further behind in areas where the facts are important. Since a teacher will rarely have the time to drill an individual student in the unlearned facts, it is often up to a tutor or the child's parents to provide the necessary practice. The formal behavior management program that follows is one way to help a child attain mastery of important basic facts. A major advantage of the program is that it is very simple to implement. For this reason, it could be used as an excellent starting point for training parents in the use of behavior management techniques.

Step-by-Step Procedures

Step 1: Identify the Problem. In order to keep the explanation simple, let us assume that the child needs to learn basic multiplication facts.

Step 2: Refine the Definition of the Problem. An efficient way to implement such a program is to purchase or construct a set of flashcards, each of which contains one of the basic facts to be learned. Then, the refined definition of the problem becomes responding to each flashcard with the correct answer. It may also be reasonable to specify a time limit such as 5 or 10 seconds initially, which can be decreased as the child's mastery improves.

Step 3: Assess the Baseline Rate. The baseline level of mastery is assessed by presenting each of the flashcards and noting whether the child can give the correct answer within the time limit. A convenience that results from the use of flashcards is that separate piles of cards can designate correct and incorrect answers. These can be easily counted after the entire deck has been presented to the child. The number of correct answers during the first pass through the set of flashcards is the baseline level of knowledge.

Step 4: Identify the Reinforcer and Contingency. The exact parameters of the reward could take on a number of values but the basic form of this program is that two behaviors are rewarded. First, the child receives a small reward for sitting down with the tutor and going through the flashcards. Second, the child receives a small reward for each increment in the total number of facts that are mastered. For example, the child might receive 10 cents for each review of the flashcards plus 25 cents for each individual fact mastered above the previous best performance. A decrease in the number of correct facts (and these are to be expected) is simply ignored, although the child still receives the scheduled reward for the review session.

Step 5: Begin the Program. To start the program, it is only necessary to inform the child that she or he will receive 10 cents (or some other reward) for reviewing flashcards with the tutor. For each fact that is missed, the child should be required to recite the missed fact (e.g., "6 times 8 equals 48"), so the tutor can be certain that a learning trial has taken place. After the baseline has been established, the child should be informed that each time the total number of learned facts increases above the previous high point, 25 cents (or some other reward) will be earned for each fact above the previous high. Note that the reward depends upon the *number* correct, not upon which particular facts are learned. It is important that all the facts be reviewed regularly because the additional practice will improve speed and confidence and will help the child perform better in the classroom. Also, each correct response should be followed by verbal praise from the tutor. The first time the child correctly recites all the facts, it would be appropriate to reward the accomplishment with a special treat.

Step 6: Observe the Effects of the Program and Take Steps to Strengthen Generalization Beyond the Training Environment. If the program does not appear to have a positive effect—that is, the child's mastery does not improve—one would probably look beyond the program itself for the reasons. It may, for instance, be possible that one of the academic problems discussed in Chapter 6 is interfering with progress. Alternately, the child's behavior during the training sessions may be interfering with learning. If progress is not made and no explanation can be found, it would be advisable that one of the tutoring sessions be observed by a person who has experience in behavior management.

Generalization of the facts to other situations should readily occur. That is, the child would be expected to easily make use of the facts in other contexts such as solving arithmetic problems. Again, if difficulty is evident, other explanations should be sought.

Step 7: Modify the Program, If Necessary. The simplicity of this program precludes flexibility in its modification. However, as with any behavior management program, it is possible to change the rewards as necessary to ensure optimal performance. Also, the program could be expanded to include more than one set of basic facts, though I suggest that each set be treated independently.

Step 8: Fade Out the Program. The program can be faded out in a number of ways once the child has attained one perfect pass through the flashcards. First, the contingency could be modified so that the reward for merely sitting down and participating in a review session is only received for a perfect pass through all the flashcards. This would assure that the facts were well learned and unlikely to be forgotten. Then the number of perfect passes through the flashcards required for receiving a reward could be slowly increased until the program is finally halted because the facts are thoroughly mastered. At the point where the child attains five or ten perfect sessions in a row, a special treat and a "graduation" certificate could be awarded.

STRATEGIES FOR IMPROVEMENT OF READING SKILL

Reading skills are essential to successful academic performance and progress. If remedial training is not provided to the reader who has fallen behind, that child's difficulties in reading will be compounded and failure in other academic areas is likely as well. Learning to read fluently is such an important skill that remediation techniques would seem to merit separate discussion.

Ryback and Staats (1970) reported on a home-based program for remediation of reading deficits. In this program, the child's parents were trained to reward correct reading responses with tokens that could be exchanged for cash. The training procedure consisted of five steps. In the individual word learning phase, the child was presented with a series of new words to be learned, each printed on a card. Each word remained in the series until it was pronounced correctly without prompting. When all the words in the series had been read without prompting, the child went to the next step, reading the paragraph from which the words had been taken. When the paragraph had been read with no errors, the procedure was repeated until all the paragraphs of the story had been completed. Then the child read the story silently and answered questions about it. If a question was missed, the child reread the relevant paragraph and responded to the question again. A vocabulary review was presented at the end of each 20 lessons. Over a 6-month period, the children who were trained with this method showed substantial gains in reading performance.

Blanchard (1981) described a similar strategy for training poor readers, which consists of concentrated flashcard drill on new words to be encountered in a story or passage. When all the words in a passage could be pronounced within 2 seconds of being presented, the pupil read the story and answered multiple choice questions about it. Any new words not already known by the pupil were given special attention until their meaning was understood. Blanchard reported two successful tests of this method. In each test, sixth-grade disabled readers who were trained in the procedure answered correctly significantly more comprehension questions than control groups of disabled readers. It was also found that the procedure was most effective for students whose reading performance was two or more grade levels below the level of the target reading material. It was interesting that most of the students in Blanchard's study reported that reading the materials was easier when the words in it were known beforehand.

In general, techniques that focus upon whole-word reading and vocabulary preparation prior to exposure to reading passages, seem to result in significantly improved reading and comprehension in disabled readers. Such findings suggest that a behavior management program for children with reading deficits that makes use of the two step-by-step programs described earlier could prove beneficial in many cases. Of course, before beginning any behavior management program to improve reading performance, a thorough assessment should be conducted to rule out any academic handicaps.

USE OF A HOME NOTE SYSTEM TO MONITOR SCHOOL PERFORMANCE

It is not always convenient for personnel in the schools to provide rewards or monitor the performance of children. The use of home-based behavior management programs can be one method of decreasing the burden upon school personnel (see the review by Atkeson & Forehand, 1979). The simplest method of conducting such a program is for the teacher to communicate with parents via a home note. School performance can then be rewarded by the parents, thus relieving the teacher of most of the tasks involved in conducting a behavior management program (e.g., Schumaker, Hovell, & Sherman, 1977). A potential problem with home-based programs is that parents may not be skilled in the application of behavior management techniques. Thus, it is important that the behavior of the parents be monitored to ensure that they follow the rules of the program (cf. Blechman, Taylor, & Schrader, 1981). If problems develop as a consequence of parental inconsistency or lack of understanding, it may be necessary to suggest additional training in parenting skills or family counseling.

Stepwise Procedures for a Home Note Program

The mechanics of the home note system are very simple. A printed report card (for examples, see Figures 10.1 and 10.2) is filled out once a day or week by the child's teacher. The child receives points according to the quality of academic and behavioral performance which are tabulated weekly by the child's parents. The child can use the points to "purchase" from a menu of rewards. The details are following.

Figure 10.1.   Sample A: Daily/Weekly Report Card

Student's Name _____ Date _____

The student's academic performance was (initial appropriate space)

        _____ Excellent (25 points)

        _____ Good (20 points)

        _____ Acceptable (10 points)

        _____ Unacceptable (0 points)

The student's general behavior was

        _____ Excellent (25 points)

        _____ Good (20 points)

        _____ Acceptable (10 points)

(continued)

_____ Unacceptable (0 points)

Teacher's comments _____

_____

_____

_____

_____

Figure 10.2.   Sample B: Daily/Weekly Report Card

Student's Name _____ Date _____

The student's academic performance was (initial appropriate space)

_____ Outstanding (30 points)

_____ Good (25 points)

_____ Above Average (20 points)

_____ Improvement Shown (15 points)

_____ Improvement Needed (10 points)

_____ Acceptable (5 points)

_____ Not Acceptable (0 points)

Teacher's comments _____

_____

_____

The student's general behavior was

_____ Outstanding (30 points)

_____ Good (25 points)

_____ Above Average (20 points)

_____ Improvement Shown (15 points)

_____ Improvement Needed (10 points)

_____ Acceptable (5 points)

_____ Not Acceptable (0 points)

Teacher's comments _____

_____

_____

Step 1: Identify the Problem. The problems are characterized as poorer than expected academic performance and noncompliance with school and classroom rules. With respect to academic performance, this type of program is most likely to be successful when the student shows inconsistent performance, doing well in "interesting" subject areas and poorly in "boring" subjects. This type of performance would indicate that the student is capable of doing well but is poorly motivated. Similarly, if the child has "good days" and "bad days" with respect to complying with school and classroom rules, one might also expect success with this type of program. Note that the underlying principle is that the child show some evidence of having the requisite skills for success. If the child lacks the skills necessary for academic and behavioral success, then a home note program is not likely to succeed. In such a case, it may be necessary to provide direct training in the deficit skills.

Step 2: Refine the Definition of the Problem. In the real world of the classroom, it is not always possible to take the time and energy to precisely define undesirable behavior and deficit academic skills. Instead, from the point of view of the teacher, the problem is that the student disobeys classroom rules and fails to complete assigned work. The home note program described here is designed for this situation, where the simplest possible behavior management program is desired. Of course, a potential problem is that the program will fail because the problem has not been concretely defined. Under many circumstances, however, this program will work very well. In those cases where the program does not work well, it is always possible to switch to a program that more directly attacks the problem behavior.

Step 3: Assess the Baseline Rate. It would be most desirable if the precise number of rule violations could be tabulated along with an accurate record of the child's academic accomplishment. Again, such precision may not always be possible. If this is the case, a useful baseline measurement can be obtained if the teacher fills out the home note for a week without providing any feedback to the child. In this way, a reasonably objective record of the teacher's impressions can be obtained, and it will be possible to determine whether the program results in any positive change in the child's behavior from the perspective of the classroom teacher. Also, this record will provide an excellent basis for determining the number of points that will be required for the rewards provided by the child's parents.

Step 4: Identify the Reinforcer and Contingency. The rules for implementing a home note program are very simple. At the end of each school day, the child's teacher fills out a note to the parents, such as shown in Figure 10.1 and 10.2. The child then takes the note home, and the parents tabulate the points earned for that day. The points earned are then exchanged for rewards as negotiated between the child and parents. Given that the child can earn up to 50 or 60 points per day, a reasonable starting point might be about 300-400 points for a reward of moderate size, such as a movie or small toy. Alternately, a reward menu as described in Chapter 4 might also be set up to provide varying rewards at a range of point values. In order to get the program off to a good start, it may be helpful to provide one or two small rewards that can be earned with relatively few points.

An important element of the home note program is the role of the child's teacher in providing social reinforcement for good performance and feedback regarding unacceptable behavior. Because the target behaviors are not precisely specified and, in addition, may vary considerably from day to day, it is important that the child's teacher provide feedback to the child regarding the reasons behind the points, if any, awarded for each day's performance. For example, if the child failed to complete an in-class assignment or failed a spelling test and therefore received a low rating for the day's performance, this should be carefully explained to the child at the end of the day. Likewise, if the child's behavior was rated as "unacceptable" for a day, the exact reasons for the rating should be explained. Hopefully, the knowledge of what behaviors resulted in poor ratings will motivate the child to improve her or his behavior the following days.

Step 5: Begin the Program. Several elements need to come together in order for a home note program to begin. First, an appropriate format for the note must be determined. Figure 10.1 shows the simplest format, while Figure 10.2 is more detailed. The latter is most appropriate when the child's behavior is generally poor and much improvement is needed. The additional rating levels allow the child to earn some points for less than optimal performance. Note that both formats request a rating of behavior *and* academic performance. Since each has an effect upon the other, it is recommended that both ratings be used even when improvement in only one area is needed. This will allow the child to receive at least some positive feedback. Finally, I suggest that the note be typed on the school's letterhead, which gives it a more "official" look.

Once a format for the home note has been determined, the next step is to meet with the child's parents to discuss the classroom situation and options for handling it. Hopefully, those involved, particularly the classroom teacher, will have met with or at least talked via phone to the parents on previous occasions. During the conference, the home note system should be offered as one method of dealing with the child's behavior and the willingness of the parents to cooperate should be assessed. If the parents are willing, then a date to begin the program should be set, allowing for a one-week baseline period. Alternately, the baseline data could be gathered prior to the conference to show the parents and provide an opportunity to set "prices" on the reward menu during the conference.

A few days prior to the start of the program, both the parents and the teacher should explain the program to the child. On the first day of the program nothing more need be said, although a blank copy of the home note might be shown to the child. At the end of the school day, the teacher should have a brief conference with the child to present the note and provide feedback regarding the day's accomplishments. Under no circumstances should the teacher get into arguments with the child over the appropriate rating for the day, although the teacher must also make every effort to be consistent and realistic in the standards that are applied. At the start of the program, a couple of phone contacts between the teacher and the child's parents are to be expected, to clarify rules and the operation of the system. In my own experience, one aspect of the program that frequently needs clarification concerns the nature of the point system. Children are likely to want to collect their rewards while holding on to the points they have earned. A good way to clarify this issue is to explain that the points are like money, once spent, it is gone. Alternately, the rewards could be tied to points by a rule that states that successively higher numbers of total points are followed by specified rewards. For example, 5000 points may be required for the child to earn a major reward, such as a new bicycle, while at the same time each 200 points earned toward the grand total results in a small reward, such as a pencil, sticker, or other school supply.

An alternate method of administering a home note program is to have a decreased level of involvement on the part of the parents. This may be needed when the family system has problems that preclude accurate, consistent administration of the program. The classroom teacher, tutor, special education teacher, or school principal could be responsible for keeping records of points earned and awarding items supplied by the parents. In some cases, parents are capable of providing large rewards, such as a new bicycle, but at other times the parents do not have the resources to supply even the smallest item. This should not prevent implementation of such a program. Even the smallest rewards, such as a pencil or eraser can be effective. Occasionally, I have administered programs where it seemed that the positive feedback was much more important than the specific reward for which the child was working.

Step 6: Observe the Effects of the Program and Take Steps to Strengthen Generalization Beyond the Training Environment. Once the program begins, the child's parents or other administrator of the program should keep a record of the number of points earned each day and the total number of points earned each week. As the number of points earned increases, subjective reports of classroom behavior should reflect the improvement represented by the points. If not, then the purposes and goals of the program should be reviewed.

Since the training environment is the classroom, it is not necessary to be concerned with generalization. However, it is desirable that the program be faded out. Techniques for accomplishing this are discussed under Step 8.

Step 7: Modify the Program, If Necessary. If the program fails to produce the expected changes, the first issue to look at is whether the child and his or her parents understand the program. For instance, parents will sometimes take away a reward that has been earned with good behavior in school when the child misbehaves at home. Such behavior on the part of the parents should be taken as a sign that they need additional help in learning to manage the behavior of their child. Another possibility is that the child does not understand the connection between the points earned in school and the promised reward. This could be remedied by a careful explanation or lowering the total number of points necessary to earn a smaller reward.

As in almost all behavior management programs, it is always possible that the rewards offered to the child are not powerful enough to bring about behavior change. A conference with the child may reveal what incentives are likely to be effective. It is also possible that the material reward is not the issue from the child's point of view. When the child's behavior shows improvement, significant adults should respond with obvious pride in the child's accomplishment. If this element is missing, the program could be doomed to failure. Again, an examination of the motives of the parents and their role in maintaining the child's behavior may be in order. For instance, if the parents are in the middle of a highly conflicted divorce or separation, the child's behavior may be an issue with which they are not able to cope effectively, given the extent of even larger problems in the marriage.

Because of its basic simplicity, a home note program may not be effective in every case. If either the child's ability or skill level was overestimated at the beginning of the program, the feedback provided by the home note points may be insufficient to improve performance. In such cases, more thorough assessment and new behavior management programs might be necessary.

Step 8: Fade Out the Program. Home note programs are not meant to be completely faded out, since periodic report cards and parent-teacher conferences are a regular occurrence as the child progresses through school. The goal, then, is to fade out the daily notes from the teacher and the reliance upon the reward system to maintain good behavior. As noted previously, an important part of making the transition to a reward-free system is that the adults involved in the original program must provide the child with positive attention and praise for good performance. As the child begins to excel, the number of points required for a reward can be increased, while the frequency of home notes is decreased. If good performance can be maintained with a weekly home note, then it would be reasonable to discuss the possibility of eliminating the point system entirely with the child. If both parents and teachers respond positively to the accomplishments of the child, it can be expected that the formal behavior management program can be completely replaced by informal behavior management techniques.

MONITORING AND REWARDING DAILY SCHOOL PERFORMANCE

Often, children having problems in school appear to possess adequate ability but apparently lack the motivation and organizational skills to function at an acceptable level. This type of student may, as a consequence of a disorganized approach to school work and achievement-ability discrepancies, be labeled as *learning disabled*. Such students may respond well to systematic monitoring of school performance on a subject-by-subject basis. Such a system can be backed up by either school- or home-based rewards and is very similar to a home note program. The difference is that a home note program does not provide such a detailed monitoring of performance. A step-by-step outline of such a program follows. It is a token reward program in which points are awarded to the student for emitting the component behaviors, which contribute to school success. The points are added and converted to a daily percent (total earned divided by total possible). A percent, rather than total number of points earned is suggested to eliminate the effects of the variability likely to be found in the academic schedule of a junior or senior high school student.

Stepwise Procedure

Step 1: Identify the Problem. Like the home note program just described, this program is designed to improve behavior and academic performance. Unlike the home note program it is designed to monitor all potential problem areas. Thus, this program is designed for the student who is not doing well in school as a result of disorganization, poor attendance, poor study habits, inappropriate behavior in class, production of low quality work, or any other problem that can be concretely defined. The program is specially suited for the junior or senior high-school resource setting, but requires the cooperation of the student's teachers who must provide daily or weekly ratings of the student's performance.

Step 2: Refine the Definition of the Problem. Unlike the home note program, which assumes that the student possesses the critical skills needed for success, the daily monitoring program can be used as a tool for teaching and rewarding academic survival skills. A Daily Performance Record is used to record the points earned by the student in each academic subject or period. Each category of behavior is worth 1-5 points, with 1 point representing unacceptable performance and 5 points representing outstanding performance. It is up to the teachers involved to establish the criteria for each level of performance. These criteria should be discussed with the student, so he or she receives daily feedback regarding the acceptability of his or her behavior. Thus, the definitions of acceptable and unacceptable behavior are determined by the teachers while working directly with the student.

The sample Daily Performance Record shown in Figure 10.3 is designed to be as flexible as possible. It allows for monitoring attendance, homework, preparation for class (having books, note-taking materials, pencil or pen, etc.), completion of in-class assignments, quality of completed work, and any other behaviors relevant to acceptable performance. The Daily Performance Record is meant to be the responsibility of the student, who should carry the record and present it to each teacher for completion at the end of the academic period. Because the Daily Performance Record provides reminders and detailed criteria for acceptable behavior, it is therefore possible that the student can learn new skills, such as appropriate organizational habits, as a consequence of this behavior management program.

Figure 10.3.   Daily Performance Record

Name									
Date				*Points*					
				5 = Outstanding Performance					
Points Earned:				4 = Good Performance					
				3 = Acceptable					
Total Possible:				2 = Improvement Needed					
				1 = Unacceptable					
Percent:									

	Period or Subject						
	1	2	3	4	5	6	7
Attendance							
Homework Completed							
Has Needed Materials							
In-class Assignments Complete							
Quality of Completed Work							
Teacher's Initials							

Comments and Upcoming
Assignments

_____

_____

_____

Step 3: Assessment of the Baseline Rate. Several methods of establishing a baseline can be employed with this behavior management program. The simplest method would be to use the records of the student's academic performance that are regularly kept by her or his teachers. This approach has some validity, even though the behaviors that are the direct target of the behavior management program may not be directly monitored, because the ultimate goal is to improve academic performance. Another approach to establishing a baseline is for the monitor of the program to survey each teacher to determine the frequency of the behaviors directly targeted for change. Finally, the student for whom the program is designed could carry the Daily Performance Record to each of his or her teachers for a period of about 1 week before the program begins. The problem with this method is that the student may not be very reliable in collecting the data. However, this behavior, itself, can become part of the baseline record.

Step 4: Identification of the Reward and Contingency. In this program, the contingency concerns the relationship between the number of points earned and whatever rewards can be mutually agreed upon by those involved in planning the program. As shown in Figure 10.3, each of the behaviors monitored in the program is given a rating of 1-5 with 5 representing outstanding performance and 1 representing unacceptable performance. For each day that the program is in effect, one of two methods can be used for computing the total number of points earned. First, if there is little variability in the behaviors expected from day to day, then the total number of points earned can simply be added up.

A second method is to use percentage points instead of the unweighted sum. Percentage points are computed by dividing the total number of points earned by the total number of possible points for a given day. The total possible points is equal to five times the total number of behavior categories that were rated summed across subjects or periods. This method is most useful when the number of applicable behavior categories changes from day to day, such as when homework is assigned irregularly in one or more classes. An additional advantage of using percentage points is that each student whose behavior is monitored on such a program will be able to earn a minimum of about 30 percentage points and a maximum of 100 points. Keeping all students on the same scale should simplify record keeping and design of programs.

Percentage points alone have little or no value to most students. However, when percentage points may be exchanged for rewards, behavior change can be expected to take place. For younger children, stickers, small toys, school supplies, and the opportunity to run errands should be sufficient to promote behavior change. For older students, the rewards used to back up the daily percentage points may include privileges, prizes, or those that are negotiated with the individual student. The backup reward may be provided by parents, school personnel, or both. Flexibility in the selection of the backup reward is a key to success.

The choice of whether the backup reward is provided on a daily, weekly, monthly, 6-week, or 9-week basis depends upon the age of the student, his or her maturity, and the size of the reward for which the student is working. When doubt exists as to how the backup reward should be delivered, it should be remembered that behavior change is easiest to obtain when the interval between rewards is shortest.

Once the time interval and backup reinforcer have been selected, their precise relationship must be determined. If a 1-week time interval has been selected, then the student could earn a maximum of 500 percentage points per week. A reasonable starting point for the management program might be that the student earns a small reward for obtaining 250 percentage points, a larger reward for obtaining more than 300 percentage points, and a highly desirable reward for obtaining 400-500 percentage points. One contingency for obtaining 400 or more percentage points might be that the student could gain some relief from the monitoring system.

Step 5: Begin the Program. To begin the program a good supply of the Daily Performance Records should be available. Records could be custom-designed for each student or one generic form for all students could be employed. To begin the program, the adult in charge simply announces the rules of the program to the student and sets the day on which the rules will take effect.

Steps 6, 7, and 8: Observe, Strengthen Generalization, Modify, If Necessary, and Fade Out the Program. Once the program has begun, two issues become important. First, the backup reward must be powerful enough to motivate the student to improve his or her behavior. This is an issue that may require repeated negotiation with the student before an adequate system is developed. The second issue is strengthening generalization of the skills, so that the student can function in school without the monitoring program. This is accomplished by employing the usual procedures for fading out a reward system and through careful evaluation, and modification, if necessary, of the particular behaviors included in the monitoring program. The behaviors monitored should contribute to the student's eventual independent functioning in the school.

BEHAVIOR CONTRACTS AS A TOOL FOR IMPROVING ACADEMIC PERFORMANCE

Behavior contracts are written agreements designed to promote behavior change. They do this by specifying target behaviors and contingencies to all involved in identification of the problem. Contracts can be a part of any formal behavior management program. In fact, a teacher who finds a particular behavior management program especially useful may wish to put the procedure into a "standard" contract, so that it may be easily implemented. Special education teachers may find that this is a useful way of setting the initial structure for their new students.

Behavior contracts have several features that can be important in the success of a behavior management program. One of their main advantages is that they clarify the roles of those involved with the student, such as teachers, biological parents, and stepparents. When a written agreement has been distributed to all involved, misunderstandings, misinterpretations, and mistakes are less likely than if the rules are described to parents over the phone. Occasionally, parents will learn new ways of dealing with their children from a written contract. Other advantages of behavior contracts are that they allow for input from all involved; they can point to problems that go beyond the immediate issues, such as abuse or chemical use/abuse; and their potential applications are almost unlimited.

A detailed discussion of general principles in writing and negotiating behavior contracts is included in Chapter 4. An example of a behavior change contract is shown in Figure 10.4. This contract includes goals for both completing classroom work and following classroom rules. It describes a fairly concrete and complicated procedure that could be simplified in a number of ways. Such a contract would probably be most useful after simpler procedures had already failed to bring about the desired changes. As with all behavior contracts, its provisions would be open to negotiation and change each review date.

Figure 10.4.   Sample Behavior Change Contract

The purpose of this contract is to help _____
learn to (a) obey classroom rules, and (b) complete seatwork for each day.

A. _____ can earn stickers by following classroom
rules. The first time a rule is violated each day his/her name will be written on the
board. For each additional time a rule is broken, a checkmark will be placed by his/her
name.

The student can earn his/her name and checkmarks off the board for following the
teacher's instructions. At the end of each day a sticker will be awarded if the student's
name is not on the board:

Name *not* on board = 1 sticker

Name or checkmarks on board = 0 stickers

B. Stickers will also be given for completing assigned seat work. One sticker will be
awarded for completing arithmetic worksheets. One sticker will be awarded for
completing all reading worksheets. One sticker will be awarded for completing all
other worksheets and projects for the day. If all written work for the day is finished a
bonus of two more stickers will be awarded.

Finish arithmetic work = 1 sticker

Finish reading work = 1 sticker

(continued)

Finish all other work = 1 sticker

Finish all work for the day = 2 bonus stickers

C. If 28 or more stickers are earned in 1 week (Mon–Fri), five bonus stickers will be awarded. If 30 stickers are earned in 1 week, an *additional* 5 stickers will be awarded.

D. Stickers earned in school may be used to "buy" rewards supplied by the student's parents from the following menu:

_____ 10 stickers

_____ 30 stickers

_____ 40 stickers

_____ 50 stickers

_____ 100 stickers

_____ 200 stickers

F. The student's teacher agrees to keep a daily and weekly record of the number of stickers earned.

G. This contract will be reviewed on _____

H. Signatures.

Student _____

Mother _____

Teacher _____

Father _____

Program Modifications

The Behavior Change Contract is fairly complex, but it could be simplified in a number of ways. One of the most obvious changes is that points could be substituted for stickers, resulting in some savings of time and money. Stickers would have the advantage of providing some degree of immediate reinforcement for younger children. The provisions for bonus stickers could also be deleted with little loss in the effectiveness of the program, depending upon the child involved. Finally, the number of behaviors targeted by the program could be reduced. For instance, if the student is busy doing assigned work, it may not be necessary to include rewards for following classroom rules, and this aspect of the contract could be deleted.

Should this version prove ineffective, two major modifications could be attempted. First, the definitions of desired and undesired behavior could be made more specific and concrete. For instance, the classroom rules could be specified in the contract and rewards could be made contingent upon following these rules.

Likewise, annoying and/or disruptive behavior not covered by classroom rules could be defined in the contract along with ways of rewarding the absence of such behavior. If the child lacks the necessary skills for succeeding in the classroom, it may be possible to carefully define the deficit skill in the contract and reward its occurrence, although other formal behavior management programs may be better suited to this type of problem.

The second way to modify the behavior contract is to change the time interval over which behavior is counted and rewarded. At one extreme, the requirement for acceptable behavior could be increased and rewards delivered on a less frequent schedule, such as once a week. At the other extreme, the time interval could be shortened so that the child begins anew after perhaps 1 hour, receiving stickers for each hour of acceptable behavior.

Behavior contracts can be very effective techniques for changing children's behavior. The number of possible variations in the form and specific provisions of contracts is infinite. Virtually any of the techniques discussed in this book can be put into writing in the form of a behavior contract. In the course of using behavior change contracts, school personnel should be aware that their first efforts may not be successful. However, this should not be interpreted as failure. Instead, it indicates that the contract needs renegotiation and change. As the age of the child with whom the contract is negotiated increases, the amount of input from the child should also increase. For instance, high-school-age students may have legitimate needs from parents and teachers that can be included in a behavior contract.

chapter 11

USING BEHAVIOR MANAGEMENT TO IMPROVE CHILDREN'S SOCIAL SKILLS

Social skills are behaviors that allow or enhance social relationships with peers or adults. Cartledge and Milburn (1986) assert that teaching of social skills is a subtle component of classroom instruction, because children who ask appropriate questions, smile at the teacher, and seek help when needed are going to be more successful than children who do not do these things.

Social skills can be conceptualized as consisting of two components: cognitions and behavior. *Cognitions* refer to the covert thoughts that mediate social behavior. For example, a child may be accidentally bumped while in the corridor or lunch line. One child may interpret the event as an accident and not react at all, while another child may see it as purposeful aggression and respond by punching and fighting. Still another child may impulsively strike back without any attempt to interpret the event. The fact that the child was bumped is not as important as the covert reasoning and thinking that occurred, or did not occur, in the situation. Cognitions also include the thinking skills to determine a reasonable course of action in various situations. An example might be a child who desires to play with a toy that another child is using. An impulsive child, with a deficit in social reasoning skills, might just take the toy without considering the consequences or other acceptable ways to reach the goal. On the other hand, a socially skilled child might consider alternative ways of obtaining the toy, such as asking for it or offering to trade it for another toy. An interesting study by Ladd and Oden (1979) showed that children who were not well accepted by their peers tended to provide unhelpful or inappropriate strategies in response to sample situations in which a need for help was evident.

The behavioral component of social skills is the overt, clearly observable components of social behavior. In the examples just cited, the relevant behaviors would be fighting and taking a toy away from another child, respectively. Either of these behaviors could be reduced with a well-designed management program. However, it is possible that such programs would miss the point if they failed to train the child in the skills necessary to behave appropriately in these or similar situations. A more lasting impact might be obtained by training the child in both the overt behavioral component (e.g., making a request) and the cognitive component (that is, the thinking skills to identify problems and generate appropriate solutions).

In this chapter techniques for accomplishing both types of training will be discussed.

WHEN IS IT APPROPRIATE TO REMEDIATE SOCIAL BEHAVIOR?

Within any group of children, one will find those who are are skilled in social situations and those for whom social interactions are a problem. An important question is: Which socially unskilled children should be candidates for programs to improve social skills?

Usually, training children in social skills is considered a parental prerogative. For instance, some parents may reinforce a child for aggressively pursuing goals. Other parents may reinforce consideration for others and kindness, while punishing or ignoring aggressive behavior. In planning a behavior management program designed to improve social skills, it is important to consider the place of the child's behavior in the home. At the same time, social skills training can be useful to counteract the negative effects of the home. As noted in Chapter 5, many specific social behaviors are negatively affected by home factors, such as divorce, alcoholism, parental conflict, abuse, or neglect. In these cases, social skills training may be useful to counteract the poor model of conflict resolution provided by the parents or to partially compensate for a parent's absence in divorced families.

One may find it necessary to remediate a social skills deficit resulting in harm to the child or others. Anger is an important emotional issue for many children from homes where conflict or disorganization is high. The outward manifestations of such anger might be frequent fighting, noncompliance, verbal aggression, or school failure. Children coming from homes in which they were abused, neglected, or subjected to the inconsistencies that accompany alcohol abuse are also likely to be angry. Learning to recognize anger, identify its source, and cope with it without harming others are tasks that can be accomplished via social skills training. The result of successful training can be a safer environment for other children in the school and improved academic performance.

Social skills training may also be useful for children who are frequently "picked on" by others. Often, these children respond to teasing in a way that reinforces the aggressors and makes the victim a more frequent target. These children may benefit from skills training that provides them with other ways of handling the situation.

In general, social skills training may be useful for many problem behaviors. Children who show deficits in social skills may benefit from programs to teach skills, while those with behavior excesses (e.g., impulsivity or aggression) may benefit from cognitive-behavioral interventions that focus on thinking and reasoning skills. Programs for dealing with both problems are discussed later in this chapter.

SOCIAL SKILLS ASSESSMENT

Kendall and Braswell (1982a) discussed two levels of assessment relevant to cognitive-behavioral interventions employed in the schools: the specifying level and the general impact level. The *specifying level* refers to the specific changes that occurred as a result of an intervention. The *general impact level* refers to the conspicuous effects of a particular intervention, such as might be observed in the classroom or on the playground.

It is important to note the distinction between the specifying and impact levels when planning social skills interventions for several reasons. First, different assessment techniques are relevant at the two levels. At the specifying level, one seeks information regarding the specific skills that were acquired or modified. At the impact level, one seeks evidence of a conspicuous impact as in parent or teacher ratings of behavior, sociometric ratings, or the return of deviant behavior to within normal limits.

Another important implication of the distinction between impact and specifying levels is that it alerts the practitioner to the importance of conducting relevant interventions. One technique for defining the relevance of a particular skill is to assess its importance in the target child's peer group. Skills that popular, socially successful peers use should improve the social adjustment of the target child. It is hoped that interventions will result in prosocial behaviors that will be "trapped" (that is, rewarded and shaped) by the natural environment.

A second important assessment issue is whether the identified problem results from a performance deficit or a skills deficit. In a performance deficit, the child possesses the skill to perform a particular behavior but simply does not perform it with satisfactory frequency. A performance deficit usually indicates that the child is not adequately motivated to behave in the desired manner, because the child is never rewarded for the desired behavior or because the child receives rewards for some other, usually undesirable, behavior. If a performance deficit is involved, then it should be possible to increase the frequency of the target behavior by arranging that a reward of sufficient value is delivered contingent upon it.

On the other hand, when the child's behavior is the result of a skill deficit, simply rewarding the target behavior will not work because the behavior is not a part of the child's repertoire. Additional measures are then necessary to assure that the child learns the behavior. Such measures may include shaping the target behavior, structuring the environment to increase the probability of the target behavior, employing models of appropriate social behavior, coaching, or conducting a structured behavior management program.

TECHNIQUES OF SOCIAL SKILLS TRAINING

A detailed review of the numerous behavior management techniques that have been employed in social skills training is beyond the scope of this chapter. However, for the reader who would like to pursue this topic further, a large number of sources are available. For an up-to-date review of techniques and principles, Ross's (1981) book is suggested. Specific issues in assessment and treatment of social skills deficits from the behavior management and other perspectives are provided by Cartledge and Milburn (1986), Conger and Keane (1981), Gresham and Nagle (1980), Kendall and Braswell, (1982b), and Wanlass and Prinz (1982). Volume 5, numbers 3/4, of *Child & Youth Services* (LeCroy, 1982) is a special issue devoted to social skills training.

The goal of this chapter is to present three techniques that can be applied to the problem of social skills deficits. First, a traditional behavior management approach to remediating social skills deficits will be outlined. Second, the cognitive-behavioral approach to remediating social skills deficits will be outlined via application of the LAHDR technique described in Chapter 7. Finally, a behavior management perspective will be used to discuss some techniques of assertion training.

Teaching Behavioral Components of Social Skills

The most straightforward use of behavior management techniques in social skills interventions is to identify a target behavior and then reward it in some manner. The goal is to increase its frequency. Increasing the frequency of one behavior may also be a tool for decreasing the frequency of an undesired behavior. For example, one may reward cooperative play with the goal of reducing the frequency of aggressive behavior. As cooperative play increases, the opportunity for aggressive acts is reduced.

As an example, consider a child with social skills deficits in two areas. First, the child has a couple of bad habits that attract the attention of peers who tend to avoid him or her. Second, the child lacks some basic skills involved in interacting positively with others. The following step-by-step program illustrates a formal behavior management program for remediating this type of problem.

Step 1: Identification of the Problem. First of all, consider what types of behavior problems are likely to cause a child's social status to be low. Many of the behaviors discussed in other chapters, such as hyperactivity, various fears and phobias, aggression, outbursts of crying, and academic deficits that attract peer attention, may lead to low social status. On the other hand, it is possible to observe a number of other "strange" characteristics that may attract negative peer attention. Such characteristics might include poor hygiene, unusual gestures, strange faces, weird noises, talking out of turn, telling strange stories, inappropriate touching of self or others, inappropriate laughter, or whatever the inventive mind of a child can come up with. In the present example, two methods of dealing with such behaviors will be discussed: a response cost procedure and the use of a "reminder," which can evolve into a form of mild punishment or be used as the basis of a program involving positive reinforcement.

At the same time a child is behaving in a way to attract the negative attention of peers, he or she may lack skills needed to take a more positive position within the social structure of a classroom. These skills would vary with the developmental age of the child, of course. Recall the discussion of child development in Chapter 2. During early childhood, which was defined as the period from birth to about 7 years, important developmental themes include learning about the consequences of actions, developing feelings of trust in adults, competence, and initiative. Numerous specific behaviors are typically expected in the social skills domain.

Among the social skills typically expected to appear in early childhood are appropriate labeling of feelings in self and others, sharing and cooperative play, following rules, taking turns and standing in line, saying please and thank you at appropriate times, requesting and giving help when needed, making relevant contributions to discussions and conversations, refraining from interrupting others, apologizing, and coping with the annoying behavior of others.

Middle childhood was defined as the period from about age 7 to 12. Within this time span, the child's ability to deal cognitively with the environment improves to allow an understanding of more complex relationships. Continuing development of a sense of competency through accomplishment in school encourages the child to do things well and carry projects through to completion. Within the social skills domain, the child is expected to learn how to participate in group activities, sensitivity to others, improved conversational skills, the skills involved in maintaining a friendship, giving gifts on special occasions, making and keeping promises and confidences, recognizing and acknowledging the positive accomplishments of others, coping with the annoying behavior of others, and making appropriate requests and refusals with peers.

Adolescence encompasses the period from age 13 to young adulthood. During this period, the child's thinking skills approach those of an adult and he or she learns to cope with the variety of roles (friend, son or daughter, student, etc.) that must be fulfilled and mold them into a cohesive identity. In the social skills domain, the adolescent should be learning the skills to deal socially with the opposite sex, responding to subtle messages in conversation, advanced conversational skills, setting and meeting goals, social dating with the opposite sex, and job-application skills.

Dodge, McClaskey, and Feldman (1985) generated a Taxonomy of Problematic Social Situations for Children by asking teachers and clinicians to identify frequent social situations that they thought were likely to result in social problems among children. The resulting list of 44 situations was subjected to factor analysis, which revealed six situation types: Peer Group Entry, Response to Peer Provocations, Response to Failure, Response to Success, Social Expectations, and Teacher Expectations. The authors suggested that the detailed assessment that may result from using their instrument can be useful in developing profiles of problematic situations and deficit skills for children who show social skill problems.

Other lists of social skills may be found in LeCroy (1982), Cartledge and Milburn (1986), and instruments for measuring adaptive behavior, such as the Vineland Adaptive Behavior Scales (Sparrow, Balla, & Cicchetti, 1984) or the School Social Skills Rating Scale (Brown, Black, & Downs, 1984). Development of systematic measures of social skills deficits has not yet reached a high level of sophistication, but promising instruments are currently available. One such instrument is the School Social Skills Rating Scale (Brown, Black, & Downs, 1984). The scale asks the rater to judge the student's typical performance of 40 behaviorally specific social skills. The manual for the scale describes a curriculum specifying components of each of the 40 skills. While the School Social Skills Rating Scale does not describe how to improve deficit skills, it does provide an outline for assessing and planning of interventions.

Given this background information, what types of behaviors are likely to bring a social skills problem to the attention of school staff members? First of all, an excess of aggressive behavior, especially on the playground, may initially attract attention. Then, as more attention is focused upon the child, it may be noticed that he or she rarely engages in positive interactions with peers and that other children tend to regard the child as an outcast or troublemaker. Academic achievement may also be poor with considerable off-task behavior, and it would not be surprising if the child were referred to special service personnel for emotional problems. In the most severe cases, the child's family history may reflect the instability of divorce, chemical abuse, or child abuse.

In addition to frequent aggressive behavior, the typical child with a social skills deficit may engage in a variety of attention-seeking behaviors. Lacking in the academic and social skills that usually result in positive attention within the school, such children may engage in less desirable behavior that is inadvertently reinforced by the attention of peers and adults. This may include being out of seat and doing silly things, making loud noises, talking out of turn, and so on. On the other hand, it is possible for children to engage in behavior that others find weird or disturbing, while being truly unaware that such behavior is unusual or results in lowered social status among peers. Poor personal hygiene is probably the most frequent behavior of this type.

As in all behavior management programs, a key to successfully remediating the problem is careful assessment of the problem behavior. In the case of potential social skills deficits, assessment takes on an even greater importance because the behavior that attracts attention often will not have an obvious relationship to the skill deficit.

Step 2: Refine the Definition of the Problem. A child's behavior is most likely to come to the attention of the professional staff of a school because it is disruptive or has some other negative characteristic. Often, a direct focus upon the problem behavior is sufficient to successfully remediate the problem. When this is not the case, one hypothesis worth considering is that a lack of social skill underlies the initially identified problem. Establishing the potential helpfulness of some sort of social skills training requires careful assessment.

The place to begin, of course, is with the original problem behavior. Although social skills deficits may manifest themselves in a number of forms, the two most common indicators are social withdrawal and acting out. Since social withdrawal is one of the major indicators of child depression, a program for remediating this behavior, or lack of it, is presented in Chapter 8. Acting out can also be a sign of a social skills deficit because the behavior is most likely under circumstances in which some other behavior would be considered more adaptive.

A detailed analysis of the problem behavior should be the first step in the assessment process. Questions of interest would include: When does the behavior tend to occur? How frequent is the behavior? What events regularly precede the behavior? Does the degree of structure in the situation seem to influence the behavior (i.e., is it more likely during free time than when all the students are working on the same assigned activity)? What is the preferred behavior in situations where the undesired behavior occurs?

Once a detailed picture of the problem behavior begins to emerge, and an idea of a more preferred behavior begins to take shape, then it is appropriate to seriously consider the potential need for social skills training. Probably the most important issue to resolve is whether the preferred behavior is ever observed. If the child, at least occasionally, emits the more desirable behavior, then it would not be necessary to teach the child a new skill. Instead, a program to increase the frequency of the desired behavior should effectively remediate the problem. On the other hand, it could be observed that the child almost never emits a socially appropriate response in the problem situation. In such a case, the child may need to be taught a new, socially acceptable way to behave in the problem situation.

A reasonable method for deciding what new social behavior should be the target of intervention is to observe other children in the same situations. The new skill taught to the target child should be one that is likely to be rewarded by other children and adults. Once a potential new skill is identified, it may be necessary to break it down into a step-by-step sequence or components so it can be effectively taught. The components or steps that are identified must be behaviorally specific if the program is to be effective.

For example, socially successful children are usually regarded as cooperative, while socially unsuccessful children are often regarded as uncooperative. What are the specific behaviors associated with cooperation? Cartledge and Milburn (1986) listed following group rules, complying with reasonable requests, taking turns, sharing appropriately, and participating in group activities as specific responses associated with cooperation. To this list one could add making reasonable requests, staying on-task, talking at appropriate times and not interrupting others, providing others with reinforcement, being able to offer alternative solutions to problems, and accepting the majority opinion on issues that affect the group.

Another area of social skill that is likely to be valued in the school is politeness. Cartledge and Milburn (1986) list eight components of this social skill: making eye contact, smiling, saying "please," saying "thank you," offering to help others, apologizing appropriately, addressing others appropriately, and making positive comments to others. Furthermore, it would be possible to be even more specific in describing these components. For instance, *offering help to others* could mean the following: First, recognizing that someone needs help or acknowledging a request for help. Second, making a relevant offer of help, and third, carrying out the help. Finally, the child might be expected to respond appropriately to thanks by saying "you're welcome" or something similar.

Thus, when a child appears to have a deficit in social skills, it is necessary to first identify the general problem and then proceed to specify the area of the skill deficit. If any acting out behavior is present, this will need to be remediated. Then, the specific behaviors associated with the social skill deficit must be further specified. Since the target child is not likely to emit these behaviors at any significant frequency, the best source of data regarding the acceptability of the specified social skill behaviors is how the popular, well-liked students of the same sex behave in similar situations.

Step 3: Assessment of the Baseline Rate. Programs to improve social skills can be very difficult to plan because social behavior is so complicated. Consequently, the initial target behaviors must be selected with great care. Baseline observations can then be used to confirm whether the behavior management program has a good chance to work as expected. Baseline observations for a program involving social skills deficits should focus on two types of behavior: any acting out, aggressive behavior, or other behavior that attracts negative attention, and observations of the social skill or behavioral component to be increased. Concurrently, it is also helpful to obtain baseline data regarding the behavior of one of the more popular students of the same sex. These observations can reveal whether the target behavior plays any role in the child's social success and whether other children reward the target behavior. Recall that a key to success in social skills training is to train new skills that will be rewarded in the natural environment.

The particular observational techniques used depend upon the nature of the problems to be remediated. With acting out or aggressive behavior, it is probably best to record the occurrence of each incident, noting the circumstances and any other relevant information. Social skill behaviors are more likely to occur in particular contexts such as class discussions, free periods, lunch period, group projects, and other relatively unstructured portions of the school day. Consequently, a time-sampling procedure might work best with the social skills component of such a behavior management program.

Since two children are being observed, it is necessary to change the typical time-sampling procedure. Instead of observing one child for the entire period, it is necessary to split the time between the target child and the control or popular child. The best way to do this may be to alternate time periods between the two children. For instance, the first 2 minutes of the observation period can be spent observing the target child, the next 2 minutes observing the other child, the next 2 minutes observing the target child, and so on until the end of the observation period. With this method, the conditions of the observations are as similar as possible for the two children.

Step 4: Identify the Reinforcer and Contingency. The primary concern of school personnel will usually be any negative behaviors such as aggression, acting out, or other unusual behavior. Several methods can be used to reduce such behavior. The use of timeout was discussed in detail in Chapter 7, and might be useful for aggression or any other behavior that involves potential harm to self or others. However, for some behaviors, timeout may not be necessary or desirable. Two other methods of reducing undesired behavior are to present something the child does not desire contingent upon the undesired behavior, or to take away something that the child desires contingent upon the undesired behavior.

Finding something undesirable, other than timeout, requires some preparation. If the child is highly motivated to change, it might not be necessary to become too elaborate. A card that can be labeled in some appropriate way, such as "Reminder Card" or anything that the child finds relevant, can be presented to the child each time the undesirable behavior occurs. If the child is highly motivated to change, a reduction in behavior may occur even if the cards are not backed up by any material reward. On the other hand, it may be necessary to back up the cards in some way. Each card presented to the child could represent a loss of points in a response cost procedure. Alternately, after a period in which the cards were simply presented to the child, he or she could be rewarded for reducing the number of cards received from some prearranged level determined by examining previous records.

If the child received 16 cards in the first week, he or she could then receive a reward contingent upon reducing the number of cards received in future weeks. The structure of such a reward program could vary from a menu of different rewards, each contingent upon a different level of performance, or it could consist of rewarding the child for each reduction in the number of cards received in a given week.

Once a program to reduce the undesirable aspects of the child's social behavior has been planned, the complementary problem of increasing desirable behavior can be approached. When the goal is to improve a highly concrete, easily defined, behavior, such as academic productivity, it is not difficult to structure a reward program. One reason is that the products of such behavior are easily defined and monitored. It is also easy to arrange delivery of rewards without interfering with the child's productivity. However, it is not so easy to reward the components of social behavior.

The problem is basically twofold. First, the exact form of positive, desirable behavior is likely to vary with the context in which it occurs, and the range of acceptable behavior is likely to be fairly broad. Second, it may be difficult to deliver a reward without interfering with the behavior and altering the ongoing interaction of which the desirable behavior is part. I suggest that the solution is to have a flexible program, which begins at a level that is least likely to intrude upon the behavior and its context. If this fails, then more and more structured interventions can be attempted until some success is experienced.

At the level of least structure, one might institute a plan similar to a home note. Recall that a home note, which was described in Chapter 10, provides a simple way of rating the acceptability of a child's behavior. Such a rating system could be tied to a reward system based upon points earned as described in Chapter 10. The key to making such a program successful would lie in the external supports provided by the person in charge. In other words, several steps could be taken to improve the viability of the program. First, generous prompts and pointing out an appropriate model to the child could illustrate desirable behaviors. Second, when the rating of behavior was communicated to the child, an explanation of the positive and negative aspects of his or her performance could be provided. Another method of helping the child would be to actually rehearse appropriate behavior, such as a simple request for help. Generous verbal praise and prompting may succeed in making up for the unstructured nature of such a program.

At a higher level of structure, it might be necessary to proceed to systematically train the child in desired behavior. This could be accomplished in a stepwise manner, beginning with one-on-one instruction in the desired behavior, followed by practice in a highly structured prearranged situation. Then, rewarding the child for emitting the desired behavior in unstructured situations, which occur regularly in the classroom, can be added to the program. The precise structure of the reward system could be determined according to the needs and desires of the child. A token program would seem best suited to such social skills training, because rewards can be delivered without interfering with an ongoing interaction. Response cost procedures can be used to suppress undesired behavior. Use of a token program also allows wide variability in the backup reward system.

Steps 5 and 6: Begin the Program, Observe Its Effects, and Take Necessary Steps to Strengthen Generalization. The program finally chosen can be started by announcing its rules to the child. Observing its effects will require an occasional return to baseline conditions, so that a valid observation can be conducted. Improvements noted in the child's behavior during formal observations (using the same technique employed to gather the baseline data) should readily generalize to the unstructured environment, if they are maintained by social reward from the child's peers. If the behavior is not rewarded by the child's peers, then a reassessment of the original program may be necessary to determine what can be done to improve generalization. It may be helpful to include other children in the observations to determine whether they are trying to keep the target child in his or her former role, perhaps because they have difficulty coping with the changes.

Step 7: Modify the Program, If Necessary. Because social skills are very complicated, success may not be immediate. If undesired behavior fails to decrease, then a careful analysis of other factors may be helpful. Often such behaviors are rewarded by peer attention, which may be stronger than the contingency presented by a classroom teacher or school psychologist. The options for changing the program are to increase the strength of the contingency or employ a group behavior management program in which all members of the group may benefit from an improvement in the target child's behavior. The Good Behavior Game plus Merit, discussed in Chapter 7, may work well in this situation.

With respect to the behavior that is desirable to increase, many options are available should the original program not be successful. First, a change in the target behavior could be beneficial. A reexamination of the baseline data for the target child and the other, more socially competent child could lead to hypotheses regarding other behaviors in which the child may need coaching or training. In the following section, an adaptation of the LAHDR approach, first described in Chapter 7, is described. The value of this technique is that it introduces a method of training a child in the cognitive skills that mediate social behavior.

Step 8: Fade Out the Program. Fading out the program consists of allowing natural contingencies to take over the function of the original structured program. At the same time, the value of tokens can be decreased or the number of points needed to earn a reward can be increased. Also, attention and praise from the classroom teacher can be substituted for material rewards, tokens, or points.

Adapting the LAHDR Technique

Richard and Dodge (1982) examined the relationship between social adjustment and social problem-solving skills in school-aged boys who were categorized as either aggressive, isolated, or popular. The most significant finding was that popular boys generated more solutions to a series of hypothetical stimulus situations than aggressive and isolated boys. Aggressive and isolated boys did not differ in the number of solutions they generated. Furthermore, all three groups generated initial solutions that were judged effective, but the subsequent solutions generated by the aggressive and isolated boys were inferior to those generated by the popular boys. Finally, it was found that all three groups were capable of selecting the most effective solution to a problem given several choices and all boys indicated that the most effective solution was the one they would try in the situation. Asarnow and Callan (1985) obtained similar results noting that differences in knowledge and/or attitudes could be contributing to the social problems of children disliked by their peers.

Thus, this research indicated that one of the cognitive deficits associated with social skills problems is the ability to generate a number of alternative solutions to a problem. The LAHDR technique, which was described in Chapter 7, provides a basic structure for remediating such a deficit. That is, children who are taught to mediate their problem-solving efforts with appropriate verbal self-instruction can show improved social skills. Such improvement would come from slowing down immediate reactions to situations, considering goals, considering the relationship of various courses of action to goals, considering consequences of various behaviors, and, in general, making better decisions regarding behavior in social contexts.

Recall that the LAHDR technique is a step-by-step technique for remediating impulsive or inattentive approaches to academic tasks. The acronym, LAHDR, stands for the five-step sequence that children are trained to follow while solving academic problems: LISTEN, ASK, HOW, DID, and REWARD. These, in turn, are the first words in a series of questions that the child asks himself or herself: LISTEN to instructions. ASK myself what I'm supposed to do. HOW do I do it? DID I do it right? REWARD myself for doing it right.

As presented in Chapter 7, this procedure would primarily be useful for remediating academic deficits characterized by inattention to key aspects of the task, acting too quickly to have processed the relevant cues, or difficulty organizing a task into its elements. The goal of such training is to teach the child a general method for approaching tasks in a thoughtful, rather than impulsive, manner. Many of the social behaviors that a child needs to succeed in school could also benefit from similar training, because social behavior is just as likely as academic behavior to be more successful when the child takes time to think about his or her actions before doing something and taking time to evaluate the consequences of his or her behavior afterwards.

Kendall and Braswell (1985) also included an affective component in their cognitive-behavioral treatment for impulsive children. Recall, from Chapter 7, that this procedure is similar to the LAHDR technique in that the child is taught to apply a systematic, stepwise approach to problem solving. The affective aspect of the treatment can begin with the assignment of homework. In Kendall and Braswell's procedure, the children could earn a bonus reward if they could remember and describe an example of how they applied the steps they were taught to a real life situation. It would not be surprising if the children at least occasionally cited examples of how they used their problem-solving skills in social situations.

In addition to the unstructured homework assignments, Kendall and Braswell also included specific training procedures to help the child learn to cope with social situations. The main feature of this component of the training is role plays of potentially problematic situations. A group of problem situations is written on index cards, from which a sample situation is drawn. Then, the child and therapist act out the situation. The goal is for the child to identify the problem and look at possible courses of action, taking into account the real limits of the situation. Typically, they encourage the child to create at least three alternative courses of action and evaluate each one in terms of its consequences and whether it would actually lead to attaining the child's goal.

The next step in the role play is for the child to choose one of the alternatives. Kendall and Braswell state that the child's choice should be respected, even if it involves hitting another child. They argue that the child is being taught *how*, not *what*, to think. On the other hand, a strong argument could also be made for making positive consequences contingent upon choosing a nonviolent alternative. This would be particularly true in school where all personnel have an interest in protecting children from harm. The final step in the sequence is for the child to reward his or her skilled problem solving or emit a coping statement that will cue better performance in the future without being punishing.

Butler, Miezitis, Friedman, and Cole (1980) employed a role play format in the treatment of depressive symptoms in preadolescents. The main objective of the treatment was to teach children a problem-solving approach to threatening or stressful situations that emphasized learning to generate as many potential solutions to problem situations as possible. The greatest amount of favorable changes was observed in the role play treatment compared to control conditions. Consequently, this type of intervention seems to represent a useful approach to a variety of social skills deficits.

The step-by-step procedure that follows is designed to illustrate these points.

Step 1: Identification of the Problem. Cognitive-behavioral training to improve thinking skills and decrease impulsive behavior may be useful under a wide variety of circumstances. More concretely, one might consider such training when the initial definition of the problem includes such behaviors as aggression, talking out in class, poor peer relationships, appearing to act too quickly given the situation, hyperactivity, being out of seat without permission, and statements indicating a low self-concept. Of course, this list of behaviors is not exhaustive. The key is to look for signs that the child is acting in an impulsive manner. Most frequently, this may be indicated by an observer's belief that there is an alternative means of dealing with a particular problem for a child who apparently is not considering that alternative.

Step 2: Refine the Definition of the Problem. The procedure that follows has two components: general training in problem-solving skills and specific training in coping with those situations that seem to lead to trouble for the child. In refining the definition of the problem, then, two questions should be considered. First, does the child behave in an impulsive manner, which might benefit from training in thinking skills? Second, what specific situations result in problems for the child?

Answering the first question has been discussed in Chapters 6 and 7, under the topic of hyperactivity, because impulsivity is one of its accepted defining characteristics. Signs of impulsivity listed in *DSM-III* (American Psychiatric Association, 1980) include often acting before thinking, shifting excessively from task to task, experiencing difficulty organizing work, needing a lot of supervision, frequent calling out in class, and difficulty awaiting turn in games or group situations. These types of behaviors would be relevant in assessing the problem at the specifying level.

Another approach to the assessment of impulsive behavior is to employ a more general instrument, such as the Self-Control Rating Scale (Kendall & Wilcox, 1979; reproduced in Kendall and Braswell, 1985). This scale consists of 33 items, which are rated on a 7-point continuum by a child's teacher. The scale covers a broad range of behaviors and was designed to measure generalization of behavior management programs beyond the specific training environment.

Impulsive behavior can be indicated when a child acts too quickly to have processed the relevant components of a problem and, in addition, typically comes up with an inappropriate solution. This may happen in a variety of social situations, ranging from participation in group activities to those that result in anger and fights. Children who require a lot of individual attention and counseling because they frequently say things that get them into trouble or hurt the feelings of others are also likely to be approaching social situations in an impulsive or inattentive manner. Impulsiveness also can be indicated when the child is unable to reconstruct a series of events that may have gained the attention of the classroom teacher, such as aggressive behavior.

Once observations have indicated that a child behaves in an impulsive manner, the next step is to identify the conditions likely to elicit such behavior. This is much more important in cognitive-behavioral programs than most other behavior management programs, because the ultimate goal is to improve the child's behavior in the situations that precede impulsive acts rather than to simply reduce the frequency of impulsive behavior. Of course, as an indirect consequence of the cognitive-behavioral training, it is assumed that impulsive acts of all kinds will decrease. Thus, refining the definition of the target behavior means to identify the situations in which improved social skill is needed.

Consider an example. Suppose that a child is aggressive and seems to be disciplined regularly for fighting. One approach to this situation would be to arrange that some type of punishment follow each act of aggression. For young children, a brief period of timeout may be appropriate. For older children, temporary removal from the situation in which fighting occurred may effectively reduce its frequency. At the same time, however, observations may show that such behavior tends to occur in a particular setting under a particular set of circumstances. For example, during team games played during physical education periods or, maybe, during group projects in the classroom. Improving behavior in these situations would be the focus of the cognitive-behavioral training.

Another approach to defining the problem situation would be to categorize behavior under a broad heading, such as impulsive acts. This might include both physical and verbal aggression, talking out of turn, breaking various classroom rules, or any other behavior that captures the child's particular problem.

As observational data are collected, it is also wise to look carefully at the child's academic performance. If academic performance is poor, it may be more efficient to consider whether the child's behavior should be regarded as hyperactive or impulsive in general, rather than just in social situations. In this case, I would suggest that the initial focus of intervention be upon academic behavior, following the program for impulsive children described in Chapter 7. Then, once problem-solving skills have been mastered on the most concrete level, training can be conducted, as described in this section, with the goal of promoting generalization of the newly acquired problem-solving skills to social situations.

Step 3: Assessment of the Baseline Rate. The refined definition of the problem may include a narrowly defined behavior which occurs in a limited number of situations, or a broader category, such as "impulsive acts." Baseline data could be collected by simply recording each instance of the problem behavior. A portable record sheet such as a 3×5, card with blocks for each hour or half-hour of the school day, might be convenient. Each time one of the target behaviors occurs, a single mark should be made in the correct time block. Additional notes, such as teacher responses to the behavior, should be made on the back of the card. The baseline period may extend for as long as necessary, but several days to 1 week should be adequate. In the case of high magnitude aggressive behavior, which may lead to injury of other children, it may be prudent to begin baseline observations and the management program, itself, at the same time. Refer to Chapter 7 or Chapter 4 for discussions of how to decrease the frequency of a behavior.

If the target behavior is restricted to a particular environment, an alternative means of collecting baseline data is to calculate the percent of times that the target behavior occurs in the problem situation. This would be appropriate when the number of opportunities to be in the problem situation varies.

At the general impact level of assessment, one may also wish to collect information regarding the child's academic performance, time on task, and social status. It might also be informative to administer the Self-Control Rating Scale (Kendall & Braswell, 1985). These measures would provide concrete evidence regarding the general impact of the training procedure and whether programming for generalization beyond the training environment was occurring as planned.

Step 4: Identification of the Reinforcer and Contingency. The goal of this behavior management program is to teach the child to stop and think about his or her social behavior. Recall that a similar procedure was described in Chapter 7. In this procedure the goal is to reward use of five verbal cues in problem solving: LISTEN, ASK, HOW, DID, and REWARD. These five words are used as cues to the following series of steps in solving problems: LISTEN to instructions. ASK myself what I'm supposed to do. HOW do I do it? DID I do it right? Finally, REWARD myself for doing it right. Each of these cues is treated as an instruction that prompts the child in how to solve problems in a systematic way. Once the sequence has been modeled for the child, he or she is taught to use it independently in solving problems and doing other school work. This technique is similar to others that have been used successfully to train children in cognitive skills (e.g., Kendall & Braswell, 1985).

In the context of improving children's social skills, the same technique could be employed with some modification. Kendall and Braswell (1985) suggest a more general problem-solving procedure consisting of defining the problem, developing a possible strategy that will lead to a solution, focusing attention on the problem at hand, choosing and implementing a possible solution, and, finally, rewarding oneself for a good job or uttering a coping statement that cues better future performance instead of being self-deprecating or punishing. This series of steps would be appropriate for both concrete worksheets and other academic work or more general problems involving social situations.

The LAHDR procedure would work just as well in this regard if the steps were modified appropriately. One version of such a modification follows:

- L   LOOK at the problem!
- A   ASK myself what I want to do (what my goal is)?
- H   HOW can I reach the goal?
- D   DECIDE what to do (upon a course of action)!
- R   REVIEW what happened and whether the goal was reached and
- R   REWARD myself for reaching my goal without hurting others!

Other versions could easily be devised by those interested in applying the procedure. The specific details of the steps the child is taught are probably not as important as teaching the child that positive results can follow slowing down and thinking before acting. Thus, if the practitioner is uncomfortable with the specifics of these procedures, the details can be changed while keeping the general approach intact.

A more important question is, what is an appropriate level of skills at which to begin training focused upon social skills? Many children who have social skills deficits are also likely to have other problems, such as poor academic performance. Would it be appropriate to ignore the academic problems and focus training on the social skills problem? If the child has an impulsive approach to classwork as well as social situations, it may be most reasonable to begin at the concrete level of teaching the child to stop and think about worksheets and other assignments before completing them. Then, once the child has shown progress in completion of concrete tasks, the training can be extended to social problem solving. This approach is recommended by Kendall and Braswell (1985), who suggest that therapists using cognitive-behavioral interventions employ a progression from concrete, impersonal tasks to more general, emotionally laden material involving interpersonal situations.

What, then, are the precise steps one would use to teach social problem-solving skills to a child using a cognitive-behavioral approach? Two components are involved in such training: first, practice in social problem solving conducted in a role play situation and, second, specific training to promote generalization of the skills to real situations within the school. Goldstein, Sprafkin, Gershaw, and Klein (1980) and McGinnis, Goldstein, Sprafkin, and Gershaw (1984) describe a systematic approach to social skills training consisting of four steps: modeling, role playing, performance feedback, and transfer of training. In addition, they provide assessment instruments, progress charts, and describe how to conduct training in a group format. The method is similar to the one that follows and these books may be consulted should more detail be needed in applying such techniques, especially in a group format.

Before role playing can begin, a group of practice situations must be selected. These situations should encompass a wide variety of social problems occurring in a number of different environments. For example, one situation could be: "You are walking down the hall when somebody bumps into you?" Another situation might be: "You are working during 'quiet' time, when your friend starts to 'bug' you." Note that the examples should be both age-appropriate and use language that the child is accustomed to hearing. A list of hypothetical situations follows:

1. "You are walking down the hall when you are bumped by someone you don't like."
2. "You are reading a fun book when someone grabs it away from you."
3. "You want to join a game and the kids won't let you."

4. "You are on the playground and your classmates start teasing you because you are too fat, ugly, tall, skinny, short, dumb, funny looking, smart, or silly (choose only one)."
5. "You worked really hard on your arithmetic worksheet, but the teacher asks you to do it over."
6. "Your friend wants you to help him cheat on a test, but you don't want to because you will get into trouble."
7. "Your best friend just told you that she has a new best friend."
8. "Your mom tells you to clean your room but you want to watch your favorite program on TV."

These hypothetical situations should be modified as needed by changing their content or adding new ones. The final set should contain hypothetical situations that are relevant to the age, sex, lifestyle, and language of the child. The situations should also contain a wide range of difficulty, since it would be best if the child experienced some success and learned the role-playing procedure before being confronted with situations that represent his or her real-life problems. Although presenting the situations to the child in order of difficulty might seem too artificial, in fact, the best starting point might be with some completely neutral situation such as how to go about writing a report (for older children) or complete a worksheet (for younger children). Then, the general approach to solving problems can be taught in a nonthreatening context.

A role play is a play-acted version of a potentially real situation in which the actors and actresses take roles and pretend that they are in the situation. Of course, the major problem with role playing as a behavioral intervention is the generalization of skills to real-life situations. This is the main reason that selection of the hypothetical situations is so important. If they are relevant and give the child practice in new ways of approaching problematic situations, the chances are greater that generalization will occur.

To conduct the actual training, a group of hypothetical situations should be carefully selected and perhaps written on some medium, such as index cards. Then, an appropriate setting should be found for the role play training. The child should be introduced to the general idea that problems can often be solved by stopping and thinking about them before doing anything. One might then talk about some specific reasons for conducting the training and express hope that the time together will help the child stop getting into trouble, learn how to be a good friend, or be happier. It is important to establish at least some rapport with the child and understand how the child perceives his or her problems, if indeed, the child sees any problems at all.

The goal is to train the child to use the steps shown above to solve each of the hypothetical problems, which should have been selected previously. It may be appropriate to illustrate the steps with a poster or put them on cards. Training is accomplished by first explaining the steps to the child and then modeling the solutions to one or two of the hypothetical situations. Then, the child is requested to attempt another situation, saying everything out loud so that the instructor can follow the child's approach.

At this point, the instructor must have a clear set of goals in mind and skillfully apply the basic principles of behavior management to direct the child toward acceptable performance. Reminders to use each of the five steps and generous social reward, praise, and encouragement are the main tools at the disposal of the instructor. Consistency in delivering these rewards is also likely to be related to success. It may be helpful to use a token reward program with response cost contingencies to gain precise control over the behavior of the child. It will be necessary to fade out the token program over time, however, if the training is to generalize to real situations. The following hypothetical schedule of activities is presented as an example:

Session 1 Introduce the child to the procedure and instructor. Use informal activities to establish rapport and introduce the child to the concept of role playing.

Session 2 Establish a set of reasonable rules with contingencies for violation. Introduce the child to the steps involved in solving problems. The instructor models for the child and then takes the child through the procedure providing as much prompting and support as necessary. Then, the child goes alone through each step in the problem-solving procedure, using cards or verbal prompts as reminders.

Sessions 3 to 8 Continue practicing role play situations of increasing difficulty.

Sessions 9 to 10 Begin introducing role play situations that are directly related to the problems the child is experiencing within the school. If the child chooses a response that is likely to lead to problems, prompt him or her to think about what would happen and whether some other response might be better. I suggest that the last response chosen by the child should be one with a realistic chance of success.

Sessions 11 to 15 Introduce activities designed to promote generalization, such as homework assignments. These assignments could consist of having the child discuss how she or he could use the problem-solving technique to deal with actual problems. Furthermore, a particular situation could be practiced one session and the actual outcome could be discussed in the following session.

Sessions 16 to 20 Review the child's accomplishments, continue to practice problematic situations, and terminate the instructor-child relationship.

For additional information regarding how to conduct the sessions, see Chapter 7 of this book and Kendall and Braswell (1985).

Step 5: Begin the Program. Once a schedule has been arranged, materials have been prepared, and a place to conduct the training has been found, the program may begin. Although baseline data would include academic records and behavioral observations from the classroom, the instructor may also find it helpful to keep records of the training sessions. This record might include notes on the general behavior of the child during the training sessions, which may reveal much that is of value to know regarding the child's personality or suggest other behavior management programs that may be more beneficial. These observations may also suggest a need for a more thorough assessment, special education programming, or evaluation by a clinical psychologist or psychiatrist.

A second source of data is the child's responses to each problem situation. The instructor should record whether the child responds appropriately to the five LAHDR steps. A prepared mimeographed sheet could be used for this purpose.

Step 6: Observe the Program's Effects and Strengthen Generalization Beyond the Training Environment. As the program progresses, effects upon the original measures should be observable. At the same time, improvement in the child's skill at using the problem-solving steps should be observable. Records of the sessions should show that fewer prompts are required and fewer response cost penalties are needed as time passes. Academic performance and time on-task might also show improvement. Readministration of the sociometric measure and any teacher-report instruments would probably be most useful prior to the end of the program, since the results may suggest program modifications.

Several components of the program designed to improve the chances that the new skills will generalize to real-life problems have already been described. However, these components are part of the training that takes place within the training sessions. It may be necessary for the instructor to go outside the training environment and into the classroom or onto the playground. What could be done in these situations? First, once the child has acquired problem-solving skills within the role play setting, it might be helpful to set up a behavior management program to reward the child for using these skills in other settings. Such a program may need to focus upon the outcome rather than the behavior that mediates the outcome. Another technique may be to have the child plan her or his behavior in a particular situation within a training session, observe the child's behavior and reward him or her according to how closely actual behavior conforms to the plan.

Another way of promoting generalization outside the training environment is to conduct group instruction in the problem-solving technique. The format of such training would be similar to that used with the individual child. The major difference would be that a much richer role playing format would be available, and it is likely that real problems will develop that can be solved by the children using a structured approach. The size of the group could vary from about five or six to an entire class. Of course, the size of the group and its composition would greatly influence the format. For more concrete guidance on the format of children's groups see Kendall and Braswell (1985, p. 172ff) and Gazda (1976).

Step 7: Modify the Program, If Necessary. The behavior management program described in this section is very complex. Consequently, when the program is not successful, there are many potential explanations. It is possible that the program, itself, requires modification (i.e., because it is too complex), or that the child is not sufficiently motivated to attempt the problem-solving procedure outside of the training environment. A simplified program, such as described in Chapter 7 might address both of these problems.

An important component of the program is the skill of the instructor. Consistent and generous use of praise and social reinforcement is necessary. However, it is possible that the child may be receiving rewards for undesired behavior or that rewards are inconsistent. Observation of training sessions by another, experienced individual could provide some valuable data. Likewise, it may be observed that some behavior of the child is interfering with progress. A special response cost program to eliminate such behavior could greatly improve the likelihood of success. Alternately, other behavior problems that require other behavior management approaches may be identified. Finally, it may be that important data were overlooked in the initial assessment, and the initial hypothesis regarding the nature of the problem could require complete or partial revision.

Another possible modification of the program is to make assertive behavior the target of the intervention. This would require only instruction in the meaning of the terms assertive, nonassertive, and aggressive in the context of the procedure just described. Then, the child would be taught to label these types of behavior and discriminate among them. Role playing of hypothetical situations involving violations of rights, refusal of unreasonable requests, and other components of assertive behavior would be conducted. This topic is covered more thoroughly in the following section.

Step 8: Fade Out the Program. Fading out an individualized program, such as described here, consists of ascertaining that generalization has indeed occurred, and reducing the frequency of individual sessions with the child. As the program draws to a close, the focus can shift from practice of role play situations to discussion of "homework" assignments and how what has been learned can or has been applied in real-life situations. The length of time between sessions can also be progressively increased, until they are essentially eliminated. Follow-up assessment to determine the persistence of the observed effects and whether additional "booster" sessions might be helpful may also be part of this step.

The Assertive Skills Approach

Assertive behavior encompasses the ability of a person to "act in his or her own best interests, to stand up for herself or himself without undue anxiety, to express honest feelings comfortably, or to exercise personal rights without denying the rights of others" (Alberti & Emmons, 1978, p. 27). Assertive behavior lies in the middle of a continuum of behavioral styles, which is anchored at one end by non-assertion and at the other end by aggression. *Nonassertion* involves violating one's own rights by failing to express honest feelings, thoughts, and beliefs, or expressing one's thoughts and feelings in such a timid, apologetic, diffident, or self-effacing manner that they can easily be disregarded or ignored. At the other end of the continuum is *aggression*. Aggression involves directly standing up for one's rights and expressing oneself in ways that are often dishonest, usually inappropriate, and always violate the rights of others. The usual goal of aggressive behavior is domination or winning, accomplished by humiliating, degrading, belittling, or overpowering other people so they become weaker and less able to express and defend their own rights and needs.

In the middle of this continuum of behavioral styles is *assertion*. Assertion involves standing up for one's personal rights and expressing thoughts, feelings, and beliefs in direct, honest, and appropriate ways that do not violate another person's rights. Messages are conveyed without dominating, humiliating, or degrading the other person. Assertive behavior is a positive approach to communication that involves respecting oneself and the adult or child with whom one is communicating.

Training in assertive skills for adults remains extremely popular and it is very common to see advertisements for workshops in assertiveness. The prototype for training adults is the book by Lange and Jakubowski (1976). It emphasizes both developing understanding of the principles of being assertive and role playing various situations requiring assertive behavior. Contracting for behavior change and homework assignments involving practice of new skills are also part of the training techniques.

Despite the popularity of assertion training classes and workshops for adults, not much has been done with respect to the possibility of teaching assertive skills to children. Vogrin and Kassinove (1979) presented groups of children with training in assertive behavior and found that third-grade children could learn to be significantly more assertive. No assessments were conducted with this group of normal children to determine the effect of the training on daily functioning, but the study did establish the potential efficacy of giving such training to children with special needs. Horan and Williams (1982) successfully employed assertion training as a drug abuse prevention strategy. Positive effects were obtained immediately after treatment and 3 years later. It seems reasonable to suggest that children who participate in social skills training groups may benefit from learning to differentiate assertive, nonassertive, and aggressive behavior.

One topic of great concern to both children and adults has been the sexual abuse of children. Programs for preventing abuse have been shown on national television and are part of the curriculum of some schools. These programs typically involve three principles: first, that the child has a right to be comfortable about what happens to his or her body; second, that some touches are uncomfortable and/or frightening and that the child has a right to say "No!" to such advances, and finally, that a child who has been exposed to an abusive situation should tell somebody and keep on telling until somebody listens. This type of teaching is very similar to the adult version of assertion training and represents a very important application.

Assertion training for adults generally employs a group format such as outlined by Lange and Jakubowski (1976), who employ self-assessment, lectures, and structured exercises to teach assertiveness skills. Vogrin and Kassinove (1979) conducted training in assertiveness with normal third-grade children in 16 sessions over 3 months. The training consisted of lectures on the nature of assertion and either role played practice of assertive skills or listening to audiotaped models behaving unassertively, assertively, or aggressively. The children were urged to play various roles in hypothetical situations. The instructor coached them using direct instruction, role reversal, and shaping to teach appropriately assertive responses. The results of several posttreatment measures showed that children in the role-playing group had the greatest positive changes in assertive skills, as measured by written tests.

According to the general principles that are the foundation of assertion training, such training would be effective for children who are regularly "picked on" and subjected to other aggressive behavior by their peers. Unfortunately, no empirical evidence for the efficacy of such training exists. However, it seems that integrating such training with the cognitive-behavioral intervention described earlier would have a positive impact, if the instructor was careful to include training that would increase generalization to real life situations.

WHEN NOT TO EMPLOY SOCIAL SKILLS INTERVENTIONS

As noted at the very beginning of this chapter, children who are socially skilled are likely to do better in school than socially unskilled children. Furthermore, training in social skills is both an overt and covert part of the regular education curriculum. When a child has an obvious deficit in social skills, it is likely to be related to both academic and interpersonal problems. For these reasons, when an assessment reveals a social skills deficit, the temptation may be to provide remediation as soon as possible. However, social skills training represents a complex, sensitive intervention that should not be undertaken lightly. Because of the very personal nature of social skills interventions, the rights of the child, the child's parents, and school personnel are all important considerations in whether to conduct such interventions.

Since many social skills interventions involve taking the child out of the regular classroom, the child's parents must be informed as to the nature of the training and its goals. Due to its complexity, social skills training may often involve special services personnel, such as a school psychologist. When special services for the handicapped are involved, parents have the ultimate say in whether any intervention will be allowed to take place, unless a due-process hearing is conducted. As noted earlier, parents are usually regarded as providing the primary training in social skills to their children. Consequently, their objections or support are crucial elements in any intervention.

On the other hand, those in the school have the right to educate the children in their charge to the best of their ability. Often, a single child can disrupt this process to an unacceptable degree. When this happens, social skills training will not be the only feasible intervention. Numerous other interventions are discussed in this book. Many of them could be valuable in bringing the most obvious problems under control. Furthermore, providing training in social skills may be going further than is necessary or practical. In the case of children from unstable and/or conflict-laden homes, the best the school may be able to do is to bring behavior within normal limits, so that learning can take place while ignoring higher-order needs of the child until useful communication can be established with the child's parents. It is an unfortunate fact of school life that not everything can be fixed as quickly as one would desire, even by the most skilled manager of behavior.

REFERENCES

Alberti, R. E., & Emmons, M. L. (1978). *Your perfect right: A guide to assertive behavior* (3rd ed.). San Luis Obispo, CA: Impact Publishers.

Alberto, P. A., & Troutman, A. C. (1986). *Applied behavior analysis for teachers* (2nd ed.). Columbus, OH: Merrill Publishing.

Alibrandi, T. (1978). *Young alcoholics*. Minneapolis, MN: Compcare Publications.

American Psychiatric Association. (1980). *Diagnostic and statistical manual of mental disorders* (3rd ed.). Washington, DC: Author.

Argulewicz, E. N., Elliott, S. N., & Spencer, D. (1982). Application of a cognitive-behavioral intervention for improving classroom attention. *School Psychology Review, 11*, 90–95.

Asarnow, J. R., & Callan, J. W. (1985). Boys with peer adjustment problems: Social cognitive processes. *Journal of Consulting and Clinical Psychology, 53*, 80–87.

Asarnow, J. R., & Carlson, G. A. (1985). Depression Self-Rating Scale: Utility with child psychiatric inpatients. *Journal of Consulting and Clinical Psychology, 53*, 491–499.

Atkeson, B. M., & Forehand, R. (1979). Homebased reinforcement programs designed to modify classroom behavior: A review and methodological evaluation. *Psychological Bulletin, 86*, 1298–1308.

Azrin, N. H., & Foxx, R. M. (1974). *Toilet training in less than a day*. New York: Pocket Books.

Azrin, N. H., & Holz, W. C. (1966). Punishment. In W. K. Honig (Ed.), *Operant behavior: Areas of application and research*. New York: Appleton-Century-Crofts.

Bandura, A. (1969). *Principles of behavior modification*. New York: Holt, Rinehart, & Winston.

Bandura, A. (1977). *Social learning theory*. Englewood Cliffs, NJ: Prentice-Hall.

Bane, M. J. (1979). Marital disruption and the lives of children. In G. Loevingen & O. C. Moles (Eds.), *Divorce and separation: Context, causes and consequences*. New York: Basic Books.

Barahal, R. M., Waterman, J., & Martin, H. P. (1981). The social cognitive development of abused children. *Journal of Consulting and Clinical Psychology, 49*, 508–516.

Barkley, R. A. (1979). Using stimulant drugs in the classroom. *School Psychology Digest, 8*, 412–425.

Barkley, R. A., Karlsson, J., Strzelecki, E., & Murphy, J. V. (1984). Effects of age and Ritalin dosage on the mother-child interactions of hyperactive children. *Journal of Consulting and Clinical Psychology, 52,* 750-758.

Bauer, W. D., & Twentyman, C. T. (1985). Abusing, neglectful, and comparison mothers' responses to child-related and non-child-related stressors. *Journal of Consulting and Clinical Psychology, 53,* 335-343.

Baumrind, D. (1983). Rejoinder to Lewis's reinterpretation of parental firm control effects: Are authoritative families really harmonious? *Psychological Bulletin, 94,* 132-142.

Beattie, J. R., & Maniscalo, G. O. (1985). Special education and divorce: Is there a link? *Techniques: A Journal for Remedial Education and Counseling, 1,* 342-345.

Bellack, A. S., & Hersen, M. (Eds.). (1985). *Dictionary of behavior therapy techniques.* New York: Pergamon Press.

Belsky, J. (1980). Child maltreatment: An ecological integration. *American Psychologist, 35,* 320-335.

Benson, H. B. (1979). *Behavior modification and the child.* Westport, CT: Greenwood Press.

Berger, M. (1981). Remediating hyperkinetic behavior with inpulse (sic) control procedures. *School Psychology Review, 10,* 405-407.

Bersoff, D. N. (1982). The legal regulation of school psychology. In C. R. Reynolds & T. B. Gutkin (Eds.), *The handbook of school psychology.* New York: John Wiley & Sons.

Biran, M., & Wilson, G. T. (1981). Treatment of phobic disorders using cognitive and exposure methods: A self-efficacy analysis. *Journal of Consulting and Clinical Psychology, 49,* 886-889.

Blagg, N. R., & Yule, W. (1984). The behavioral treatment of school refusal—A comparative study. *Behavior Research and Therapy, 22,* 119-127.

Blanchard, J. S. (1981). A comprehension strategy for disabled readers in the middle school. *Journal of Reading, 24,* 331-336.

Blechman, E. A., Taylor, C. J., & Schrader, S. M. (1981). Family problem solving versus home notes as early intervention with high-risk children. *Journal of Consulting and Clinical Psychology, 49,* 919-926.

Bolles, R. C. (1975). *Learning theory.* New York: Holt, Rinehart, & Winston.

Bower, G. H., & Hilgard, E. R. (1981). *Theories of learning.* Englewood Cliffs, NJ: Prentice-Hall.

Bowman, P., & Goldberg, M. (1983). "Reframing:" A tool for the school psychologist. *Psychology in the Schools, 20,* 210-214.

Brown, C. M., Meyers, A. W., & Cohen, R. (1984). Self-instruction training with preschoolers: Generalization to proximal and distal problem-solving tasks. *Cognitive Therapy and Research, 8,* 427-438.

Brown, L. J., Black, D. D., & Downs, J. C. (1984). *School Social Skills (S-3) manual.* East Aurora, NY: Slosson Educational Publications.

Brown, P., & Elliot, R. (1965). Control of aggression in a nursery school class. *Journal of Experimental Child Psychology, 2,* 103-107.

Brown, R. T., & Conrad, K. J. (1982). Impulse control or selective attention: Remedial programs for hyperactivity. *Psychology in the Schools, 19,* 92-97.

Butler, G., Cullington, A., Munby, M., Amies, P., & Gelder, M. (1984). Exposure and anxiety management in the treatment of social phobia. *Journal of Consulting and Clinical Psychology, 52,* 642-650.

Butler, L., Miezitis, S., Friedman, R., & Cole, E. (1980). The effect of two school-based intervention programs on depressive symptoms in preadolescents. *American Educational Research Journal, 17,* 111-119.

Cantor, P. (1983). Depression and suicide in children. In C. E. Walker & M. C. Roberts (Eds.), *Handbook of clinical child psychology*. New York: John Wiley & Sons.

Carlson, J. G., & Wielkiewicz, R. M. (1976). Mediators of the effects of magnitude of reinforcement. *Learning and Motivation, 7*, 184–196.

Carson, T. P., & Adams, H. E. (1981). Affective disorders: Behavioral perspectives. In S. M. Turner, K. S. Calhoun, & H. E. Adams (Eds.), *Handbook of clinical behavior therapy*. New York: John Wiley & Sons.

Carstens, A. A. (1985). Retention and social promotion for the exceptional child. *School Psychology Review, 14*, 48–63.

Cartledge, G., & Milburn, J. F. (Eds.). (1986). *Teaching social skills to children* (2nd ed.). New York: Pergamon Press.

Cautela, J. R. (1982). Covert conditioning with children. *Journal of Behavior Therapy and Experimental Psychiatry, 13*, 209–214.

Christian, B. (1983). A practical reinforcement hierarchy for classroom behavior modification. *Psychology in the Schools, 20*, 83–84.

Conger, J. C., & Keane, S. P. (1981). Social skills intervention in the treatment of isolated or withdrawn children. *Psychological Bulletin, 90*, 478–495.

Darley, J. M., Glucksberg, S., Kamin, L., & Kinchla, R. A. (1981). *Psychology*. Englewood Cliffs, NJ: Prentice-Hall.

Darveaux, D. X. (1984). The Good Behavior Game plus Merit: Controlling disruptive behavior and improving student motivation. *School Psychology Review, 13*, 510–514.

Dobson, J. (1970). *Dare to discipline*. Wheaton, IL: Tyndale House Publishers.

Dodge, K. A., McClaskey, C. L., & Feldman, E. (1985). Situational approach to the assessment of social competence in children. *Journal of Consulting and Clinical Psychology, 53*, 344–353.

Dollard, J., & Miller, N. E. (1950). *Personality and psychotherapy*. New York: McGraw-Hill.

Drake, E. A. (1981). Helping children cope with divorce: The role of the school. In I. R. Stuart & L. E. Abt (Eds.), *Children of separation and divorce: Management and treatment*. New York: Van Nostrand Reinhold.

Dreikurs, R., & Grey, L. (1970). *A parents' guide to child discipline*. New York: Hawthorn/Dutton.

Ehrlich, V. Z. (1982). *Gifted children: A guide for parents and teachers*. Englewood Cliffs, NJ: Prentice-Hall.

Eimers, R., & Aitchison, R. (1977). *Effective parents/responsible children*. New York: McGraw-Hill.

Elliott, C., & Ozolins, M. (1983). Use of imagery and imagination in treatment of children. In C. E. Walker & M. C. Roberts (Eds.), *Handbook of clinical child psychology*. New York: John Wiley & Sons.

Emery, R. E. (1982). Interparental conflict and the children of discord and divorce. *Psychological Bulletin, 92*, 310–330.

Eron, L. D. (1980). Prescription for the reduction of aggression. *American Psychologist, 35*, 244–252.

Ferritor, D. E., Buckholdt, D., Hamblin, R. L., & Smith, L. (1972). The non-effects of contingent reinforcement for attending behavior upon work accomplishment. *Journal of Applied Behavior Analysis, 5*, 7–17.

Finch, A. J., Saylor, C. F., & Edwards, G. L. (1985). Children's depression inventory: Sex and grade norms for normal children. *Journal of Consulting and Clinical Psychology, 53*, 424–425.

Finch, M., & Hops, H. (1982). Remediation of social withdrawal in young children: Considerations for the practitioner. *Child and Youth Services, 5* (nos. 3/4), 29–42.

Fine, M. J., & Holt, P. (1983a). Intervening with school problems: A family systems perspective. *Psychology in the Schools, 20,* 59–66.

Fine, M. J., & Holt, P. (1983b). Corporal punishment in the family: A systems perspective. *Psychology in the Schools, 20,* 85–92.

Forman, S. G., & O'Malley, P. L. (1984). School stress and anxiety interventions. *School Psychology Review, 13,* 162–170.

Foxx, R. M., & Shapiro, S. T. (1978). The timeout ribbon: A nonexclusionary timeout procedure. *Journal of Applied Behavior Analysis, 11,* 125–136.

Frame, C., Matson, J. L., Sonis, W. A., Fialkov, M. J., & Kazdin, A. E. (1982). Behavioral treatment of depression in a prepubertal child. *Journal of Behavior Therapy and Experimental Psychiatry, 13,* 239–243.

Garman, G. C. (1983). *Taking a look at discipline.* Elizabethtown, PA: The Continental Press.

Gazda, G. M. (Ed.). (1976). *Theories and methods of group counseling in the schools* (2nd ed.). Springfield, IL: Charles C Thomas.

Germain, R. B., & Merlo, M. (1985). Best practices in assisting in promotion and retention decisions. In A. Thomas & J. Grimes (Eds.), *Best practices in school psychology.* Kent, OH: The National Association of School Psychologists.

Goldstein, A. P., & Pentz, M. A. (1984). Psychological skill training and the aggressive adolescent. *School Psychology Review, 13,* 311–323.

Goldstein, A. P., Sprafkin, R. P., Gershaw, N. J., & Klein, P. (1980). *Skill-streaming the adolescent.* Champaign, IL: Research Press.

Gresham, F. M., & Nagle, R. J. (1980). Social skills training with children: Responsiveness to modeling and coaching as a function of peer orientation. *Journal of Consulting and Clinical Psychology, 48,* 718–729.

Guidubaldi, J., Cleminshaw, H. K., Perry, J. D., & Mcloughlin, C. S. (1983). The impact of parental divorce on children: Report of the nationwide NASP study. *School Psychology Review, 12,* 300–323.

Guidubaldi, J., & Perry, J. D. (1984). Divorce, socioeconomic status, and children's cognitive-social competence at school entry. *American Journal of Orthopsychiatry, 54,* 459–468.

Guyer, M. J. (1982). Child abuse and neglect statutes: Legal and clinical implications. *American Journal of Orthopsychiatry, 52,* 73–81.

Hall, R. V., Lund, D., & Jackson, D. (1968). Effects of teacher attention on study behavior. *Journal of Applied Behavior Analysis, 1,* 1–12.

Harris, K. R., Wong, B. Y. L., & Keogh, B. K. (1985). Cognitive-behavior modification with children: A critical review of the state-of-the-art. *Journal of Abnormal Child Psychology, 13,* 327–476.

Harris, S. L., & Fong, P. L. (1985). Developmental disabilities: The family and the school. *School Psychology Review, 14,* 162–165.

Harvey, J. H., & Weary, G. (1984). Current issues in attribution theory and research. *Annual Review of Psychology, 35,* 427–459.

Hatzenbuehler, L. C., & Schroeder, H. E. (1978). Desensitization procedures in the treatment of childhood disorders. *Psychological Bulletin, 85,* 831–844.

Hearst, E. (Ed.). (1979). *The first century of experimental psychology.* Hillsdale, NJ: Lawrence Erlbaum Associates.

Hetherington, E. M. (1979). Divorce: A child's perspective. *American Psychologist, 34,* 851–858.

Hinshaw, S. P., Henker, B., & Whalen, C. K. (1984). Cognitive-behavioral and pharmacologic interventions for hyperactive boys: Comparative and combined effects. *Journal of Consulting and Clinical Psychology, 52,* 739–749.

Hollon, S. D. (1984, Oct. 11). *Cognitive therapy: An advanced workshop.* Presented at the Annual Convention of the North Dakota Psychological Association.

Homatidis, S., & Konstantareas, M. M. (1981). Assessment of hyperactivity: Isolating measures of high discriminant validity. *Journal of Consulting and Clinical Psychology, 49,* 533–541.

Hops, H. (1983). Children's social competence and skill: Current research practices and future directions. *Behavior Therapy, 14,* 3–18.

Horan, J. J., & Williams, J. M. (1982). Longitudinal study of assertion training as a drug abuse prevention strategy. *American Educational Research Journal, 19,* 341–351.

Hyman, I. A., & Wise, J. H. (Eds.). (1979). *Corporal punishment in American education.* Philadelphia, PA: Temple University Press.

Jacobson, R. H., Lahey, B. B., & Strauss, C. C. (1983). Correlates of depressed mood in normal children. *Journal of Abnormal Child Psychology, 11,* 29–40.

Jones, R. T., & Kazdin, A. E. (1981). Childhood behavior problems in the school. In S. M. Turner, K. S. Calhoun, & H. E. Adams (Eds.), *Handbook of clinical behavior therapy.* New York: John Wiley & Sons.

Kalter, N., Pickar, J., & Lesowitz, M. (1984). School-based developmental facilitation groups for children of divorce: A preventive intervention. *American Journal of Orthopsychiatry, 54,* 613–623.

Kanfer, F. H., Karoly, P., & Newman, A. (1975). Reduction of children's fear of the dark by competence-related and situational threat-related verbal cues. *Journal of Consulting and Clinical Psychology, 43,* 251–258.

Kanfer, F. H., & Phillips, J. S. (1970). *Learning foundations of behavior therapy.* New York: John Wiley & Sons.

Kazdin, A. E., Esveldt-Dawson, K., Sherick, R. B., & Colbus, D. (1985). Assessment of overt behavior and childhood depression among psychiatrically disturbed children. *Journal of Consulting and Clinical Psychology, 53,* 201–210.

Kazdin, A. E., French, N. E., & Unis, A. S. (1983). Child, mother, and father evaluations of depression in psychiatric inpatient children. *Journal of Abnormal Child Psychology, 11,* 167–180.

Kazdin, A. E., French, N. E., Unis, A. S., Esveldt-Dawson, K., & Sherick, R. B. (1983). Hopelessness, depression, and suicidal intent among psychiatrically disturbed inpatient children. *Journal of Consulting and Clinical Psychology, 51,* 504–510.

Kazdin, A. E., Moser, J., Colbus, D., & Bell, R. (1985). Depressive symptoms among physically abused and psychiatrically disturbed children. *Journal of Abnormal Psychology, 94,* 298–307.

Kendall, P. C., & Braswell, L. (1982a). Assessment for cognitive-behavioral interventions in the schools. *School Psychology Review, 11,* 21–31.

Kendall, P. C., & Braswell, L. (1982b). Cognitive-behavioral self-control therapy for children: A components analysis. *Journal of Consulting and Clinical Psychology, 50,* 672–689.

Kendall, P. C., & Braswell, L. (1985). *Cognitive-behavioral therapy for impulsive children.* New York: The Guilford Press.

Kendall, P. C., & Wilcox, L. C. (1979). Self-control in children: Development of a rating scale. *Journal of Consulting and Clinical Psychology, 47,* 1020–1029.

Kerasotes, D., & Walker, C. E. (1983). Hyperactive behavior in children. In C. E. Walker & M. C. Roberts (Eds.), *Handbook of clinical child psychology.* New York: John Wiley & Sons.

King, H. E., & Kleemeier, C. P. (1983). The effect of divorce on parents and children. In C. E. Walker & M. C. Roberts (Eds.), *Handbook of clinical child psychology.* New York: John Wiley & Sons.

Kirk, S. A., & Chalfant, J. C. (1984). *Academic and developmental learning disabilities.* Denver, CO: Love Publishing Company.

Kovacs, M. (1980/1981). Rating scales to assess depression in school-aged children. *Acta Paedopsychiatry, 46,* 305–315.

Kübler-Ross, E. (1969). *On death and dying.* New York: Macmillan.

Ladd, G. W., & Mize, J. (1982). Social skills training and assessment with children: A cognitive-social learning approach. *Child and Youth Services, 5,* 61–74.

Ladd, G. W., & Oden, S. (1979). The relationship between peer acceptance and children's ideas about helpfulness. *Child Development, 50,* 402–408.

Lahey, B. B., Delamater, A., & Kupfer, D. (1981). Intervention strategies with hyperactive and learning disabled children. In S. M. Turner, K. S. Calhoun, & H. E. Adams (Eds.), *Handbook of clinical behavior therapy.* New York: John Wiley & Sons.

Lange, A. J., & Jakubowski, P. (1976). *Responsible assertive behavior.* Champaign, IL: Research Press.

Lazarus, A. A., & Abramovitz, A. (1962). The use of "emotive imagery" in the treatment of children's phobias. *Journal of Mental Science, 108,* 191–195.

LeCroy, C. W. (Ed.). (1982). Social skills training for children and youth. *Child and Youth Services, 5,* 1–152.

Leon, G. R., Kendall, P. C., & Garber, J. (1980). Depression in children: Parent, teacher, and child perspectives. *Journal of Abnormal Child Psychology, 8,* 221–235.

Lewis, R. O., & Blampied, N. M. (1985). Self-management in a special class. *Techniques: A Journal for Remedial Education and Counseling, 1,* 346–354.

Linn, R. T., & Hodge, G. K. (1982). Locus of control in childhood hyperactivity. *Journal of Consulting and Clinical Psychology, 50,* 592–593.

Madsen, C. H., Becker, W. C., & Thomas, D. R. (1968). Rules, praise, and ignoring: Elements of elementary classroom control. *Journal of Applied Behavior Analysis, 1,* 139–150.

Maser, J. D., & Seligman, M. E. P. (Eds.). (1981). *Psychopathology: Experimental models.* San Francisco, CA: W. H. Freeman & Co.

McCarney, S. B., Leigh, J. E., & Cornbleet, J. A. (1983). *Behavior Evaluation Scale.* Columbia, MO: Educational Services.

McClannahan, L. E., & Krantz, P. J. (1985). Some next steps in rights protection for developmentally disabled children. *School Psychology Review, 14,* 143–149.

McGee, R., Williams, S., & Silva, P. A. (1985). Factor structure and correlates of ratings of inattention, hyperactivity, and antisocial behavior in a large sample of 9-year-old children from the general population. *Journal of Consulting and Clinical Psychology, 53,* 480–490.

McGinnis, E., Goldstein, A. P., Sprafkin, R. P., & Gershaw, N. J. (1984). *Skill-streaming the elementary school child.* Champaign, IL: Research Press.

McMahon, R. J., Forehand, R., & Griest, D. L. (1981). Effects of knowledge of social learning principles on enhancing treatment outcome and generalization in a parent training program. *Journal of Consulting and Clinical Psychology, 49,* 526–532.

Meichenbaum, D. H., & Goodman, J. (1971). Training impulsive children to talk to themselves: A means of developing self-control. *Journal of Abnormal Psychology, 77,* 115–126.

Miller, L. C. (1983). Fears and anxiety in children. In C. E. Walker & M. C. Roberts (Eds.), *Handbook of clinical child psychology.* New York: John Wiley & Sons.

Miller, P. M. (1983). *Theories of developmental psychology.* San Francisco, CA: W. H. Freeman and Company.

Millman, H. L., Schaefer, C. E., & Cohen, J. J. (1980). *Therapies for school behavior problems.* San Francisco, CA: Jossey-Bass Publishers.

Morris, C. G. (1982). *Psychology: An introduction* (4th ed.). Englewood Cliffs, NJ: Prentice-Hall.

Morris, R. J., & Kratochwill, T. R. (Eds.) (1983a). *The practice of child therapy.* New York: Pergamon Press.

Morris, R. J., & Kratochwill, T. R. (1983b). *Treating children's fears and phobias.* New York: Pergamon Press.

Morris, R. J., & Kratochwill, T. R. (1985). Behavioral treatment of children's fears and phobias. *School Psychology Review, 14,* 84–93.

Newman, B. M., & Newman, P. R. (1979). *Development through life: A psychosocial perspective.* Homewood, IL: The Dorsey Press.

Oden, S., & Asher, S. R. (1977). Coaching children in skills for friendship making. *Child Development, 48,* 495–506.

Ollendick, T. H., & Cerny, J. A. (1981). *Clinical behavior therapy with children.* New York: Pergamon Press.

Ollendick, T. H., Matson, J. L., & Helsel, W. J. (1985). Fears in children and adolescents: Normative data. *Behavior Research and Therapy, 23,* 465–467.

Palkes, H., Stewart, M., & Freedman, J. (1972). Improvement in maze performance of hyperactive boys as a function of verbal training procedures. *The Journal of Special Education, 5,* 337–342.

Patterson, G. R., Cobb, J. A., & Ray, R. S. (1973). A social engineering technology for retraining the families of aggressive boys. In H. E. Adams & I. P. Unikel (Eds.), *Issues and trends in behavior therapy.* Springfield, IL: Charles C Thomas.

Peterson, N. J., & Moe, G. L. (1984). A multimethod assessment and intervention with a socially rejected child. *School Psychology Review, 13,* 391–396.

Pfeffer, C. R. (1981). Developmental issues among children of separation and divorce. In I. R. Stuart & L. E. Abt (Eds.), *Children of separation and divorce: Management and treatment.* New York: Van Nostrand Reinhold Company.

Phillips, R. H. (1984). Increasing positive self-referent statements to improve self-esteem in low-income elementary school children. *Journal of School Psychology, 22,* 155–163.

Piers, E. V. (1984). *The Piers-Harris Children's Self-Concept Scale: Revised manual.* Los Angeles, CA: Western Psychological Services.

Prout, H. T. (1984). A comparative review of child behavior therapy books. *School Psychology Review, 13,* 533–534.

Reynolds, C. R., & Gutkin, T. B., (Eds.). (1982). *The handbook of school psychology.* New York: John Wiley & Sons.

Reynolds, W. M. (1984). Depression in children and adolescents: Phenomenology, evaluation and treatment. *School Psychology Review, 13,* 171–182.

Richard, B. A., & Dodge, K. A. (1982). Social maladjustment and problem solving in school-aged children. *Journal of Consulting and Clinical Psychology, 50,* 226–233.

Richter, N. C. (1984). The efficacy of relaxation training with children. *Journal of Abnormal Child Psychology, 12,* 319–344.

Rose, J. S., Medway, F. J., Cantrell, V. L. & Marus, S. H. (1983). A fresh look at the retention-promotion controversy. *Journal of School Psychology, 21,* 201–211.

Ross, A. O. (1981). *Child behavior therapy.* New York: John Wiley & Sons.

Ryback, D., & Staats, A. W. (1970). Parents as behavior therapy-technicians in treating reading deficits (dyslexia). *Journal of Behavior Therapy Research and Experimental Psychiatry, 1,* 109–119.

Saigh, P. S., & Antoun, F. T. (1984). Endemic images and the desensitization process. *Journal of School Psychology, 22,* 177–183.

Salend, S. J., & Allen, E. M. (1985). Comparative effects of externally managed and self-managed response-cost systems on inappropriate classroom behavior. *Journal of School Psychology, 23,* 59–67.

Schacht, T. E. (1985). DSM-III and the politics of truth. *American Psychologist, 40,* 513–521.

Schaefer, C. E., & Millman, H. L. (1981). *How to help children with common problems.* New York: Litton Educational Publishing. (Paperback edition published by Plume Books, New American Library.)

Schumaker, J. B., Hovell, M. F., & Sherman, J. A. (1977). An analysis of daily report cards and parent-managed privileges in the improvement of adolescents' classroom performance. *Journal of Applied Behavior Analysis, 10,* 449–464.

Schwartz, M., Friedman, R., Lindsay, P., & Narrol, H. (1982). The relationship between conceptual tempo and depression in children. *Journal of Consulting and Clinical Psychology, 50,* 488–490.

Schwartz, S., & Johnson, J. H. (1985). *Psychopathology of childhood* (2nd ed.). New York: Pergamon Press.

Seligman, M. E. P., Abramson, L. Y., Semmel, A., & Von Baeyer, C. (1979). Depressive attribution style. *Journal of Abnormal Psychology, 88,* 242–247.

Shaw, W. J. (1983). Delinquency and criminal behavior. In C. E. Walker & M. C. Roberts (Eds.), *Handbook of clinical child psychology.* New York: John Wiley & Sons.

Silberman, M. L., & Wheelan, S. A. (1980). *How to discipline without feeling guilty.* Champaign, IL: Research Press.

Slater, E. J., & Haber, J. D. (1984). Adolescent adjustment following divorce as a function of family conflict. *Journal of Consulting and Clinical Psychology, 52,* 920–921.

Smith, D., & Kraft, W. A. (1983). DSM-III: Do psychologists really want an alternative? *American Psychologist, 38,* 777–785.

Solnick, J. V., Rincover, A., & Peterson, C. R. (1977). Some determinants of the reinforcing and punishing effects of timeout. *Journal of Applied Behavior Analysis, 10,* 415–424.

Sparrow, S. S., Balla, D. A., & Cicchetti, D. V. (1984). *Vineland Adaptive Behavior Scales, interview edition, survey form manual.* Circle Pines, MN: American Guidance Service.

Spitzer, R. L. (1985). DSM-III and the politics-science dichotomy syndrome. *American Psychologist, 40,* 522–526.

Staats, A. W. (1963). *Complex human behavior.* New York: Holt, Rinehart, & Winston.

Staats, A. W. (1971). *Child learning, intelligence, and personality.* New York: Harper and Row.

Staats, A. W. (1975). *Social behaviorism.* Homewood, IL: The Dorsey Press.

Stokes, T. F., & Baer, D. M. (1977). An implicit technology of generalization. *Journal of Applied Behavior Analysis, 10,* 349–368.

Swanson, H. L. (1985). Effects of cognitive-behavior training on emotionally disturbed children's academic performance. *Cognitive Therapy and Research, 9,* 201–216.

Swift, M. S., & Spivack, G. (1975). *Alternative teaching strategies.* Champaign, IL: Research Press.

Thackwray, D., Meyers, A., Schleser, R., Cohen, R. (1985). Achieving generalization with general versus specific instructions: Effects on academically deficient children. *Cognitive Therapy and Research, 9,* 297–308.

Thomas, R. M. (1979). *Comparing theories of child development.* Belmont, CA: Wadsworth Publishing Company.

Thorndike, E. L. (1898). Animal intelligence: An experimental study of the associative processes in animals. *Psychological Review Monograph Supplement, 2* (Whole No. 8).

Townsend, R. B. (1984). *School corporal punishment, home discipline, and violence: Some unhealthy relationships.* Paper presented at the Annual Convention of the National Association of School Psychologists, Philadelphia.

Turner, S. M., Calhoun, K. S., & Adams, H. E. (1981). *Handbook of clinical behavior therapy.* New York: John Wiley & Sons.

Ullman, L. P., & Krasner, L. (1975). *A psychological approach to abnormal behavior* (2nd ed.). Englewood Cliffs, NJ: Prentice-Hall.

Vogrin, D., & Kassinove, H. (1979). Effects of behavior rehearsal, audiotaped observation, and intelligence on assertiveness and adjustment in third-grade children. *Psychology in the Schools, 16,* 422–429.

Wahler, R. G. (1980). The insular mother: Her problem in parent-child treatment. *Journal of Applied Behavior Analysis, 13,* 207–219.

Wanlass, R. L., & Prinz, R. J. (1982). Methodological issues in conceptualizing and treating childhood social isolation. *Psychological Bulletin, 92,* 39–55.

Walker, C. E., & Roberts, M. C. (Eds.). (1983). *Handbook of clinical child psychology.* New York: John Wiley & Sons.

Waterman, J. (1982). Assessment of the family system. In G. Ulrey & S. J. Rogers (Eds.), *Psychological assessment of handicapped infants and young children.* New York: Thiene-Stratton Inc.

Webster-Stratton, C. (1985). Predictors of treatment outcome in parent training for conduct disordered children. *Behavior Therapy, 16,* 223–243.

Weller, E. B., & Weller, R. A. (1984). *Current perspectives on major depressive disorders in children.* Washington, DC: American Psychiatric Press.

Welsh, R. S. (1976). Severe parental punishment and delinquency: A developmental theory. *Journal of Clinical Child Psychology, 5,* 17–23.

Wherry, J. N. (1983). Some legal considerations and implications for the use of behavior modification in the schools. *Psychology in the Schools, 20,* 46–51.

Whitmore, J. R. (1980). *Giftedness, conflict, and underachievement.* Boston, MA: Allyn & Bacon.

Williams, G. J. R. (1983). Child abuse. In C. E. Walker & M. C. Roberts (Eds.), *Handbook of clinical child psychology.* New York: John Wiley & Sons.

Wirt, R. D., Lachar, D., Klinedinst, J. K., & Seat, P. D. (1977). *Multidimensional description of child personality: A manual for the Personality Inventory for Children.* Los Angeles, CA: Western Psychological Services.

Witt, J. C., & Elliott, S. N. (1982). The response cost lottery: A time efficient and effective classroom intervention. *Journal of School Psychology, 20,* 155–161.

Witt, J. C., & Martens, B. K. (1984). Adaptive behavior: Tests and assessment issues. *School Psychology Review, 13,* 478–484.

Wolfe, D. A. (1985). Child-abusive parents: An empirical review and analysis. *Psychological Bulletin, 97,* 462–482.

Workman, E. A. (1982). *Teaching behavioral self-control to students.* Austin, TX: Pro-Ed.

Zatz, S., & Chassin, L. (1983). Cognitions of test-anxious children. *Journal of Consulting and Clinical Psychology, 51,* 526–534.

Zatz, S., & Chassin, L. (1985). Cognitions of test-anxious children under naturalistic test-taking conditions. *Journal of Consulting and Clincial Psychology, 53,* 393–401.

Zimmerman, J., & Sims, D. (1983). Family therapy. In C. E. Walker & M. C. Roberts (Eds.), *Handbook of clinical child psychology.* New York: John Wiley & Sons.

GLOSSARY OF BEHAVIOR MANAGEMENT TERMS

Appetitive: describes a stimulus, such as food or drink, that a child will tend to approach and that can serve as a reinforcer.

Assessment: careful observation of the frequency, typology, precursors, and consequences of a particular behavior.

Aversive: describes a stimulus, such as a spanking or other painful event, that a child will tend to avoid and that can serve as a punisher.

Avoidance: a contingency in which a behavior postpones a punishing event.

Behavior: an observable response.

Classical conditioning: the process of having an appetitive or aversive stimulus occur, contingent upon the presentation of a stimulus.

Contingency: a rule that relates behavior to its consequences.

Continuous reinforcement: the delivery of reinforcement for a particular response following every such response performed by the child.

Discriminative stimulus: a stimulus that signals that reinforcement is available or not available for a particular behavior.

DSM-III: the most generally recognized manual of diagnostic criteria for psychological/psychiatric disorders; published by the American Psychiatric Association (1980).

Extinction: the process of ceasing to deliver a consequence for behavior; the predicted result is that the behavior will eventually cease occurring.

Incompatible response: a response that cannot be emitted at the same time as some other response; reinforcement of an incompatible response is one method of eliminating undesired behavior.

Interval schedules: schedules of reinforcement, in which the delivery of reinforcement depends upon the amount of time since the last reinforcer was delivered.

Negative punishment: the process of removing a pleasant stimulus (food, attention) contingent upon a behavior, causing it to decrease in frequency.

Negative reinforcement: the process of removing an unpleasant stimulus (pain, boredom) contingent upon a behavior, causing it to increase in frequency.

Partial reinforcement: the process of following a behavior by a contingent event only a fraction of the times that the behavior occurs; behavior that has been subject to partial reinforcement is much more resistant to change (extinction) than behavior that has been reinforced each time it occurred.

Positive reinforcement: the process of following a behavior by an appetitive stimulus (food, attention) causing the behavior to increase in frequency.

Premack principle: a general law of behavior that states that a low probability behavior (i.e., cleaning room) can be reinforced by allowing access to a high probability behavior (i.e., playing).

Punishment: the application of an unpleasant stimulus (i.e., spanking) contingent upon a behavior causing it to decrease in frequency.

Ratio schedules: schedules of reinforcement in which reinforcement is delivered contingent upon the *number* of responses emitted by the child.

Timeout: similar to negative punishment; the process of removing a child to a boring place where reinforcement is unavailable, contingent upon a behavior, causing it to decrease in frequency.

Token reward: rewarding behavior with a token (gold star, points, poker chip) that has value because it can be exchanged for other, more desirable rewards.

AUTHOR INDEX

SUBJECT INDEX

Ability, 113, 114, 118
Abuse, 153
　See also, physical abuse, sexual abuse
Academic performance, 113–120
　and ability, 114
　and achievement, 114
　and motivation, 114
　and sensory capacity, 115
　improvement of, 200–221
Achievement, 113, 114, 118
Adaptive behavior, 116
Adolescence, 26–27
Aggressive behavior, 5, 8, 121–122
Alcoholism, in children, 123–124
Alphabet, teaching, 201–205
Anger, 223–224
Anxiety, 108–113
　techniques of management, 180–185
　test, 112–113
　See also, phobia
Appetitive stimulus
　definition, 30
Assertive behavior, 8–9, 121, 242–244
　importance in behavior management, 9
Assessment
　general impact level of, 224
　informal vs. formal, 40
　of family systems, 91–95
　specifying level of, 224
　step-by-step procedure for, 42–48

summary of procedures, 47–48
Attention, 28, 67, 103, 104, 138–141
Attention deficit disorder, 104, 138
　See also, hyperactivity
Attribution theory, importance in communication with parents, 89
Aversive stimulus,
　definition, 30
Avoidance, 33

Baseline data, techniques of collecting, 51–55, 143, 157–158
Basic behavioral repertoire, 28, 200
　improvement of, 200–205
Basic facts, mastery of, 201, 205, 205–207
Basketball, 148
Behavior chains, 65
Behavior contracts, 218–221
Behavior management, 3
　books, 75
　defined, 3, 4
　judging effectiveness of, 34
　journals, 76
　of parenting behavior, 96–97
　reasons for ineffectiveness of, 59
　steps in conducting program, 49–60
Behavior modification, 3
Behavior shaping. See shaping.
Behavior therapy, 3

ABOUT THE AUTHOR

Richard M. Wielkiewicz obtained his PhD from the University of Hawaii in 1977, specializing in experimental psychology and learning theory. Later, he attended Moorhead State University in Moorhead, Minnesota, for additional training in school psychology. He presently works as a school psychologist for the Fargo Public Schools in Fargo, North Dakota.